From Peterborough to Faëry
The Poetics and Mechanics of Secondary Worlds

From Peterborough to Faëry: The Poetics and Mechanics of Secondary Worlds

Essays in honour of
Dr. Allan G. Turner's 65th Birthday

edited by
Thomas Honegger & Dirk Vanderbeke

2014

Cormarë Series No. 31

Series Editors: Peter Buchs • Thomas Honegger • Andrew Moglestue • Johanna Schön

Series Editor responsible for this volume: Thomas Honegger

Library of Congress Cataloging-in-Publication Data

From Peterborough to Faëry: The Poetics and Mechanics of Secondary Worlds – Essays in honour of Dr. Allan G. Turner's 65th Birthday
edited by Thomas Honegger and Dirk Vanderbeke
ISBN 978-3-905703-31-3

Subject headings:
Burns, Robert, 1759-1796
Fforde, Jasper, 1961-
Gaiman, Neil, 1960-
Geoffrey Chaucer, 1340-1400
Miéville, China, 1972-
Pratchett, Terry, 1948-
Tolkien, J.R.R. (John Ronald Reuel), 1892-1973
Vance, Jack, 1916-2013

Cormarë Series No. 31

First published 2014

© Walking Tree Publishers, Zurich and Jena, 2014

All rights reserved. No portion of this book may be reproduced, by any process or technique, without the express written consent of the publisher

Cover illustration *From Peterborough to Faëry* by Anke Eißmann.
Reproduced by permission of the artist. Copyright Anke Eißmann 2014.

Set in Adobe Garamond Pro and Shannon by Walking Tree Publishers
Printed by Lightning Source in the United Kingdom and United States

BOARD OF ADVISORS

ACADEMIC ADVISORS

Douglas A. Anderson (independent scholar)

Dieter Bachmann (Universität Zürich)

Patrick Curry (independent scholar)

Michael D.C. Drout (Wheaton College)

Vincent Ferré (Université de Paris-Est Créteil UPEC)

Verlyn Flieger (University of Maryland)

Thomas Fornet-Ponse (Rheinische Friedrich-Wilhelms-Universität Bonn)

Christopher Garbowski (University of Lublin, Poland)

Mark T. Hooker (Indiana University)

Andrew James Johnston (Freie Universität Berlin)

Rainer Nagel (Johannes Gutenberg-Universität Mainz)

Helmut W. Pesch (independent scholar)

Tom A. Shippey (University of Winchester)

Allan G. Turner (Friedrich-Schiller-Universität Jena)

Frank Weinreich (independent scholar)

GENERAL READERS

Johan Boots

Jean Chausse

Friedhelm Schneidewind

Isaac Juan Tomas

Patrick Van den hole

Johan Vanhecke (Letterenhuis, Antwerp)

Acknowledgments

Many thanks to all those who worked with us to make this volume possible – and who were able to keep a secret for so long!

Special thanks to the WTP interns who helped proofreading the text and who proved expert typo-hunters: Stephanie Luther, Olga Pisanaia, Luise Wendler, and Stefanie Schneider.

Contents

Introduction i

List of Publications by Allan Turner vii

Wolfram R. Keller
Geoffrey Chaucer's Mind Games:
Household Management and Aesthetics
in the Prologue to the *Legend of Good Women* 1

Andrew 'Chunky' Liston
Burns's Bogles 25

Julian Eilmann
Romantic World Building:
J.R.R. Tolkien's Concept of Sub-creation and the Romantic Spirit ... 37

Tom A. Shippey
Jack Vance: Il ottimo fabbro 57

Doreen Triebel
Stories that Last: Storytelling in
Terry Pratchett's *The Amazing Maurice and His Educated Rodents* ... 75

James Fanning
Thursday Next, or: Metalepsis Galore – and More 99

Thomas Honegger
From Faëry to Madness:
The Facts in the Case of Howard Phillips Lovecraft 113

Dirk Vanderbeke
The Sub-creation of Sub-London:
Neil Gaiman's and China Miéville's Urban Fantasy 141

Allan G. Turner anno aetatis suae LXV
(picture courtesy of Anna Prosowska)

Thomas Honegger & Dirk Vanderbeke

Introduction

It all began with St Peter, fisherman and also patron saint of fishermen, the profession most often associated with high levels of imagination and almost unbelievable yarns. It is he who performed some of the fantastic deeds of the gospels, like walking on water, until he was caught in the trap that imperils both the religiously faithful and aficionados of fantastic literature, the Todorovian momentary hesitancy and loss of 'a willing suspension of disbelief'. And it was St Peter who finally became the archetype of one of the most important stock figures of fantastic literature, the gatekeeper who allows or denies access to the land of promise from which no man returns.

But then he is not only important for fantastic literature as a person but also as a name giver and patron of locations, and the places named after St Peter are usually also closely connected to the uncanny, the mysterious, the magical and the fantastic. First, of course, there is the Russian St Petersburg, a city as inexplicable, labyrinthine and unknowable as Prague or Venice, and home to the masters of fantastic literature Gogol and Pushkin. It is a place where noses detach themselves from bodies and ride in carriages or where a dead duchess reappears in the image of the queen of spades. In his book *Universe of the Mind: A Semiotic Theory of Culture* (New York: I.B. Tauris, 2001), Yuri Lotman included a chapter on "The Symbolism of St Petersburg" in which he writes: "The city hewn in the air and without foundation – this is Petersburg, the supernatural and phantasmagoric space" (Lotman, 196). He then evokes a "genre of the scary or fantastic story with a 'Petersburg local colour'" (ibid.), and suggests that in the time of Pushkin St Petersburg was "a place where the mysterious and fantastic was the norm" (ibid.).

In the Western hemisphere, there is yet another St Petersburg, home to all the fantastic stories that ever were written. It is a place where pirates roam and haunted houses are "dissected, plank by plank, and [their] foundations dug up and ransacked for hidden treasure." It is a place of enchantment, where gangs of robbers swear oaths signed with blood, where magicians turn Arabs and elephants into a Sunday school picnic and where young boys who are willing to believe in all the fantastic yarns not only ultimately find the box of gold but also free a runaway slave, quite possibly the most fantastic element of all. And, what is best, the city itself is purely imaginary, the dream vision of eternal childhood where Mark Twain located his tales about Tom Sawyer and Huck Finn.

And then there is Peterborough, Cambridgeshire, a city that is certainly one of those places where the membrane between our world and the Perilous Realm is particularly thin and transparent. Just west of the fens, a region where earth and water mingle, this location has been inhabited since the Bronze Age. It was first mentioned in the eighth century by Bede in his *Ecclesiastical History*, when the town was still called Medeshamstede, and Hugh Candidus, a monk at Peterborough Abbey in the 12th century, wrote that it was founded in the territory of the North Gyrwas, the people of the fens.

Peterborough is also home to the *Peterborough Chronicle*. At first sight, this book does not really seem to belong to the genre of fantasy and imagination – among other things it tells how through the monks' "own carelessness, and through their drunkenness, in one night the church and all that was therein was consumed by fire", obviously a piece of early realism. But then medieval histories are also known for their flights into the realm of fancy and the supernatural, and the *Chronicle* also contains the first account of the Wild Hunt in English, an event that was interpreted as a bad omen when an obviously incompetent and greedy new abbot was appointed by the king:

> Þa son þaeraefter þa saegon & herdon fela men feole huntes hunten. Þa huntes waeron swarte & micele & laðlice, & here hundes ealle swarte & bradegede and laðlice, & hi ridone on swarte hors & on swarte bucces. Þis waes segon on the selue derfald in þa tune on Burch & on ealle þa wudes ða waeron fram þa selue tune to Stanforde; and þa muneces herdon ða horn blawen þat hi blewen on nihtes. Soðfeste men heom kepten on nihtes; saeidon, þes þe heom þuhte, þet þaer mihte wel ben abuton twenti other þritti hornblaweres.

> Immediately after [Henry of Poitou came to Peterborough as a new abbot], several persons saw and heard many huntsmen hunting. The hunters were swarthy, and huge, and ugly; and their hounds were all swarthy, and broad-eyed, and ugly. And they rode on swarthy horses, and swarthy bucks. This was seen in the very deer-fold in the town of Burch [Peterborough], and in all the woods

from that same town to Stamford. And the monks heard the horn blow that they blew in the night. Credible men, who watched them in the night, said that they thought there might well be about twenty or thirty horn-blowers.

Peterborough Cathedral, the original home of the *Peterborough Chronicle*, dates from the 12th and 13th centuries. It is only a brisk walk's distance (2.4 miles) from Dogsthorpe, a residential area of Peterborough, which in the 1960s became the new home of Deacon's Grammar School. The institution had been founded in 1722 in Cowgate with money assigned for this purpose in the will of the late Thomas Deacon. Maybe the wild hunt had passed this way on their ride through Peterborough and left some beneficial impression on the inhabitants. It is against the backdrop of this rich historical tapestry that we have enter Allan Turner, a young lad of tender age, to receive the benefit of an education at Deacon's School; an education that laid the foundations for his long and fruitful academic career. After taking his A-Levels in French, German, Latin and Music, he continued his education at the University of Reading where, after a BA (1st Class Honours) in German, he later received his M.Phil. for his dissertation consisting of an edition of a medieval German manuscript (*Christi Leiden*, MS Nürnberg Stadtbibliothek Cent. IV 31). In the following years he added additional strings to his academic and didactic rather than Elvish bow by studying for the Postgraduate Certificate of Education (with Commendation in Practical Teaching) at the University of Leeds and for an M.Phil. in Linguistics at St. John's College (University of Cambridge). At a later stage he rounded off his professional formation with the Cambridge/RSA Diploma in the Teaching of English as a Foreign Language and a Ph.D. in Translation Studies at the University of Newcastle. It may not be amiss to add that Allan has been appreciated for his skill as both a choirmaster and a singer. Moreover, his research has taken him beyond philology into the Elysian Fields of oenology, although his book on German wine never did get finished.

His professional and academic appointments took him to Basel, Trier, Greifswald, Marburg, and, finally, Jena, inspiring and motivating several generations of students. Simultaneously Allan made incessant excursions into the Perilous Realm, not of faculty meetings but of Faëry. The works of J.R.R. Tolkien as well as the medieval (and post-medieval) literatures and languages of Northern Europe, which inspired much of Tolkien's work, have had a profound and lasting impact on his personal and professional formation. Thus his students could not only profit from his expertise in language teaching, but also from his encyclopaedic knowledge of things "English" in particular and things "cultural" and "folkloristic" in general. Less frequent, but still with a profound impact, have been his seminars on Tolkien and medieval literature and languages. Allan has also made a point of attending (and mostly enjoying) academic conferences on his favourite subjects, and his active and sustained involvement with the British and the German Tolkien Societies (TS and DTG respectively) has earned him a substantial reputation. This was particularly evident when the organiser of the 2008 DTG conference in Jena made the mistake of scheduling Allan's paper in competition with that of another scholar – who found himself lecturing to less than the proverbial handful since everybody else among the more than fourscore attendants wanted to hear Allan's paper.

Yet Allan has not only contributed to Tolkien and translation studies by means of his academic papers or his monograph *Translating Tolkien* (Peter Lang, 2005), but has also written numerous reviews for *Hither Shore* and acted as a sounding board for many of his colleagues' ideas and as a critical proof-reader of their papers. And, last but not least, we must mention his involvement with Walking Tree Publishers – variously as author, (co-)editor, and member of the Board of Advisors. Walking Tree Publishers were, predictably, very pleased to undertake the publication of this volume in his honour.

The eight papers of this volume focus on one specific aspect of his broad range of scholarly interests: the creation of secondary worlds in literature. The specification "in literature" – or maybe better: by means of poetic language – is a crucial one, since Allan is very much a man of the written and spoken (and sung) word. Others may find enchantment in pictures or movies, but for him it is the poet or *scop* unlocking the word-hoard who weaves the spells of enchantment. We have always suspected that Tolkien's description of the recitations in the Hall of Fire at Rivendell depicts quite accurately his idea of an ideal evening entertainment.

We cannot offer Elvish poetry, but the eight papers written by former and present colleagues make up for this by means of their thematic and chronological breadth. It is the "father of English literature" who stands at the head of our volume and Wolfram R. Keller discusses the representation of the workings of imagination in Geoffrey Chaucer's works. He is followed by Andrew "Chunky" Liston, who takes a closer look at the supernatural in Burns's "Tam O'Shanter". Remaining within the Romantic period, Julian M. Eilmann's account of "Romantic world-building" discloses striking parallels between some of the central ideas of the Romantic movement and Tolkien's theory of "secondary worlds" and "sub-creation". The remaining papers focus on the literature of the 20th and 21st centuries. Tom Shippey's contribution introduces us to the astoundingly fertile imagination of Jack Vance, who has been one of the 20th century's most prolific world-builders. Terry Pratchett, another very productive and prominent author of fantasy, is the subject of Doreen Triebel's essay. She provides a close and informed eco-critical reading of Pratchett's fantasy-novel *Maurice and the Rodents*. The (narrative) mechanics and complications of multiple secondary worlds is the subject of James Fanning's contribution on Jasper Fforde's *Thursday Next* novels, and Thomas Honegger's study of the reception of H. P. Lovecraft's "anti-mythos" illustrates the strong mythologizing pull on secondary creations. The final paper by Dirk Vanderbeke investigates the role of London in some central texts of "urban fantasy".

We wish our readers – and Allan in particular – much pleasure in these excursions into the Perilous Realm.

Jena, March 2014

Thomas Honegger & Dirk Vanderbeke

List of Publications by Allan G. Turner

Papers, monographs and books edited

'A Theoretical Model for Tolkien Translation Criticism'. In *Tolkien in Translation* (Cormarë Series 4), ed. Thomas Honegger. Zurich and Berne: Walking Tree Publishers, 1-30. 2003.

'Fronting in Tolkien's Archaising Style and its Translation'. In *English Core Linguistics. Essays in Honour of D.J. Allerton*, ed. Cornelia Tschichold. Berne: Peter Lang, 301-321. 2003.

(together with Francis Jones). 'Archaisation, Modernisation and Reference in the Translation of Older Texts'. In *Across Languages and Cultures* 5.2:159-185. 2004.

Translating Tolkien: Philological Elements in The Lord of the Rings. Duisburger Arbeiten zu Sprach-und Kulturwissenschaft. Frankfurt am Main: Peter Lang. 2005.

'Translation and Criticism: The Stylistic Mirror'. In *Yearbook of English Studies* 36.1:168-176. 2006.

'Jewels'. In *The J.R.R. Tolkien Encyclopedia: Scholarship and Critical Assessment*, ed. Michael Drout. New York: Routledge, 311. 2006.

'Language'. In *The J.R.R. Tolkien Encyclopedia: Scholarship and Critical Assessment*, ed. Michael Drout. New York: Routledge, 328. 2006.

'Prose Style'. In *The J.R.R. Tolkien Encyclopedia: Scholarship and Critical Assessment*, ed. Michael Drout. New York: Routledge, 545. 2006.

'Rhetoric'. In *The J.R.R. Tolkien Encyclopedia: Scholarship and Critical Assessment*, ed. Michael Drout. New York: Routledge, 567. 2006.

(as editor). *The Silmarillion: Thirty Years On*. (Cormarë Series 15). Zurich and Berne: Walking Tree Publishers. 2007.

'The Lays of Beleriand: Epic and Romance'. In *Hither Shore* 3:27-36. 2007.

'Putting the Paratext in Context'. In *The Ring Goes Ever on, Proceedings of the Tolkien 2005 Conference: 50 Years of The Lord of the Rings*, ed. Sarah Wells. Coventry, England: The Tolkien Society, 283-288. 2008.

'Tom Bombadil: Poetry and Accretion'. In *Tolkien's Shorter Works*. (Cormarë Series 17), eds. Margaret Hiley and Frank Weinreich. Zurich and Jena: Walking Tree Publishers, 1-16. 2008.

'Tom Bombadil: The Sins of his Youth'. In *Hither Shore* 4:119-127. 2008.

'The Hobbit and Desire'. In *Hither Shore* 5:83-92. 2009.

(together with Dirk Vanderbeke). 'The One or the Many? Authorship, Voice and Corpus'. In *Sub-creating Middle-earth: Constructions of Authorship and the Works of J.R.R. Tolkien*. (Cormarë Series 27), ed. Judith Klinger. Zurich and Jena: Walking Tree Publishers, 1-20. 2012.

(as editor together with Julian Eilmann). *Tolkien's Poetry*. (Cormarë Series 28). Zurich and Jena: Walking Tree Publishers, 2013.

'Early Influences on Tolkien's Poetry'. In *Tolkien's Poetry*. (Cormarë Series 28), eds. Julian Eilmann and Allan Turner. Zurich and Jena: Walking Tree Publishers, 205-221. 2013.

Reviews

Review of Lucie Armitt. 2005. *Fantasy Fiction: An Introduction*. London: Continuum, in *Hither Shore* 5:243. 2009.

Review of J.R.R Tolkien. 2009. *The Legend of Sigurd and Gudrún*. London: HarperCollins, in *Hither Shore* 6:253. 2010.

Review of Cécile van Zon (ed.). 2009. *Lembas Extra: Tolkien in Poetry and Song*, in *Hither Shore* 7:238. 2011.

Review of Steve Walker. 2009. *The Power of Tolkien's Prose: Middle-Earth's Magical Style*. New York: Palgrave Macmillan, in *Hither Shore* 7:242. 2011.

Review of *Tolkien Studies 7*, in *Hither Shore* 8:289. 2012.

Review of Jason Fisher (ed.). 2011. *Tolkien and the Study of his Sources*. Jefferson NC/London: McFarland, in *Hither Shore* 8:298. 2012.

Review of Christopher MacLachlan. 2012. *Tolkien and Wagner: The Ring and Der Ring*. Zurich and Jena: Walking Tree Publishers, and Renée Vink. 2012. *Wagner and Tolkien: Mythmakers*. Zurich and Jena: Walking Tree Publishers, in *Hither Shore* 9:173-175. 2013.

Review of Mark T. Hooker. 2012. *Tolkien and Welsh*. [no place]: Llyfrawr, in *Hither Shore* 9:182-183. 2013.

Review of Michael Saler. 2012. *As If: Modern Enchantment and the Literary Prehistory of Virtual Reality*. Oxford: Oxford University Press, in *Hither Shore* 9:188-189. 2013.

Review of Barbara Kowalik (ed.). 2013. *O What a Tangled Web: Tolkien and Medieval Literature – A View from Poland*. Zürich and Jena: Walking Tree Publishers, in *Hither Shore* 10. 2014.

Review of *Tolkien Studies* 10, in *Hither Shore* 10. 2014.

Wolfram R. Keller

Geoffrey Chaucer's Mind Games: Household Management and Literary Aesthetics in the Prologue to the *Legend of Good Women*

Abstract

This article investigates Geoffrey Chaucer's advancement of a playful poetics of dissonance as represented in and legitimated by ventricular mind games, that is, representations of the three ventricles in *The House of Fame* and the Prologue to the *Legend of Good Women*. In both works, Chaucer stages the journeys of dissonant literary tidings through a mismanaged mental apparatus. In the course of the journey the dissonant images furnished by the imagination cannot be resolved by higher cognitive faculties of logic and memory. Ultimately, the cacophonous journey is epitomized as the *modus operandi* of Chaucerian poetry.

Granted: Geoffrey Chaucer's representation of faculty psychology can probably not be described in terms of what Tolkien referred to as a "secondary world." And yet, it was one of those long hallway conversations about Tolkien with Allan Turner at Marburg University's English department that prompted my interest in the ways in which Chaucer fictionalizes mental processes in his dream visions and the ways in which he represents the mental capacities associated with the three ventricles of the poet's brain. While scholars have begun to pay attention to such representations, the scope of Chaucer's representation of mental processes as forms of household management, the poet's concomitant recalibration of the mental apparatus in order to privilege invention (in the modern sense rather than the classical rhetorical meaning of *inventio*), and the aesthetics of such a ventricular poetry have not yet been sufficiently recognized. This may be due to the playfulness with which Chaucer deeply embeds questions of poetics and literary authorship within his works. These embedded representations of literary authorship are slowly coming into view, as scholars are becoming more interested in "how [...] authorship function[s] internally, not as a condition of writing but as a part of its meaning" (Edwards, "Authorship" 52). Chaucer transfers pressing questions of literary authorship, of literary invention from the extradiegetic level (e.g., Minnis, *Medieval Theory*;

Trigg, *Congenial Souls*) to the intradiegetic level (e.g., Minnis, *Fallible Authors*), even to the level of characters (Keller, "Chaucer"; for strategies of authorial representation, see also Schlesier and Trînca). Such dislocated representations of authorship are perhaps best grasped in terms of the games Chaucer plays with representations of authorship, with the audience, and with contemporary authors like John Gower. What follows, however, is not a game theory reading of the Prologue to the *Legend*, although the framework of games appears to be helpful in understanding Chaucer's representation of ventricular processes, as they consistently manifest themselves in his dream visions – and beyond.

Literary games are rule-governed events that usually involve authors and readers or readers and texts. Like other games, literary games are social and cultural products, as Betsy McCormick emphasizes with respect to the *Legend*. Games are remembered, become institutionalized qua re-enactment and re-play, and as such contribute to the formation of cultural traditions. Games, that is, have a social function beyond the duration of the game itself. The most important social function, as Johan Huizinga observes, is an experimental "ethical testing," in which transgressions can ensue without real-world consequences (McCormick 105-110; Huizinga 9-10). The *Legend* has already been read with respect to the game it plays with a view to the "debate on women" (McCormick) and with regard to the game Chaucer appears to play with palinodes, observed by Jamie Fumo in a parallel reading of Chaucer's "Retraction" to the *Canterbury Tales* and the Prologue to the *Legend*. My interest, however, lies particularly in Chaucer's concurrent game of representing authorship by means of depicting the poet's brain at work. While this seems to be an oblique game Chaucer primarily plays with himself, insofar as the *Legend* can be read as a playful response to Chaucer's earlier representations of ventricular poetics, it appears that other poets, John Gower and Chaucer's fifteenth-century successors were eager to play both with and against the "father of English poesy", negotiating their variously transgressive poetics in the playful realm of dream-games.

In what follows, I argue that Chaucer uses the doubly secure arena of the dream-game in order to test his transgressive conception of literary authorship by means of deeply embedded representations of the author's poetological journeys through the three ventricles of his brain. Such representations are not merely humorous mappings of cognitive processes; they involve problematic analogies between authoritative textual and philosophical knowledge, entailing not only a metamorphosis of the faculties itself, but a concurrent (and ethically problematic) revaluation of the place of imagination, an advancement of an aesthetics of disharmony, of the noise emerging from unresolved (and unresolvable) contradictions. In order to evince these points, I first illustrate how medieval medical/philosophical authorities conceptualized the human brain's structure and the functions associated with the individual parts of the ventricles, and how scholars have thus far discussed Chaucer's interest in faculty psychology. In the second part of this essay, I illustrate how the *House of Fame* takes the audience through the three ventricles of the brain – and how the persistence of imaginational disharmony is epitomized not only as a desirable aesthetic quality, but is, to a large extent, inevitable, given that historiographical and literary narratives are inherently cacophonous. In the Prologue to the *Legend of Good Women*, Chaucer replicates the poet's journey through his own noisy mental apparatus, adopting, as it were, a slanted perspective on the judgment of his own works. While the Prologue to some extent problematizes imaginational disharmony, it nevertheless leaves audiences with the hermeneutic effort to enjoy – and make sense – of contradictory images.

1

Medieval medical authorities and philosophers believed that, anatomically, the brain consisted of three interlinked cells, or three ventricles. The theory of the three ventricles was widely known in late-medieval England and is succinctly summarized in John Trevisa's vernacular translation of Bartholomaeus Anglicus's *De proprietatibus rerum*. Bartholomaeus presents an Aristotelian-derived model of the mind that divides the inward wit into three small cells:

> The innere witte is departid aþre by þre regiouns of þe brayn, for in þe brayn beþ þre smale celles. þe formest hatte *ymaginatiua*, þerin þingis þat þe vttir witte apprehendiþ withoute beþ i-ordeyned and input togedres withinne, *vt dicitur Johannico I*. þe middil chambre hatte *logica* þerin þe vertu estimatiue is maister. þe þridde and þe laste is *memoratiua*, þe vertu of mynde. þat vertu holdiþ and kepiþ in þe tresour of mynde þingis þat beþ apprehendid and iknowe bi þe ymaginatif and *racio*. (Trevisa 1: 98)

These three ventricles were associated with five capacities: in the cell of imagination, these are the *sensus communis*, responsible for the reception of sensory input, and *imaginatio* for retaining these images; in the cell of *logica* or *cogitatio*, the *virtus imaginativa* compares and assembles images, while the *virtus extimativa* evaluates these images; and, finally, with the cell of memory scholars associated the capacity to store the images as they arrive. The structural set-up of the three ventricles itself remained a commonplace in medical and philosophical discourses well into the Renaissance, while medieval (and early modern) scholars differed occasionally on the precise functions of the individual ventricles (see Bundy; Wolfson; Harvey), especially concerning the place of the imagination (see, e.g., summary in Lobsien and Lobsien). Not infrequently, medieval Latin as well as vernacular literary texts attest to the wide knowledge of the workings of the ventricles among literary authors, Chaucer included (*Boece* 5.pr. 4; see also Burnley 99-115; Edwards, *Dream* 4-11). Moreover, Latin and vernacular texts occasionally chart journeys through the mental apparatus, that is, protagonists travel through the cells of their own brains, concomitantly reflecting upon the functions associated with the respective ventricles (see esp. Lynch, *High Medieval Dream Vision* 21-76, Scheuer, "Bildintensität" and "Cerebrale Räume").

That Chaucer's poetological dream visions engage with faculty psychology is not a new observation. Robert Edwards's *Dream of Chaucer*, for instance, details how Chaucer deals with questions of memory and imagination in his dream poetry. That the narrators of Chaucer's dream visions consistently parallel the dreamer's journey through an imaginary topography with a journey through the three ventricles has been observed occasionally, but the epistemological-poetological implications remain largely underappreciated. Unfortunately so, since the study of Chaucer's concomitant representation of epistemological and poetological processes may suggest important insights not only into Chaucer's conceptualization of literary authorship, but also into his successors' attempts to renegotiate the place of the author in a quickly changing literary field, which forced poets to rethink their implication in Lancastrian propaganda, their place in systems of patronage, and their position vis-à-vis classical and near-contemporary literary authorities, especially Chaucer.

Important contributions to Chaucer's journeys through ventricular mindscapes have been offered by Mario Klarer and Frank G. Hoffman. Klarer's focus has been on questions of ekphrasis in Chaucer's *House of Fame*, which he sees as charting the dreamer's journey from the cell of memory to the ventricle of imagination. Frank Hoffman's unpublished 2004 dissertation *The Dream and the Book* offers a more sustained reading of Chaucer's representation of cognitive processes. He argues (19) that:

> While it would be going too far to say that Chaucer's dream-poems are all neatly structured by adherence to a three-part ventricular model of these spaces, he is at some pains to present the imagery, processes and content of his poetic dreamwork as feasible and identifiable in terms of medieval descriptive psychology. [...] medieval psychology found that dreams consisted of remembered images from the third ventricle (*memoria*) recombined by the creative powers of the second ventricle (*vis formativa*). The ability to actually "see" the resulting dream was, again, dependent on the *imaginatio* of the first ventricle.

Hoffman's account calls attention to the consistency with which Chaucer's dream visions engage with faculty psychology and ventricular processes, while it also spotlights the re-combinative nature of Chaucerian poetry, in his view, the combination of different classical sources (esp. 58). As will emerge below, my focus is less on the recombination of authorized sources but rather lies on the question of how Chaucer fits the work of the poet into the world of ventricular processes. Moreover, I have reservations about the way in which Klarer and Hoffman map Chaucer's journey through the ventricles, a disagreement that is perhaps instructive inasmuch as it draws attention to the way Chaucer's deviates from the orthodox identifications of the cells with particular functions. Klarer's and Hoffman's views of a journey from *memoria* to *imaginatio* basically follow the order of the ventricles as delineated in Chaucer's *Canterbury Tales*. In the *Second Nun's Tale*, the ventricles are listed back to front: "Memorie, engyn [= *logica*], and intellect also" (338-339), but, as Edwards observes, in contrast to Chaucer's source for this passage, the *Legenda aurea*, the three faculties are represented as "relatively independent powers" (*Dream* 7). Edwards's account of Chaucer's representation of faculty psychology is generally focused more on the processes and capacities associated with the ventricles rather than the ventricles themselves: "the faculties serve Chaucer as topoi for discussing the nature of poetic creation" (*Dream* 8). Text internal references suggest, as I show below, that the dreamer does travel through the mental apparatus, albeit in the other direction, from *imaginatio* to *memoria* (and back into the world; for direction of travel through the apparatus, see also Lynch, *Chaucer's Philosophical Visions*

62-63). While sleep is widely and rightly seen as impairing or modifying the work of the ventricles, as suspending judgment, the poems nonetheless appear to depict journeys of the dreamers (with disharmonious images as their baggage) through the apparatus after they were experienced. Audiences, that is, deal with written accounts of the dreams rather than the dreams themselves; the poem doubles upon the audience precisely the experience of judging which the poem itself attempts to judge on the plot level. What one witnesses on the plot level seems to be a transformation of the work of the ventricles themselves, insofar as what is characteristic of Chaucer's depiction of the ventricle of imagination (i.e., sensual overload) becomes a feature also of the ventricle of memory – which goes some way, I believe, to explain how scholars have come to a different mapping of the journey's direction. On the poetological level, then, this suggests that the *House of Fame* epitomizes ventricular disorder as the gold standard of literary innovation. Poetry, the *House of Fame* suggests, is conscious disorder – legitimated by the observation that disorder is always already inherent in historiographical and literary discourses in the first place. This is conceptualized by a third interest of the poem – actually, a third discourse – that is aligned with the dreamer's journey, that of traveling towards the sweet melody of the heavenly spheres, Boethian *musica mundana*.[1]

2

Disharmony, especially disharmonic images, are the main feature of the *House of Fame*.[2] The short warning at the beginning of the poem that a disharmonious relationship between body and soul will lead to nightmares (Pro. 21-52) could not be more suitable. Audiences perceptive to questions of harmony might thus be unsurprised when the dreamer wakes up in the temple of Venus, ambivalently associated in late-medieval England with the music of "the spirit and the flesh in harmony with created nature" and the "music of the flesh as it seeks inferior satisfactions" (Robertson 126; Chamberlain, "Musical Signs" 63). In terms of

---

1 Incidentally, a fourth layer (which thus renders many of the dream visions as [un-conventional] allegories) is that of questions of household management, the opposition of *oikonomia* and *chrematistike*, which will be occasionally alluded to, but will have to be the subject of a separate inquiry.
2 In the following sketch of ventricular processes in the *House of Fame*, the emphasis is on cognitive processes. For a more detailed investigation of the attendant soundscape, see Keller, "Chaucers Klang(t)räume", which forms the basis for this section.

cognitive processes, the dreamer-protagonist Geffrey has arrived in the first ventricle with its function of "feling" and "vertu ymaginatif," with sensing and retaining images. The description of the temple is not only dominated by verbs referring to sense perception, but also by an obvious mismatch between what the dreamer *sees* and what he *hears*. First of all, he sees "writen" on the wall the beginning of the *Aeneid*, which discusses poetry in terms of song: "I wol now synge, yif I kan, / The armes and also the man" (1.142-144). The *Aeneid* is here presented as a visual narrative, as the dreamer "First sawgh […] the destruction / Of Troye" (1.151-152). The summary of the *Aeneid* continues until the dreamer gets to the Dido episode. Here, he is confronted with two different "images" of Aeneas and Dido, one in keeping with Virgil, the other ultimately stemming from Ovid's *Heroides*. The latter, the dreamer does not see as much as he hears it: he hears Dido's lament (1.300-310, 315-360). Moreover, what he hears is incompatible with that which he has seen: the Virgilian Aeneas, who legitimately places empire over love, contrasts sharply with the Ovidian Aeneas, who is renounced for scandalizing Dido's reputation, prompting her suicide. Incidentally, these over-layered, contradictory images literally lead to a new narrative, in which Dido wonders about the nature of men – and, significantly, the fact that male poets appear to invest in the ill-repute of women to further their literary fame. There is no authority for this part of Dido's speech, and Geffrey himself is the only authority for it, the only *auctor*: "Non other auctor allege I" (1.314).

While Geffrey sees the rest of the *Aeneid* depicted, he feels very disoriented about what he beheld, and finally exits the temple, only to find himself in a desert, which does not help him in locating his whereabouts. Finally, he is picked up by a gigantic and excessively verbose eagle which marks, however, the shift from the ventricle of *imaginatio* to *logica*, from the perception of images to the judgment thereof. The plot of the second book is admittedly not associated with a cell-like structure, a vessel or container. And yet, that what is depicted appears to be associated with the ventricle of *logica*; in a sense, the depiction is in keeping with the "vertu estimatiue," the combinatory function of the ventricle, since it is an intermediary, insofar as it has access to both the first and third ventricles. The shift from *imaginatio* to higher cognitive functions is also signaled by the proem to the second book, notably with the first reference to the nine muses in the English vernacular:

> And ye, me to endite and ryme
> Helpeth, that on Parnaso duelle,
> Be Elicon, the clere welle.
> O *Thought* [*logica*], that wrote al that I mette,
> And in the *tresory hyt shette*
> *Of my brayn* [= *memoratiua*], now shal me se
> Yf any vertu in the be
> To tellen al my drem aryght.
> Now kythe thyn *engine* and myght!
> (2.520-528, my italics; and see 1.468-472)

The dreamer's appeal to *logica* for order also furthers the audience's Ciceronian-Boethian expectations, as the dreamer journeys higher and higher into heaven, with the expectation that Geffrey shall experience the melodious music of the spheres. Boethian expectations of reaching enlightenment are furthered also by explications as to how speech is nothing but sound, broken air that, in keeping with its nature (the multiplication of "kynde"), rises up so Fama can process it (2.762, 765-768), and the comparison of the diffusion of sound with ripples caused by a stone thrown into water is likewise Boethian (2.782-822). The dreamer now likens his upward movement explicitly with the feathered Thoughts of Philosophy, paralleling the journey into the spheres with the movement of the image of sense perception into deeper layers of the soul: "And thoo thoughte y upon Boece, / That writ, 'A thought may flee so hye / Wyth fetheres of Philosophye [...]'" (2.972-974). What is omitted, though, is Boethius's eventual experience of the Platonic realm of Ideas (Fyler 46), which leads to a transformation of Boethius's and Scipio's spheres, a transformation that replicates the disharmonies of the Aeneas-Dido plot witnessed by the senses (in the first book of the poem).

The main analogy between the eagle's flight and the processes associated with the second ventricle is the judgment that ensues at the beginning of Book 2. The eagle, on behalf of Jove, passes judgment on Geffrey – and, implicitly, on the hybrid Ovidian-Virgilian narrative Geffrey's *imaginatio* had furnished. The eagle explains that the journey is a reward for Geffrey's dedicated service to Venus, for his ability "To make bookys, songes, dytees, / In ryme or elles in cadence." Notwithstanding Chaucer's "cadence," what is problematic about Geffrey, quips the eagle, is his isolation: as he returns from his "reckonings" at work, he turns merely to books – what he lacks is real-life experience about love, a lack that a visit to the realm of fame will cure, since he will witness all manner tidings, written or spoken narratives, including "Mo love-dayes and acordes / Then on instrumentes be cordes" (2.622-623, 647-696). The problem with Geffrey's poetry, in other words, is that there is too little of the man in the poet.

If Geffrey's own, un-authorized narrative of Dido and Aeneas is any indication as to what such poetry based on experience would be like, it is barely surprising that the universe of tidings that the dreamer is going to behold in the course of his journey is equally noisy and disharmonious. Instead of the "great and pleasing sound that fills" Scipio's ears as the latter travels through the heavenly spheres in the *Somnium Scipionis* (Macrobius 5.3), Chaucer's dreamer beholds nothing but noise; the eagle directs the dreamer's attention to the "The grete soun [… / …] that rumbleth up and doun / In Fames Hous, full of tydynges, / Bothe of feir speche and chidynges, / And of fals and soth compouned. / Herke wel; hyt is not rouned. / Herestow not the grete swogh?" (2.1024-1031). While he witnesses the consonance of narratives in analogy to the Boethian consonance of low and high tones, what results in Geffrey's heaven ("fals and soth compouned") is far from *pleasing* harmony. At the end of the second book, Geffrey's confusion about the hybrid narrative he perceived in the temple of Venus is due to the fact that his logical faculty is not creating any order, but rather passes the noisy data on to an equally cacophonous ventricle of memory.

The third book begins with the dreamer's exploration of the palace of Fama, which resembles a Gothic cathedral that, in turn, represents a formal memory system, embodying "the metaphor of musical harmony in its architectural proportions" (Edwards, *Dream* 114; see also Robertson 121; Carruthers 89-98, 279-280). Geffrey has reached the most important ventricle of his brain, the "tresour of mynde." Already outside the palace, cacophony is apparent everywhere, as the dreamer espies a vast multitude of minstrels and musicians, playing their various instruments simultaneously, mirrored on the narrative level by means of an excessively long enumeration (3.1214-1258). This rambunctious assembly aptly prefaces the greater disorder the dreamer witnesses inside the palace, which, I believe, represents his artificial memory. As standard reference works on the art of memory advise, whatever one wishes to remember needs to be placed in a luminous spot, preferably in an architectural space, a house or a church. Geffrey's memory represents a particularly disorganized architectural mnemonic, an astoundingly untidy mental household, in which many things are not found where they should be, where they are *dis*placed. The pillared authorities of Trojan history which the dreamer first notices seem to be in the right place. Even here, however, the dreamer notices "envye" between them and is struck by Homer's subjective take on Trojan history, his Greek bias (3.1464-1480). The noisiness continues as the dreamer sees the goddess Fama at work. He witnesses nine groups of petitioners approaching the goddess in order to receive their reputations in what turns out to be a parody of *musica mundana*, whether understood in terms of the movement of nine sounding spheres (as in Chaucer's *Parlement of Foules* or *The Man of Law's Tale*) or the harmony of seven tones caused by the movement of the seven planets or the planets' spheres (Cicero, Macrobius): nine groups of petitioners ask for fame, which is problematically awarded arbitrarily, and seven times Fama asks Eolus to trumpet their reputations out into the world (for a detailed reading, see Keller, "Chaucers Klang(t)räume"). The disharmonious narratives arriving from the ventricle of imagination are judged in the second ventricle, but the judgment is arbitrary, a mere parody of divine harmony, and the valuation of the narratives is equally disharmonious given the arbitrariness of Fama's judgment.

Cacophony is likewise characteristic of the dreamer's natural memory, which is represented by Daedalus's wicker labyrinth of Rumor, which Lee Patterson has identified as being based on Orosius's labyrinth of history (101). It is here that the dreamer experiences the troubling consonance of the compounding of "fals and soth" as potentially inherent in any narrative. In the wicker cage, he perceives personified tidings whirling around so loudly that, had the structure been located in Paris, one could have easily heard the noise in Rome (3.1927-1934). As the tidings multiply, they eventually intend to exit the wicker house; and here, the dreamer beholds an astounding hybridization of tidings, which Katherine Zieman, in a different context, identifies as the "the raw materials for contemporary vernacular fiction" (85). Two tidings reach an opening at the same time, wanting to leave the labyrinth first. Having to decide who should go first, the tidings decide to compromise; they shall leave the wicker cage together, as *one* tiding: "I shal never fro the go, / But be thyn owne sworen brother! /

We wil medle us ech withother, / That no man, be they never so wrothe, / Shal han on [of us] two, but bothe / At ones [...]" (3.2100-2105). Echoing the Platonic-Boethian conception of concord, according to which sounds either desire to blend harmoniously or go separate ways (Boethius, *De inst. mus.* 1.28; Plato, *Timaeus* 67 a-c), what ensues in the dreamer's memory is the problematic concord of two radically discordant things, which, as Chaucer knew from translating Boethius, should never go together: "fals and soth compouned / Togeder fle for oon tydynge" (3.2108-2109; *Boece* 2 metr. 8). Truth and falsehood chime together in a way that precludes the possibility of separating one from the other. This is surely a form of consonance, but one that could not be more disharmonious on an ethical level. As such, the new tiding is released back into the world, first traveling towards Fama, whose arbitrary allocation of reputation suddenly emerges as a highly rational act: if literary-historiographical narratives are always already inherently true and false at the same time, how could Fama's judgment be anything but arbitrary.

More importantly, the noisy hybridizing of literary-historiographical discourse retroactively legitimizes the kind of poetical innovation witnessed in the dreamer's initial fabrication of a new narrative of Dido and Aeneas, the result of disharmonious images perceived by the senses.[3] The poetological points raised by the poem ultimately find a correlative on the plot level, the plot of the poem representing itself as the product of such a theory of poetry: it enacts the processes it describes, offering an aesthetical theory as a work of art. In this *ars poetica*, lower cognitive processes associated with the imagination become central and cause the transformation of ventricular processes – more precisely, a shift in the valuation of these processes – in which the noise resulting from contradictory perceptions is the cornerstone of his poetics, is his poetry. Such an authorization of the author's mental topography in turn (because of the inevitably circularity of the poem's argument) authorizes a mode of authorship that acknowledges the witnessed cacophony inherent in discourse; it is endemic

---

3 As my reading of the *House of Fame* anticipates, I would push the recombinative nature of Chaucer's poetry further. What I believe is at stake in Chaucerian poetics is the way in which contradictions and the partial incoherence of authoritative accounts push poets towards re-imagining things with a difference. The question as to the competing Virgilian and Ovidian accounts of Aeneas and Dido in the *House of Fame* ultimately cannot be resolved by an either/or, but by both: both accounts can be used for the making of new narratives, notably narratives *like* the *House of Fame* itself. Such disharmonies cannot and should not yield to harmony; imaginational noise is what poetry is.

to the structure of an individual conceptual apparatus in the filtering of the world through experience.

The Chaucerian poetics of imaginational noise is not restricted to the *House of Fame*; it is tangible in many other of Chaucer's works, especially (but not exclusively) in his dream visions. The *Parlement of Foules*, which, in the light of Cooper's dating of the *House of Fame*, possibly predates the *House of Fame*, anticipates the poetological issues raised in the later poem. Here, too, the audience travels through the ventricles. While the *Parlement* certainly seems more harmonious on account of its initial experience of divine harmony and its numerology (seven-line stanzas added up to a seven hundred-line poem, for which see Chamberlain), a second representation of the seven planets and nine spheres qua the number of debating birds, ultimately undercuts visions of harmony, in this case in a context that is arguably more political than poetical. Politics also plays into Chaucer's last representation of the three ventricles in a dream vision, in the Prologue to the *Legend of Good Women*, which passes judgment not only on the poet's own oeuvre, but does so by means of recapitulating, evaluating, and reaffirming Chaucer's poetics of cognitive dissonance.

3

The Prologue to the *Legend of Good Women* is a dream vision that reflects more explicitly on authorship and the role of imagination than Chaucer's other dream visions. Like other dream visions, it does so by means of taking the audience – and the dreamer – through the ventricles of the brain, continuing Chaucer's authorial mind game. More explicitly than the *House of Fame*, the Prologue privileges personal experience and the innovative over-layering of images rather than seemingly authoritative accounts, significantly and retroactively legitimating Chaucer's literary output. The Prologue to the *Legend of Good Women* depicts only the first two of the three ventricles, namely, *imaginatio* and *logica*; the legends themselves stand in for the writer's memory. The role of experience is emphasized from the outset, when the narrator observes that while people frequently tell one another that there is joy in heaven and pain in hell, no-one has ever returned from either heaven or hell to tell the tale: "That ther nis noon dwellyng in this contree / That eyther hath in hevene or helle ybe, / Ne may of hit noon other weyes witen / But as he hath herd seyd or founde it writen; / For by assay [=experience] ther may no man it preve" (F 5-9). Precluded from knowing certain things by experience, one is left with books, "Thurgh whiche that olde thinges ben in minde, / [...] / That tellen of these olde appreved stories" (F 18-21; for experience vs. book knowledge, see Burlin). Book knowledge is thus equated with (cultural) memory – and as adequate substitute for subjective experience. Immediately, the poem underscores the traditional evaluation of memory as *the* repository of religious, historical, personal knowledge (F 20-28), a world with which the narrator is intimately familiar.

Echoing the eagle's allegation in the *House of Fame* that Geffrey spends too much time with his books, the Prologue's narrator – who obviously stands in for Chaucer again (e.g., Payne 202) – also spends too much time reading. Except, he tells the audience, when May comes around. Then, he willingly turns away from his books and yields to pleasures afforded by the senses. The poem now emphasizes those processes of cognition associated with the first ventricle: the dreamer listens to the birds, he enjoys the sight of the flowers. The narrator is partial to a particular kind of flower which is, however, described with a curious local inflection, as the daisies "in our toun" (F 43). No one, the audience learns, loves daisies more hotly than the narrator (F 59, not in G). Unfortunately, his English, he says, is not nearly good enough to adequately praise his daisies. Accordingly, he can only assert his poetic belatedness. The field is already well tilled, the harvest brought in: "For wel I wot that ye han her-biforn / Of makyng ropen, and lad awey the corn, / And I come after, glenyng here and there, / And am ful glad yf I may fynde an ere / Of any goodly word that ye han left" (F 73-77). The passage has traditionally been read as registering Chaucer's debt to contemporary poets in the marguerite-tradition, for instance, Machaut's *Dit de la marguerite* (Chaucer's indebtedness and transformation of this tradition is discussed by Percival 23-42). Daisies, that is, can be found in other towns, too, even though they might receive a different literary treatment. Chaucer does more than simply reference French predecessors, though, insofar as he highlights his deviation from and transformation of tradition. First of all, he rather conventionally compares the writing of poetry with field work, the agricultural work characteristic of classical and medieval households, of *oikonomia*. Second, since the poet is imagining himself as searching for left-overs on fields that have already been tilled by others, poetry becomes a form of parasitical household management. Third, the praise of his predecessors' poetry and the acknowledgement of their authority is quickly undermined, given the poet's observation that *there are* left-overs. His predecessors may have harvested the crops, but not very thoroughly: they are very neglectful householders (which, following the logic of the *House of Fame*, is not an undesirable state after all). Finally, the poet implicitly brings into play the work of the inner wits. On the one hand, as Hoffman has observed (134-137, with reference to Carruthers), the passage discusses flowers in terms of books, in terms of memory; on the other hand, the poet emphasizes the work of sense perception: he *sees* what others have left over, and what has been left over are the homophone *ears*, both bringing the poet back into the realm of *imaginatio*, while at the same time anticipating the transformative nature of his noisy poetry.

First, though, the dreamer reasserts that he has to write poetry, however ineptly. In the course thereof he provides the audience with a poetic ideal of service which he appropriates simultaneously as a viable cognitive model. He writes in the service of love and, therefore, in the service of the flower, "Whom that I serve as I have wit or myght," who is the clear light in an otherwise dark world (F 83). The daisy, as has been anticipated by the dreamer's narrow focus on a particular kind of flower, becomes all consuming, becomes the center of his mental household. She becomes "The maistresse of my wit, and nothing I." The relationship between the flower and him is thus represented in terms of the dreamer's devoted courtly service which is also – as in the *House of Fame* – musically inflected: his service and devotion is so knit in the bond of the flower "as an harpe obeieth to the hond / And maketh it soune after his fyngerynge." In this manner, the daisy brings forth from the poet's heart "Swich vois" as she pleases (F 88, 90-91, 93). In terms of cognition, this may seem to figure a harmonious relationship between inner and outer wits, albeit a circular relationship in which the daisy, insofar as she assumes control of the poet's mental household, controls what he sees and, more problematically, what he writes, leaving the poet bereft of his (authorial) identity: "Be ye my gide and lady sovereyne! / As to myn erthly god to yow I calle […]" (F 94-95). With this adoption of the daisy as his sovereign, the narrator returns to the argument with which he set out, emphasizing the primacy of book knowledge and belief – belief in "autoritees" in the G-version – over the evidence furnished by the external wits (F 99-100; G 83).

Yet, the experience of the daisy is, perhaps on account of his adoption of the daisy as his guide or the etymology of the daisy as the eye of the day (F 184), overwhelmingly dominated by references to sense perception. As the narrator sets out to gaze upon the flower, kneeling in front of it, the primacy of sense experience is reasserted by means of the description of the narrator's devotion, his immediate experience of the odors, the temperate sun, the small birds, who sing in defiance of the fowler who did not catch them. Other birds are singing lays of love, echoing the bird song and the debates in the *Parlement*. Everything ultimately gives way to harmony as the "tydif," a notoriously inconstant bird, asks for forgiveness for his "unkyndenesse." This inconstant bird anticipates the poet's trespassing against the God of Love on account of his alleged misrepresentation of the trespassing of "unkynde" Criseyde (F 153, TC 4.16). The birds' final "acord" (F 159) leads the dreamer to an allegorizing of their lives: from Danger through Pity to Mercy and Courtesy. Finally, all are singing of "oon acord" (F 169), which recalls the allegorizing of the *Roman de la Rose* (the second work criticized by Cupid) as well as the disharmonious birds in the *Parlement*. In sum, the dreamer's witnessing of his own adoption of the daisy as a sovereign imagines a first movement back-and-forth between the first and second ventricle: from the ventricle of *imaginatio* the image of the daisy imprints itself more deeply in the poet's brain, assuming control of his mental activities as well as his literary output, ultimately leading to a harmony, the fragility of which is anticipated already by the preceding unruliness of the birds and the image of the parasitical poet.

As a harmonious day ends, the dreamer, with the image of the flower (literally impressed) on his mind, goes home, has a bed prepared for him in his little garden, and falls asleep. In his dream, he finds himself in a meadow by the daisy he worshipped during the day. He also notices the coming of the God of Love and his queen, who appears "ryght as a dayesye" (F 218). In the ventricle of *logica*, the narrator's daytime view of the daisy is abstracted as a symbolic representation of Alceste. As he was struck by the beauty of the daisy during the day, he is now struck by the beauty of Queen Alceste in his dream. He is so impressed, in fact, that he spontaneously sings a song, replicating his daytime attempt to praise the daisy and possibly conflated with the (not entirely) harmonious bird song.⁴ At this point, however, the replication of the waking adoption of the daisy and the dreamer's concurrent adoption of the daisy as his sovereign does not work out anymore. While Alceste admittedly retains control of the dreamer's destiny, this control is not as harmonious as figured during the day. The contradictions and disagreements that affected the dreamer's imagination and memory in the *House of Fame* are now transferred to the ventricle of judgment and evaluation, in which contradictory estimations and misreadings begin to multiply.

Once the dreamer has finished his song of praise (in rhyme royal stanzas that again anticipate the ensuing problems with the *Troilus*), he notices how nineteen women kneel down and sing the praises of the daisy. The entire household of the God of Love appears to literally crowd the poet's second ventricle. Worse still, he is discovered by the God of Love, who sees him sitting by "his" daisy. Initially self-confident, perhaps on account of the foregoing devotion to the daisy queen, the dreamer asserts his own identity "Sir, it am I" (F 314), but is immediately confronted with the God of Love's wrath. The God of Love looks upon Chaucer as his enemy, who slanders his court, who hinders his followers in their devotion with works such as Chaucer's translation of the *Roman de la Rose*, which he offered without a gloss (i.e. without the accompanying hermeneutic; for Cupid's possible problems with the *Roman*, see Percival 101-103; Minnis, *Fallible Authors* 33), and his misrepresentation of Criseyde which causes men to trust women less, who are really true as steel. In the G version of the Prologue, this passage includes the God's question as to whether Chaucer really was unable to find "in thy mynde, / Ne in alle they bokes" stories of good women (G 270-271).

Both, the allegation that Chaucer misrepresented women and the question as to whether he did not have access, in his memory, to stories of good women, naturally come as a surprise for the dreamer, especially in the light of his previous adoption of Alceste as his "guide". The complaint also comes as a surprise

---

4 One of the main differences between the F and G versions of the Prologue concerns what occurs within and outside the dream. In G, the song of the birds is already part of the dream, which would explain why the dreamer understands what they sing (Kiser 22n; Hoffman 102). In F, it appears as if the narrative is more consistent with the replication of how the waking "images" are transformed and judged in the central ventricles: here, the birdsong witnessed before falling asleep transforms into the dreamer's praise of Alceste.

for readers of Chaucer. The God's judgment, though, brings into play several aspects of a Chaucerian poetics as it articulates itself in the *House of Fame* and the *Parlement*, and as it is practiced also in works like *Troilus and Criseyde*. What is at stake is the poet's exploitation of the aesthetic potential of over-layered, contradictory images, the poetics of noise advanced and epitomized in many of Chaucer's works. Chaucer's characterization of Criseyde is precisely the result of the exploitation of disharmonious, incongruent images. Chaucer, that is, tells a completely new story of Criseyde, whose name was blemished long before Chaucer penned his Troy story (roughly at the same time as the *House of Fame*, for which see Cooper). As such, Criseyde becomes the locus of poetic invention in a modern sense, insofar as Chaucer imagines and explores Criseyde's feelings and thoughts – aspects on which tradition is remarkably silent. His presentation of Criseyde's inner life does not ensue by means of a complete abandonment of tradition. Audiences, that is, are to imagine two Criseydes. Readers have to reconcile two contradictory views of the Greco-Trojan heroine that complicate ethical judgments, prompting a disharmony which, as Chaucer suggest time and again in his dream poetry, is hardly avoidable. As the God of Love chides Chaucer for his very subjective representation of Criseyde, the double image of Criseyde emerges forcefully within the cell of judgment. The God of Love condemns Chaucer for not offering the view on Criseyde that Chaucer actually does offer. This suggests, not without an ironic twist, that the God of Love would have legitimated the transgression against tradition that Chaucer is, in fact, guilty of.

The effect of the God of Love's judgment is primarily that the two images of Criseyde are presented and offered for the poet and the audience to judge. The image of Chaucer's Criseyde is thus placed in a poetological context that underscores the poet's earlier elaborations on poetic fame, in general, and his poetic fame, in particular. Chaucer's illusionary desire to have his own reputation in his hands (as voiced in the Palace of Fama) is again challenged, since the passage confirms all of the Poet's worries offered at the end of the *Troilus*: he worries that he will be misunderstood, that his reputation will be tarnished (just like Criseyde worries about the loss of her reputation for a different kind of transgression). In other words, Chaucer uses "his" Criseyde as a means to investigate questions of literary authorship and authorial invention (for an extended argument, see Keller, "Chaucer und Boccaccio"), the kind of noisy authorial invention that constitutes the *House of Fame* and *Troilus and Criseyde*. A kind of noisy invention, however, that may lead to misperceptions and misjudgments of his works. Ironically, the poet's adopted sovereign, Queen Alceste, similarly misreads Chaucer's work, even though she seems to defend the poet by rehearsing numerous reasons as to what may have caused Chaucer's transgression.

Alceste's first line of defense is the God's household in the framework of which Chaucer's literary activity takes place. Chaucer's fellow courtiers, she observes, may have spread rumors about Chaucer, "Ryght after hire ymagynacioun" and possibly on account of their "envie" (F 355-356), which recalls the disagreement between the authorities listed in the *House of Fame* (see above). Alceste's defense also underscores the arbitrary workings of humor and literary fame as outlined in the *House of Fame*. It further leads to the less flattering assumption that the authorities have not actually read Chaucer's books. Alternatively, as Alceste allows, Chaucer may have acted upon the bonds of patronage, which inevitably constrain literary activity: "Or him was boden maken thilke tweye / Of som persone, and durste yt nat withseye" (F 366-367). This figures the work of literature precisely in terms of the relationship the dreamer imagined earlier, when he accepted Alceste as the sovereign. Now that she rules (almost) authoritatively, one cannot miss the irony that Alceste is about to impose a task on Chaucer that he dares not "withseye." And she imposes this task, not without telling the God of Love (who is sometimes read as a representation of Richard II; *Riverside* 1064n) not to act tyrannically, but mercifully towards the poet. After all, the poet is an important asset in the King's portfolio (F 380). On balance, Alceste concludes, Chaucer has furthered the God of Love's reputation: "Al be hit that he kan nat wel endite, / Yet hath he maked lewed folk delyte / To serve yow, in preysinge of your name" (F 414-416). To underscore just how important his service was, she lists Chaucer's works, the products of his noisy imagination. The closing argument is probably most persuasive, since the surprised God of Love is willing to heed her advice. In a sense, her assertion that, his transgression notwithstanding, Chaucer has furthered his name, is in keeping with Chaucer's view of a kind of poetry that does not strive to represent supernal numbers and ultimate truths, but operates on a lower level. Transgressions in the realm of poetic discourse, Alceste's argument suggests, may not be nice, but they still serve the right end, anyway.

The two instances of irony of the judgment passed on Chaucer mentioned before – poet condemned for something he did not do; contradictory defenses offered by Alceste – are topped by a third, as the dreamer steps up to the plate to defend himself: he will always gratefully remember Alceste's intervention, but really, he is not guilty of any "trespas" (F 463). Whatever he says of Criseyde or the *Rose*: "what so myn auctour mente, / Algate, God woot, yt was myn entente, / To forthren trouthe in love and yt cheryce, / And to ben war fro falsnesse and fro vice / By swich ensample; this was my menynge" (F 470-474). The poet who defied tradition in creating his Criseyde now wants Alceste and his audience to believe that he had the opposite in mind. In effect, he argues for a poetics that analogizes his devotion to Alceste and his devotion to his sources, muting his earlier, more accurate description of a parasitic poetry: no offence, he says, I merely meant to imitate. It is, naturally, the kind of poetry favored by Alceste, who commands him to retell legends of betrayed women, year in, year out, copied from the books the God of Love knows are at the dreamer's disposal. He should write poetry that so transparently aligns source and translation, poet and patron that Chaucer most likely "abandon[ed] the project before it was complete" (Cannon 47; possibly, Chaucer offers a different, more noisy hermeneutic to read the legends [see below]). Unsurprisingly, then, the God of Love brings the judgment back to Chaucer's memory, albeit with an interesting inflection that calls into question the very task the dreamer has been set: "Hastow nat in a book, lyth in thy cheste, / The grete goodness of the quene Alceste, / That turned was into a dayesye" (F 510-512; for chests as memory, see Carruthers 37-38). Certainly, Chaucer was familiar with the story of Alceste, but the transformation into a daisy appears to be Chaucer's invention (*Riverside* 1065n; Percival esp. 49-55, with reference to faculty psychology and literary invention). More importantly, Chaucer's version of Alceste, that is, the Prologue to the *Legend of Good Women* itself, is highly innovative, insofar as it is a new story of Alceste's transformation, even if Alceste emerges in the end as a problematic "kalender" of steadfastness (F 542), presumably in contradistinction to Criseyde, whose "unkind" actions and words are seen by

Troilus in terms of a "kalendes of chaunge" (TC 5.1634); the shallowness of her defense of the poet certainly puts her in a less flattering light.

Where the waking thoughts of the narrator in the first part of the Prologue to the *Legend of Good Women* appear to present a rather straightforward, if somewhat circular mental processing of images, the judgment scene, which begins to replicate the daytime setting, ultimately demonstrates the impossibility of harmonious relationships of service (input-output, source-translation, poet-patron) and unfolds a panoply of contradictory readings, of ever-increasing ironies. To unravel the complex network of intertwined discourses and intra- and intertextual references lies beyond the scope of this essay. In terms of Chaucer's conceptualizing and paralleling of mental and poetic work, however, some preliminary conclusions can be formulated.

In the Prologue, Chaucer shifts the disharmonies that overwhelm the dreamer's imagination and memory in the *House of Fame* to the Prologue's second ventricle, in which, fittingly, the poet's own works become judged (or rather: become judged by the poet himself). As opposed to the *House of Fame*, the second ventricle is presented with (relatively) unambiguous images to process. And yet, the minor disturbances witnessed initially – especially, the poet's view of parasitic literary work – reassert themselves rather disharmoniously in the realm of judgment. As in the *House of Fame*, literary quality alone emerges to be no sufficient basis for the judgment of literary work. Literary judgment is based on subjective *imaginatio*, matched by the operations of *logica* against that which is stored in memory, even if it is the kind of disorganized memory as depicted in the *House of Fame*. This entails the inevitability of misrepresentation and misperception. Such misreadings, the poem suggests (along with Alceste) are ethically perhaps less problematic in the domain of poetry than in other domains of life, at least for a poet like Chaucer who works unconstrained by the bonds of patronage. If one depends on patronage, however, transgressions can have severe consequences, of course. The main point of Chaucer's return to representations of the ventricles towards the end of his career is, I believe, the strategy by which the transfer from images furnished by the faculty of imagination to the faculty of logic and evaluation is figured in the poem, namely, as metamorphosis. Chaucer's reticence to represent metamorphosis on the plot level is well known (Fyler 17; Wetherbee 93; cf. Calabrese 53). In the Prologue, however, the metamorphosis of the daisy into Alceste is not only innovative insofar as Chaucer's ventricle of cognition sets side-by-side flower and queen, but also in terms of the concomitant noise, the ensuing debate and contradictions. Chaucer may present himself as a belated poet, the parasitical poet looking for any "ears" left by others, or as the pedestrian poet as which Alceste describes him; ultimately, the Prologue itself represents Chaucer as a transformative poet, as a writer striving to dissolve harmony into imaginational disharmony, a literary author who seeks out the contradictions inevitably inherent in literary tradition. As the double Criseyde emerges as the bone of contention in the judgment of Chaucer's works, contradictions begin to proliferate in the very mental arena in which contradictions should be eliminated. Literary judgment, Chaucer's last move in his ventricular mind game suggests, should be a matter of the same disharmonies that make good – that is, innovative – poetry in the first place. And perhaps it is with a poetics of cognitive dissonance in mind that the legends proper have to be approached.[5]

About the author

WOLFRAM R. KELLER is Assistant Professor of English at Humboldt University Berlin. His research interests include medieval and early modern English literature, the reception and transformation of antiquity in the nineteenth century, and contemporary Canadian literature. He is author of *Selves & Nations* (2008) and co-editor of several essay collections, most recently *Bi-directionality in the Cognitive Sciences* (with Marcus Callies and Astrid Lohöfer, 2011) and *Europa zwischen Antike und Moderne* (with Claus Uhlig, 2014).

---

5 This essay is part of a larger project that takes on questions of medieval literary authorship at the nexus of faculty psychology, harmony, and economics. For inspiration and valuable feedback, I am indebted to Iris Därmann, Robert Edwards, Andrew James Johnston, Jocelyn Keller, Verena Olejniczak Lobsien, Cornelia Wilde, and, of course, Allan Turner.

Bibliography

BOETHIUS. *Ancii Manlii Torquati Severini Boetii De Institutione Arithmetica Libri Duo: De Institutione Musica Libri Quinque; Accedit Geometria Quae Fertur Boetii*. Ed. Gottfried FRIEDLEIN. Leipzig, 1867.

BUNDY, Murray W. *The Theory of Imagination in Classical and Medieval Thought*. Urbana, IL: University of Illinois Press, 1927.

BURLIN, Robert B. *Chaucerian Fiction*. Princeton, NJ: Princeton University Press, 1977.

BURNLEY, J. D. *Chaucer's Language and the Philosopher's Tradition*. Cambridge: Brewer, 1979.

CALABRESE, Michael A. *Chaucer's Ovidian Arts of Love*. Gainesville, FL: University Press of Florida, 1994.

CANNON, Christopher. "The Lives of Geoffrey Chaucer." *The Yale Companion to Chaucer*. Ed. Seth LERER. New Haven, CT: Yale University Press, 2006. 31-54.

CARRUTHERS, Mary. *The Book of Memory: A Study of Memory in Medieval Culture*. 2nd ed. Cambridge: Cambridge University Press, 2008.

CHAMBERLAIN, David. "Musical Signs and Symbols in Chaucer: Convention and Originality" *Signs and Symbols in Chaucer's Poetry*. Ed. John P. HERMANN and John J. BURKE, Jr. Tuscaloosa, AL: University of Alabama Press, 1981. 43-80.

CHAUCER, Geoffrey. *The Riverside Chaucer*. Gen. ed. Larry D. BENSON. 3rd ed. Boston, MA: Houghton Mifflin, 1987.

COLLETTE, Carolyn P. (ed.). *The Legend of Good Women: Context and Reception*. Cambridge: Brewer, 2006.

COOPER, Helen. "Chaucerian Poetics." *New Readings of Chaucer's Poetry*. Ed. Robert G. BENSON and Susan J. RIDYARD. Cambridge: Brewer, 2003. 31-50.

EDWARDS, Robert R. 1989. *The Dream of Chaucer: Representation and Reflection in the Early Narratives*. Durham, NC: Duke University Press, 1989.

"Ricardian Dreamwork: Chaucer, Cupid and Loyal Lovers." *The Legend of Good Women: Context and Reception*. Ed. Carolyn P. COLLETTE. Cambridge: Brewer, 2006. 59-82.

"Authorship, Imitation, and Refusal in Late-Medieval England." *Medieval and Early Modern Authorship*. Ed. Guillemette BOLENS and Lukas ERNE. Tübingen: Narr, 2011. 51-73.

FUMO, Jamie C. "The God of Love and the Love of God: Palinodic Exchange in the Prologue of the *Legend of Good Women* and the 'Retraction.'" *The Legend of Good Women: Context and Reception*. Ed. Carolyn P. COLLETTE. Cambridge: Brewer, 2006. 157-175.

FYLER, John M. *Chaucer and Ovid*. New Haven, CT: Yale University Press, 1979.

HARVEY, E. Ruth. *The Inward Wits: Psychological Theory in the Middle Ages and the Renaissance*. London: Warburg Institute, 1975.

HOFFMAN, Frank G. *The Dream and the Book: Chaucer's Dream-Poetry, Faculty Psychology, and the Poetics of Recombination*. Unpublished dissertation. Philadelphia, PA: University of Pennsylvania, 2004.

HUIZINGA, Johan. *Homo Ludens: A Study of the Play-Element in Culture*. Boston, MA: Beacon Press, 1950.

KELLER, Wolfram R. "Chaucers Klang(t)räume: Chaucer, Boethius und die Harmonie." *Europa zwischen Antike und Moderne: Beiträge zur Philosophie, Literaturwissenschaft und Philologie*. Ed. Claus UHLIG and Wolfram R. KELLER. Heidelberg: Winter, 2014. 99-124.

"Chaucer und Boccaccio: Literarische Autorschaft zwischen Mittelalter und Moderne." *Giovanni Boccaccio in Europa: Studien zu seiner Rezeption in Spätmittelalter und Früher Neuzeit*. Ed. Achim AURNHAMMER and Rainer STILLERS. Wiesbaden: Harrassowitz, 2014. 265-79.

KISER, Lisa J. *Telling Classical Tales: Chaucer and the "Legend of Good Women."* Ithaca, NY: Cornell University Press, 1983.

KLARER, Mario. "Immaterial Images: Ekphrasis and Medieval Brain Anatomy." Address at the workshop "The Art of Vision – Ekphrasis in Medieval Literature and Culture." Berlin: Free University of Berlin, 26 Feb. 2010.

LOBSIEN, Verena Olejniczak and Eckhard LOBSIEN. *Die unsichtbare Imagination: Literarisches Denken im 16. Jahrhundert*. Munich: Fink, 2003.

LYNCH, Kathryn L. *The High Medieval Dream Vision: Poetry, Philosophy, and Literary Form*. Stanford, CA: Stanford University Press, 1988.

Chaucer's Philosophical Visions. Cambridge: Brewer, 2000.

MACROBIUS. *Commentarii in Somnium Scipionis*. Ed. Jakob WILLIS. Leipzig: Teubner, 1963.

Commentary on the Dream of Scipio. Trans. William Harris STAHL. New York, NY: Columbia University Press, 1952.

MCCORMICK, Betsy. "Remembering the Game: Debating the *Legend's* Women." *The Legend of Good Women: Context and Reception*. Ed. Carolyn P. COLLETTE. Cambridge: Brewer, 2006. 105-131.

MINNIS, Alastair. *Fallible Authors: Chaucer's Pardoner and the Wife of Bath.* Philadelphia, PA: University of Pennsylvania Press, 2008.

Medieval Theory of Authorship: Scholastic Literary Attitudes in the Later Middle Ages. 2nd ed. Philadelphia, PA: University of Pennsylvania Press, 2010.

PATTERSON, Lee. *Chaucer and the Subject of History.* Madison, WI: University of Wisconsin Press, 1991.

PAYNE, Robert O. "Making His Own Myth: The Prologue to Chaucer's *Legend of Good Women.*" *Chaucer Review* 9 (1975): 197-211.

PERCIVAL, Florence. *Chaucer's Legendary Good Women.* Cambridge: Cambridge University Press, 1998.

PLATO, *Timaeus, Critias, Cleitophon, Menexenus, Epistles.* Ed. and trans. R. G. Bury. Cambridge, MA: Loeb Classical Library, 1960.

ROBERTSON, D.W. *A Preface to Chaucer: Studies in Medieval Perspectives.* Princeton, NJ: Princeton University Press, 1962.

SCHEUER, Hans Jürgen. "Bildintensität: Eine imaginationstheoretische Lektüre des Strickerschen Artus-Romans *Daniel von dem Blühenden Tal.*" *Zeitschrift für deutsche Philologie* 124.1 (2005): 23-46.

"Cerebrale Räume: Internalisierte Topographie in Literatur und Kartographie des 12./13. Jahrhunderts (Hereford-Karte, *Straßburger Alexander*)." *Topographien der Literatur: Deutsche Literatur im transnationalen Kontext.* Ed. Hartmut BÖHME. Stuttgart: Metzler, 2005. 12-36.

SCHLESIER, Renate, and Beatrice TRÎNCA (eds.). *Inspiration und Adaptation: Tarnkappen mittelalterlicher Autorschaft.* Hildesheim: Olms, 2008.

TOLKIEN, J.R.R. *The Monsters and the Critics and Other Essays.* Edited by Christopher TOLKIEN. London: HarperCollins, 1983.

TREVISA, John. *On the Properties of Things: John Trevisa's Translation of Bartholomaeus Anglicus "De Proprietatibus Rerum"; A Critical Text.* Ed. M. C. SEYMOUR. 2 vols. Oxford: Clarendon Press, 1975.

TRIGG, Stephanie. *Congenial Souls: Reading Chaucer from Medieval to Postmodern.* Minneapolis, MN: University of Minnesota Press, 2002.

WETHERBEE, Winthrop. *Chaucer and the Poets: An Essay on "Troilus and Criseyde".* Ithaca, NY: Cornell University Press, 1984.

WOLFSON, Harry Austryn. "The Internal Senses in Latin, Arabic, and Hebrew Philosophical Texts." *Harvard Theological Review* 28.2 (1935): 69-133.

ZIEMAN, Katherine. "Chaucer's *Voys.*" *Representations* 60 (1997): 70-91.

Andrew 'Chunky' Liston

Burns's Bogles

Abstract

"Burns's Bogles" is an assessment of the supernatural in Robert Burns's classic poem "Tam o' Shanter". Better known for his treatment of the natural world, Burns nevertheless employs the supernatural at key moments in his poetry, most famously in "Tam o' Shanter". The critical response to his use of the supernatural is broad and very diverse. This paper attempts to steer a course through choppy critical waters avoiding the reefs and shoals of a reductive analysis of the supernatural in a work that defies simplistic interpretation: Burns has an ambivalent relationship to his bogles.

Robert Burns has primarily been celebrated as a poet of the natural world. A survey of the titles of some of his best known works immediately suggests why this might be the case: "To a Mouse", "To a Louse", "Twa Dogs" and "The Banks of Doon" to name but a few. Indeed, according to John Young, his interest in the natural world – with some 2,880 references to landscapes, trees, flowers, birds, the seasons and mammals – exceeds that of any other poet (ix). In addition to this, Burns and his work are often seen as the product of nature. Saying himself in his "Epistle to J. Lapraik", "Gie me a spark o' nature's fire/ That's all the learning I desire" and prefacing his first edition of poems with a profession of rustic innocence (Crawford/MacLachlan 38, 198-199), it is little wonder that in 1786 Henry Mackenzie was to suggest Burns was a natural genius and baptised him the "heaven-taught ploughman" (403). Since Mackenzie's article, Burns criticism has focused on the heavy influence of reality in Burns's writing: he appears to write from experience of the real world and to reveal that real world to his readers. As Carol McGuirk puts it "the shibboleth of Burns criticism continues to be his native (and naïve) earthiness" (xxv). Indeed the links between the biography of the man and his work can be found to be traced even in the work of the few critics who seek to separate the two.[1]

---

1 See for example Carol McGuirk, *Robert Burns and the Sentimental Era*, pp. 150-155.

While this reception remains the standard prism for viewing the Lallans bard, significantly different perspectives have been taken, notably by Carol McGuirk, Raymond Bentman and, more recently, Nigel Leask. In her book *Burns and the Sentimental Era*, McGuirk straight away points out why we cannot commit what C.S. Lewis calls the "personal heresy" of attributing Burns's protagonists' experiences directly to Burns, however much it seems tempting to do so. The artifice in Burns's poetry is plain to see in his occasional use of a first-person female protagonist (McGuirk xix): if the biographers are to be trusted and Burns did not enjoy any Tiresian enlightenment, it would seem odd to claim that Burns only speaks of his own experience when speaking with the voice of a woman. McGuirk's major achievement is the mapping of the contours of influence of the sentimental era on Burns, illustrating that it was a little more than just "a spark o' nature's fire" that informed this particular ploughman. Bentman too has argued that to take Burns at face value is to miss a lot. In the face of the widespread assumption that Burns wrote as he spoke, Bentman stresses the artifice in Burns's language, flagging up the learning that lies behind such a deft interpolation of standard English and Scots (*Burns* 79-86). Leask also writes against the grain in that Burns has generally been seen as a proto-Romantic writer. In his 2010 work *Robert Burns and Pastoral*, Leask posits Burns as an Enlightenment man, tracing the clear imprint of the ideas of improvement on the poet. In doing so, he draws attention to Burns's erudition and subtle engagement with a number of the key discourses of his age.

One key element of Robert Burns's work which also undermines the notion of Burns as simply documenting his immediate environment is the supernatural. While the number of references to supernatural elements is hardly dramatic, and Burns will never be known as a creator of a secondary world, the otherworldly is nonetheless crucial to his poetics. In a much quoted letter to Dr John Moore as early as 1787, Burns himself points out how important the thrill of the spooky was for him.

> In my infant boyish days too, I owed much to an old Maid of my Mother's, remarkable for her ignorance, credulity and superstition. – She had, I suppose, the largest collection in the country of tales and songs concerning devils, ghosts, fairies, brownies, witches, warlocks, spunkies, kelpies, elf-candles, dead-lights, wraiths, apparitions, cantraips, giants, enchanted towers, dragons and other trumpery. – This cultivated the latent seeds of Poesy; but had so strong an effect

on my imagination, that to this hour in my nocturnal rambles, I sometimes keep a sharp look-out in suspicious places; and though nobody can be more skeptical in these matters than I, yet it often takes an effort of Philosophy to shake off these idle terrors. (Crawford/MacLachlan 204)

If we turn to "Tam o' Shanter", widely perceived as one of the finest poems by Burns (R. Crawford 328; Leask 261), we find "the idle terrors" at the heart of the poem: the central action of the poem is the witches' dance and their subsequent chasing of the protagonist through the woods of Alloway. These elements have attracted critical attention: McGuirk reckons that the supernatural in "Tam o' Shanter" is merely "local color" included in order to satisfy Captain Grose (155), a friend of Burns's who was compiling an antiquarian collection and had agreed to include a depiction and description of Kirk Alloway on the condition that Burns provide a suitable story. Nigel Leask bends over backwards in an attempt to realign the superstitious elements in Burns with the Enlightenment (256-275). Furthermore, there are a number of works which treat the supernatural elements at face value, proclaiming their spine-chilling effect on the reader.[2] This paper is conceived as an attempt to analyse the role of the other-worldly in Burns's work as something more than just a cap-doffing towards a publisher. The details in the eleventh stanza of "Tam o' Shanter" of a variety of allegedly real criminal deeds (see Burnet 25-27) alongside the supernatural elements in what nevertheless seems a parodistically long list of horrors lend an edge of realistic horror to the poem. If the references to drunken Charlie breaking his neck, the discovery of a murdered child near to Alloway and Mungo's mother hanging herself had referents in the real world of Burns's contemporary readers, then the poem must have had a frightening side to it. However, to reduce the supernatural simply to a blood-curdling special effect also seems simplistic; nevertheless, there is enough of a frisson of excitement resulting from these elements that the notion of Burns as an Enlightenment man is problematised. Indeed, it would appear that the supernatural is one of a number of ways in which Burns defies categorisation, leaving norms and expectations foundering in his wake.

As one might divine from the introduction to this paper, the central poem when investigating the supernatural in Burns is "Tam o' Shanter", so Burns's "most

---

2 See for example Tom Douglas, *Death, the Devil and Tam o' Shanter*.

iconic and most commemorated poem" (Mackay 27) provides the main focus for this paper. Furthermore, given that the title of this volume includes the notion of "secondary worlds" it seems appropriate to begin with a poem which seems to revolve around the number two. At the heart of "Tam o' Shanter" is the interplay between the dualities, doublings and symmetries in the poem. On the surface level the tale is a kind of parable, finishing with a clearly identifiable moral warning against excessive alcohol consumption and dabbling with hags: after market-day, a farmer named Tam whiles away the evening in a pub. When he finally leaves the cosy pub and sets off on his long ride home, a storm is raging. Whilst passing a ruined church, he chances upon a witches' dance, which he stops to watch. Excited by a nubile young witch in her shirt-tails, Tam lets out a cry upon which the dance stops and our protagonist is chased home, escaping thanks to the nous and speed of his horse, Maggie. However, she unfortunately loses her tail to the leading witch of the chasing "hellish legion" as they cross the river. Some readers of the story argue that the moral should indeed be taken at face value.[3] However, the majority subscribe to the notion that this moral is "a mock moral, a deliberately absurd over-simplification of the meaning of the tale to make it a warning against drinking and wenching" (Daiches 292). On close inspection of the dualities in the poem, it seems a persuasive conclusion, and one can see why it has often been drawn (McGuirk 155; Leask 262; T. Crawford 235; Crawford/MacLachlan xxxii; Robert Burns, in conversation with the author, Kirk Alloway, 11.8.2013).

The most obvious duality – or apparent polarity – in the poem is created through the juxtaposition of the cosy pub scene and the witches' ceilidh in Kirk Alloway. The narrator takes his time to set the pub scene in realistic terms, painting an almost universally and timelessly familiar picture, as has been remarked upon by commentators. It has a clear referent beyond the fictive world. Thomas Crawford has drawn attention to the fact that Burns's job as an exciseman meant that the situation of having a few drinks before a long ride home will have been very familiar to the poet; he suggests that this close knowledge informs "the strain of realism" in his poetry and lends it authority (221). Subsequent to this depiction of a familiar world, we are confronted with an array of supernatural characters – the Devil, warlocks, witches and living corpses – characters who

---

3 See for example Christina Keith, *The Russet Coat*.

we certainly have not come across in real life. As Alexander Fraser Tytler said in a letter to Burns on 12th March 1791:

> In the introductory part, where you paint the character of your hero and exhibit him at the ale-house *ingle*, with his tippling cronies, you have delineated nature with a humour and *naiveté* that would do honour to Matthew Prior; but when you describe the infernal orgies of the witches' Sabbath and the hellish scenery in which they are exhibited, you display a power of imagination that Shakespeare himself could not have exceeded. (Chambers 256)

This juxtaposition is delineated by Burns in a number of ways. Most obvious is the *chiaroscuro* of the atmospheric setting. The pub is warm and bright: "Tam had got planted unco right/ Fast by an ingle bleezing finely [...]/ The storm without might rair and rustle/ Tam did na mind the storm a whistle" (Crawford/MacLachlan 137). While the tempest fails to perturb him in the pub, outside the scene is bleaker and darker: "That hour, o' night's black arch the keystane/ That dreary hour he mounts his beast in/ And sic a night he taks the road in/ As ne'er a poor sinner was abroad in/ The wind blew as twad blawn its last/ The rattling showers rose on the blast [...]/ That night a child would understand/ The Deil had business on his hand." (Crawford/MacLachlan 138).

A further key difference is the gender division. There are admittedly both male and female characters in both scenes, but the pub is overridingly male, with the camaraderie between Souter Johnny and Tam at the heart of the picture, while at the centre of the action in the ruined church are the female witches, albeit with the devil on the bagpipes in the background.

It would seem therefore that the real world is a male domain and the supernatural world female. This buys into a long tradition of seeing women as connected with the supernatural, and indeed it has been suggested that Burns is exploiting "an acute fear of the typically female witch[, which] remained very present in 18th-century folk and religious culture" (Mackay 34). The sexual overtones of the poem are at their most obvious here. The witches gradually strip as the dance progresses and the Devil's efforts on the bagpipes are decidedly suggestive: "Even Satan glowr'd and fidg'd fu' fain/ And hotched and blew wi' might and main" (Crawford/MacLachlan 141). Couple the suggestiveness of these lines with the knowledge that the antiquarian Grose had included an entry on bagpiping in his *Classical Dictionary of the Vulgar Tongue* saying a metaphorical usage existed which was too lascivious to explain (Leask 268) and one can see why Raymond Bentman goes as far as to say that, "Satan is in a frenzy of sexual desire" (*Burns* 133). Given that in the 18th century even the sight of an ankle could be considered licentious (Harvey 21), the inclusion of a near-naked witch puts "Tam o' Shanter" on the borders of pornography. This too ties into widespread superstitions about women, whose sexual insatiability was linked to the supernatural in the popular imagination (Mackay 34).

So far, so evil: not only do we have a congregation of servants of Satan in a church, but they are dancing – something which the Church of Scotland saw as sinful in itself – and what is more, there is a whiff of fornication in the air. On the surface, the message about the supernatural (and the female) seems clear.

The split between the supernatural and the real world is also underpinned by the duality of the narrative voice. On the one hand, we encounter an ironised narrator who apostrophises Tam at regular intervals throughout the narrative, giving him retrospective advice and finally trotting out the trite moral at the end: in stanza three, for example, he says, "*O Tam*! Hadst thou but been sae wise/ As ta'en thy ain wife *Kate's* advice"; in stanza fifteen, "Now *Tam*, O *Tam*! had thae been queans,/ A' plump and strapping in their teens"; again in stanza twenty, "Ah, Tam! Ah, Tam! thou'll get thy fairin!/ In hell they'll roast thee like a herrin!" (Crawford/MacLachlan 136, 140, 141). On the other hand, rather than condemning the crapulence in Ayr, there seems to be another narrative voice in the poem, which remains generally close to Tam and depicts the scene in the pub in a largely favourable light, as we have seen. Furthermore, the witches' ceilidh scene is recounted with mounting excitement, expressing the thrill Tam experiences in observing the dance. It has been noted that Burns is on the fine line between "Gothic horror and nimble glee" here (Crawford/MacLachlan xxxii). The rhythm accelerates through the simple method of the repetition of adjectives in the comparative form: "The piper loud and louder blew/ The dancers quick and quicker flew". Furthermore, an alliterative symmetry seems to emerge – the witches "reel'd […] set […] crossed […] cleekit […] swat […] reekit" – creating a palindromic pattern RSCCSR. It all leads up to the climax of the scene when Tam cannot contain his excitement any longer and yells out "'Weel done, Cutty-sark!'" (Crawford/MacLachlan 141). The fact that this is the protagonist's only line of the whole poem adds narrative emphasis to his yell, suggesting that Tam has sided with the dancers. It is only once the chase is on that the know-it-all narrator resorts to his beseeching sententious tone ("Ah, Tam! Ah, Tam!").

Ostensibly, we have a split: we seem to have two points of view in the narrative perspective. This duality is reinforced by instances of doubling in the poem. For example, in the first lines of the poem Burns primes his reader for this kind of doubling through simple repetition: "When chapman billies leave the street/ And drouthy *neebors, neebors* meet, [...] Whare sits our sulky sullen dame/ *Gathering* her brows like *gathering* storm," (Crawford/MacLachlan 136; my emphasis).

The clarity of the duality in the narrative position is muddied, however, by a number of key aspects of the poem. Firstly, in the opening stanza the proliferation of references to the first person plural not only underlines the feeling of camaraderie generated in the scene, but also ties the narrator into the jolly "bousing at the nappy" (Crawford/MacLachlan 136). He may stand back from Tam's capers every now and again but essentially he is caught up in them. Indeed, the question arises of when precisely the narrative perspective actually moves from the generally participatory to the more judgemental. The ambiguity increases when we examine just what our sententious narrator says: while he rounds off the poem with a warning ("Whene'er to drink you are inclin'd/, Or cutty-sarks run in your mind, / Think ye may buy the joys o'er dear/ Remember Tam o' Shanter's mare" (Crawford/MacLachlan 142), he is clearly guilty of the same inclination towards voyeurism as Tam. In stanza fifteen, he says that if the women had been more attractive he too would have played the Peeping Tom/ Tam – in fact, he says he would have taken his trousers off. The narrator thus proves himself to be a hypocrite.

This element of voyeurism may also be perceived to extend beyond the text: the use of "we" and "us" in the opening lines not only includes the narrator, but the reader too. Furthermore, the simple act of reading such a titillating tale bordering on the pornographic, at least by 18th-century publishing standards, could also be equated as a type of voyeurism. If we side with the narrator and agree with his moral, then we too are hypocrites. With this sleight of hand

Burns reveals the Tam in everyone and, for the attentive reader, the hypocrite in most of us.

Burns undermines the duality in further subtle ways. One recurrent motif in his work is the bee (Young 181). In Tam o' Shanter, bees are mentioned twice in quite different situations; this again initially seems to underline the dichotomy in the poem. They are used to describe the happy scene in the pub: "As bees flee hame with lades o' treasure/ The minutes wing'd their way wi' pleasure" (Crawford/MacLachlan 137). However, they are also used to describe the angry reaction of the witches when they discover the Peeping Tam: "As bees bizz out with angry fyke/ When plundering herds assail their byke" (Crawford/MacLachlan 141). As Thomas Crawford notes, "the continuity of the imagery serves to reinforce the imaginative connexion" between the supernatural and pleasure (225). By means of this image pattern, Burns suggests links between the supernatural and the real, too.

The symmetry generated by these apian similes can be found elsewhere in the poem too. For example, the narrator's urge to undress, which has already been mentioned, directly prefigures the undressing of the witches. A desire from the real world foreshadows an action in the supernatural one. Furthermore, there is a symmetry to be found in the hosts of the two party scenes: in the pub, the only female character is the landlady; at the heart of the female scene in the church is the male devil. What is more, both are charged with sexual energy: the implications of the devil's piping have been dealt with above; the landlady also indulges in "favours, secret, sweet and precious" with Tam (Crawford/MacLachlan 137). Just as the narrator's wish to flash is given in the conditional, these favours are not made explicit. In this way, the urge for licentiousness is downplayed in areas where it seems almost *de rigueur*. A little flirting is part and parcel of the generally positively depicted tavern scene. Thus Burns deftly employs symmetries to draw the careful reader's attention to the fact that the hedonistic pleasures depicted in the church, which might cause moral outrage, are in fact also present, if not so flagrantly, in what is considered by the moral-making narrator as acceptable.

Perhaps the most obvious embodiment of the stultifying aspect of morality is Tam's wife, Kate. The lines with which the spouse is introduced quickly disabuse anybody who might have thought married life would be celebrated in this poem: "Whare sits our sulky sullen dame/ Gathering her brows like gathering storm/ Nursing her wrath to keep it warm." The limits of conjugality are another identifiable polarity within the poem: Tam's general direction is from a situation with an eased moral code – the pub – via the witches' dance over the River Doon to his home. Indeed, it has been suggested that the witches' chase is a trope representing Tam's guilty conscience. The repeated references that the narrator makes to her advice to Tam could be read as the occasional flashes of conscience in a mind that is otherwise focused on guilty pleasures.

Underlying the symmetries outlined above is the Calvinist notion that pleasures are bound up in some way with evil. The image of the devil presented in the poem also relates to this. William Montgomerie puts it as follows:

> Auld Nick's place in the poem is significantly in the Kirk, though in opposition to it. [...] He is part of the human personality suppressed by Calvinism, Burns the poet and fornicator, the creator of music, the inspirer of dancing (the Kirk for centuries discouraged dancing) summing up in himself all the elements in the Scotsman that the Kirk [...] has suppressed. He is "a touzie tyke", the animal in us. (79)

We have already seen that the dance of the witches seems to be presented in a generally positive light – our protagonist is so impressed that he has to cry out his praise, after all – and this is true for the Devil in Burns's work too. In his "Address to the Deil", the devil is a familiar figure more than a horrifying one. The poem opens with a range of nicknames, something which in itself suggests a level of familiarity or intimacy: "Auld Hornie, Satan, Nick or Clootie" and finishes on a similar note – one of sympathy for Satan in his hell: "But fare-you-weel, auld Nickie-ben!/ O wad ye tak a thought an' men'!/ Ye aiblins might – I dinnae ken – / Still hae a stake – / I'm wae to think upo' yon den,/ Ev'n for your sake! (Crawford/MacLachlan 71, 74). The Devil is not entirely an enemy then.

Like the Devil, who seems to hover between the horrible and the familiar in Burns, the witches – even if they chase Tam and maim his horse – clearly also have positive merits above and beyond their sexual appeal. For example, they frolic with patriotic dances: "Nae cotillion brent new frae *France*/ But hornpipes, jigs, strathspeys and reels," (Crawford/MacLachlan 139). This unobtrusive patriotic note sounded by the representatives of the supernatural chimes with the epigraph of the poem, which is taken from the Scots translation of *The Aneid* by the medieval writer Gawin Douglas: "*Of Brownies and of Bogillis full is this buke*" (Crawford/MacLachlan 136). The choice of a nation-building text as backdrop coupled with the fact that it is the Scots version quoted also contributes to the patriotic undertone. And once again a link is made between the supernatural and patriotism (brownies and bogles being supernatural beings in Scottish folklore). Given the clear strand of patriotism to be found elsewhere in his work, for Burns to demonise it here would be highly anomalous. Instead, the understated patriotic tone also adds to the rehabilitation of the witches.

One final point to be made concerning Burns's use of the supernatural concerns the publishing history. As mentioned above, the poem was written for one of Francis Grose's antiquarian publications to accompany an entry on Kirk Alloway. As such, it is a footnote – something to add native colour to the piece. Burns submitted two prose versions which he said were folk tales before submitting his poem, which as such is already one remove from the original. Further complicating matters, "Tam o' Shanter" gives a description of a witches' sabbath which is uncannily close to the description of one in a previous antiquarian publication of Grose's (Leask 271-272). While the supernatural and the eery setting in the poem provide enough of a frisson of the sublime to fulfill that Romantic role, the knowledge that the native colour is referring back to a publication aiming to document native colour allows us to see that the supernatural in this poem is not all that it seems. If we can understand antiquarianism as broadly belonging to the spirit of the Enlightenment in that it seeks to catalogue and systematise a body of knowledge, this little joke of Burns to his publisher (and it is unlikely that anyone else got it until Nigel Leask's painstaking reading of Grose) can be seen as a subversion of the spirit of the Enlightenment, which is here cataloguing and systematising itself.

To conclude, Burns uses the supernatural in "Tam o' Shanter" for many ends. It works on the superficial level as a special effect, creating a certain excited energy in the poem. But if we look more closely, lurking in the mirk of the kirk, we also find a positive celebration of what the supernatural represents. That seems to be in part elements of the human psyche with which the Calvinist morality of Burns's day took umbrage. Among these elements, pleasure figures highly. By using a viewer of the viewer – the narrator observing Tam, the voyeur – Burns gives the poem a self-referential dimension, creating parallels with the act of reading the poem. Once we have identified the moral as a mock moral, we, as readers, are obliged to ask ourselves to what extent the hypocrisy delineated transcends the borders of the text: is the hypocrisy apparent in the sliding values of the narrator also our own? While hypocrisy is quite clearly at the heart of Burns's unpublishable "Holy Willy's Prayer" and is even personified in "The Holy Fair", in "Tam o' Shanter" Burns relies on his readers positively appreciating the supernatural in order that this central theme of his work emerges. If the supernatural here is a catalyst to the liberation from religious hypocrisy, it also has a liberating function for women: with the exception of Kate, Tam's wife, the females in the poem – from the landlady to the witches to Maggie – are all portrayed largely positively. The repositioning of the supernatural comes hand in hand with a re-assessment of the negative associations of female insatiability. Finally and perhaps most significantly, if we regard the publication history of the poem, we can identify an element of self-irony in Burns's use of the supernatural in "Tam o' Shanter": through the reference to Grose's own publication, Burns not only strikes an ironic stance towards his own witches, but also mocks the Enlightenment endeavour of universal classification and in so doing liberates his subject matter from the strictures of categorisation.

About the author

ANDREW 'CHUNKY' LISTON is a lecturer in English at Friedrich Schiller University, Jena. He was raised in Edinburgh and attended Durham University, the Humboldt University in Berlin, Zurich University and the University of St Andrews. He is currently working on a book which investigates the work of Robert Burns from an ecological perspective.

Bibliography

BENTMAN, Raymond. *Robert Burns*. Boston: Twayne Publishers, 1987.

— "Burns's Use of Scottish Diction." *Critical Essays on Robert Burns*. Carol McGuirk (ed.). New York: G.K. Hall and Co., 1998. 79-94.

BURNET, John. *Robert Burns and the Hellish Legion*. Edinburgh: National Museums of Scotland, 2009.

CHAMBERS, Robert (ed.). *The Life and Works of Robert Burns*. 4 vols. Edinburgh: Waverley, 1896.

CRAWFORD, Robert. *The Bard*. London: Jonathan Cape, 2009.

— and Christopher MACLACHLAN (eds.). *The Best Laid Schemes: Selected Poetry and Prose of Robert Burns*. Edinburgh: Polygon, 2009.

CRAWFORD, Thomas. *Burns: A Study of the Poems and Songs*. Edinburgh: Cannongate Academic, 1994 (first published 1964).

DAICHES, David. *Robert Burns*. New York: Rinehart & Co., 1950.

DOUGLAS, Tom. *Death, the Devil and Tam o' Shanter*. Hove: The Book Guild, 2002.

HARVEY, A. D. *Sex in Georgian England: Attitudes and Prejudices from the 1720s to the 1820s*. London: Phoenix Press, 2001.

KEITH, Christina. *The Russet Coat*. Hale: London, 1956.

LEASK, Nigel. *Robert Burns and Pastoral: Poetry and Improvement in Late Eighteenth-Century Scotland*. Oxford: Oxford University Press, 2010.

MACKAY, Pauline Anne. "Objects of Desire: Robert Burns the 'Man's Man' and Material Culture." *Anglistik: International Journal of English Studies* 23.3 (September 2012): 27-39.

MACKENZIE, Henry. "Extraordinary Account of Robert Burns the Ayrshire Ploughman; with Extracts from his Poems." *The Lounger* (1786): 396-405.

McGUIRK, Carol. *Robert Burns and the Sentimental Era*. East Linton: Tuckwell, 1997 (first published 1985).

MONTGOMERIE, William. *Robert Burns: New Judgements*. Glasgow: William MacLellan, 1947.

YOUNG, John. *Robert Burns: A Man for All Seasons*. Aberdeen: Scottish Cultural Press, 1996.

Julian Eilmann

Romantic world building: J.R.R. Tolkien's concept of sub-creation and the Romantic spirit

Abstract

The interpretation of Tolkien's work in the context of the Romantic literary movement is not very common among Tolkien scholars. Apart from a handful of papers – some written by the author of the present essay – Tolkien scholarship has not yet taken adequate notice of the Romantic spirit that underlies his Middle-earth mythology. In this paper Julian Eilmann continues his exploration of the Romantic tradition in Tolkien's literary work by focusing on Romantic poetology and its manifestation in Middle-earth and shows how Tolkien's praise of the fairy-story as the ideal vehicle to transport his poetological ideas concurs with central ideas of the Romantic poets who rediscovered fairy-stories as a genuinely Romantic literary form.

"Fantasy remains a human right." (Tolkien in "On Fairy-stories")

J.R.R. Tolkien is well known for his creation of a convincing fantastic world that found its most prominent realization in *The Hobbit* and *The Lord of the Rings*, which themselves were based on an even more ambitious mythological concept that readers could discover only in the posthumously published texts edited by Tolkien's son Christopher.

A volume like the present one focussing on concepts of fantastic worlds would be lacking a central element without at least one paper featuring the work of J.R.R. Tolkien. We can be sure that the amount of detail and (pseudo-historical) depth of Tolkien's literary creation have inspired many of the authors and artists who followed the new creative trail he had blazed. As is generally known, Tolkien himself reflected on his creative impulse in his influential Andrew Lang lecture, which was later published in a revised form as "On Fairy-stories". He tries to explain why the creation of fantastic worlds – Tolkien calls it the "Sub-creative Art" (OFS 47) – is of utmost importance for human beings, and his poetological essay has become a major reference point for many subsequent studies. However, my aim for this study is to take a new look at Tolkien's concept of sub-creation by connecting his thoughts with ideas and conceptions that form the basis of the literary and philosophical tradition we have come to know as Romanticism. By comparing Tolkien's ideas about imagination and enchantment with the Romantic approach to these themes I hope to deepen our understanding of Tolkien as a writer of fantasy. Furthermore, it is my conviction that Tolkien can and should be understood as an artist in the Romantic tradition. The present paper will pick up and accentuate ideas I have developed elsewhere over the last years (cf. the list of my essays in the bibliography). Beyond that the interpretation given here is part of a much broader project that will present an in-depth study of Tolkien as a Romantic writer and poet.

As I have already pointed out in my other publications, the interpretation of Tolkien's work within a Romantic framework is not very widespread in Tolkien studies. Apart from R.J. Reilly's study published in 1971,[1] Romanticism has hardly ever been the focus of Tolkien studies over the last decades. In recent years the topic slowly receives the attention it deserves, not least due to the German Tolkien Society Seminar (2010) on Tolkien and Romanticism.[2]

Awake the sleeping song: Romantic poetology

If we want to understand the way Tolkien's approach to sub-creation and fantasy shares elements with Romantic concepts, we first have to discuss the philosophical and poetological framework of the Romantic ideology. Romanticism must, of course, be understood as an international phenomenon of Western culture gaining prominence in the 19th century. For the context of this paper, however, I will limit the scope to German Romanticism because German intellectuals such as Novalis, Friedrich Schlegel, Ludwig Tieck and others played a crucial role in formulating the Romantic concepts at the end of the 18th and the beginning of the 19th centuries, and thus influenced the whole Romantic movement in Europe (cf. Eilmann, "Sleeps a song" 169).

The element of Romantic philosophy that I want to highlight here, and which is at the very heart of Romanticism, is imagination. Of course, imagination has

---

[1] Reilly basically argues that the Inklings, including Tolkien, shared a belief in what he called *Romantic Religion*.
[2] Cf. the proceedings of the seminar on "Tolkien and Romanticism" which are published in the German Tolkien Society's academic yearbook *Hither Shore*; see Eilmann "Romantische Nostalgie".

been discussed before by philosophers and poets in other periods of European intellectual history, yet it was the Romanticists who – like no other cultural movement before – emphasized the power of human imagination so as to elevate it to the status of an existential force (cf. Korff 271). The emphatic glorification of imagination in Romantic literature and art (cf. Beil 938) has to be understood as the consequence of the shift in philosophy instigated by major proponents of German idealism such as Johann Gottlieb Fichte (1762-1814) or Friedrich Schelling (1775-1854). Their writings inspired Romantic authors and thus – although adapted and modified – their ideas were incorporated in the literary works of the first generation of Romantics (cf. Korff 246). It is not my intention to explore the nature and impact of the philosophy of Fichte and his successors here, but would merely like to identify the central ideas that the Romantic authors were eager to engage with. Fichte himself followed the path opened up by the groundbreaking philosophy of Immanuel Kant. Yet Fichte, in contrast to his famous precursor, proposed the radical idea that human beings cannot legitimately base their perception and worldview on the so-called "real world". What we call reality has to be understood, according to Fichte, as the product of human consciousness. As a consequence, we have to accept that perception does not have a basis in objective reality and we can no longer naively trust in the perceived world as having an existence outside and independently of our perception. The revolutionary conclusion implied is that the material world as such arises from human consciousness. More would have to be said about Fichte's ideas, but even this short glance at Fichte's idealistic philosophy explains why Romantic artists felt attracted to his philosophy (cf. Korff 243, Zeltner 123).

Fichte's ideas allow us to see even the basic human act of perception as an imaginative or creative act, which is why the Romanticists used Fichte's philosophy (often in a bastardized form) as a legitimization for their praise of imagination. Hermann August Korff, in his insightful and still valid interpretation of Romantic thinking, argues that the Romantic authors wanted to transfer these current philosophical insights to their poetic works and express them in their texts (cf. Korff 246f). The proponents of a Romantic poetology, especially Friedrich Schlegel and Novalis, found a strong authoritative legitimization for their ambitious attempt to promote imagination in literature by referring to Fichte's major work, the *Wissenschaftslehre*. The important, and for our purpose crucial element, is that the philosophical foundation provided the Romanticists with a legitimization for their claim that those individuals endowed with the greatest imaginative intuition – poets – are the exemplary representatives of man on the highest level. The poets, with their imaginative potential, are "Weltenschöpfer" ("creators of worlds"; Korff 265). They are able of envisaging and creating anything dream- or imaginable in their minds and of giving vivid shape to these visions in their specific sphere of artistic activity:

> Novalis combines Fichte's classification with a Renaissance tradition, which understands imagination as a power of aesthetic world building. Thus "poetry" becomes direct "world-creation", and transcendental poetry should grasp and change reality in its constitutive nature. (Simon 66)[3]

The Romanticist sees the artist as the "prototype of a human being" (Schanze 557)[4] and thus as the model for what man is able to achieve aesthetically. However, the poet-artist is not completely cut off from the rest of humanity, but merely represents the pinnacle of an elemental force shared by all human beings. Each individual is theoretically able to create or at least appreciate aesthetic efforts or the wonders of the natural world. Yet this does not mean that everyone can be considered an artist or a sensitive mind. The Romanticists rather felt impelled to fight the antagonistic force of those philistines who obstinately adhered to a purely materialist worldview. The opposition and conflict between Romantic and prosaic worldviews is thus a general element in the literary work of Romanticism (cf. Beil 939) and well-known Romantic writers such as E.T.A. Hoffmann created an entire corpus

---

3 All translations from German are, unless indicated otherwise, my own. "Bei Novalis wird [Fichtes] Bestimmung mit einer solchen aus der Renaissance kommenden Traditionslinie kombiniert, die Einbildungskraft als Vermögen der ästhetischen Weltproduktion versteht. Somit wird 'Poesie' unmittelbar zur 'Welterzeugung', soll als 'Transzendentalpoesie' die Wirklichkeit in ihren konstitutiven Zügen ergreifen und verändern." (Simon 66)
4 "Vorstellung vom Künstler als Prototyp des Menschen" (Schanze 557).

of stories in which the conflict between Romantic thinking and philistine behaviour is a dominant element.[5]

Romantic texts often illustrate this opposition between the prosaic and the Romantic. Yet at the same time they stress the fact that the basic Romantic concept of imagination, with its quality transcending reality, is not something dangerous. Imagination, contrary to common belief, is not something extraordinary but a natural, essential human condition (cf. Korff 269), as the poet Klingsohr explains in Novalis's *Heinrich von Ofterdingen*. In a long discussion on art and the artist's mission, the old master poet Klingsohr tells Heinrich:

> It is rather unfortunate that imagination has a specific name and the poet has a specific guild, [...] it is nothing special. It is the original method of the human mind. Does not each human being create poetry every minute? (Novalis, *Werke* 335)[6]

The next step in the Romantic chain of thought consists in the realisation that the poetic spirit essential to the human condition is not restricted to mankind, but can be found in the whole cosmos of nature. The world itself is permeated with a poetic strain that transcends the material world (cf. Korff 271 and Eilmann, "Sleeps" 167-169). The Romanticists, in their various philosophical and literary texts, refer to this universal poetic element by different names. Sometimes it is called "poetry" or "spell", sometimes the authors use more philosophical terms such as "the Absolute" or "the Divine". In the following passage from 1807, the author Ludwig Uhland uses the term "the Eternal" to refer to the mystery he hopes to unravel:

> The Eternal surrounds man, the secret of divinity and the world. What he himself was, is and will be, is veiled to him. Sweet and fruitful are

---

5 See, for example, Hoffmann's most famous stories such as *Der Goldene Topf, Der Artushof, Die Bergwerke zu Falun* and others. In each of these stories the protagonist is torn between his artistic ambitions as a sensitive Romantic spirit and the prosaic claims and seductions of a mercantile world. This conflict is often expressed in the form of two women, one representing art and Romantic fulfillment, the other standing for the mere philistine haven of a happy yet constricting marriage. It is interesting to note that E.T.A. Hoffmann, in his personal life, was confronted with a similar conflict: Working daytime as a court jurist to make his living, he created his fantastic stories in his sparse free time, especially at night. Speaking of Tolkien it is a well-known biographical fact that he also was not a full time writer but a dedicated Oxford professor who had to find time to work on his literary project. Next to the restrictions imposed on his literary activities by his professional life as university don, he was also husband and father, which further affected his literary production.
6 "Es ist recht übel, sagte Klingsohr, daß die Poesie einen besonderen Namen hat, und die Dichter eine besondere Zunft ausmachen. Es ist gar nichts besonderes. Es ist die eigentümliche Handlungsweise des menschlichen Geistes. Dichtet und trachtet nicht jeder Mensch in jeder Minute?" (Novalis, *Werke* 335)

these secrets. [...] But the human spirit, knowing that he will never comprehend eternity in himself in full clarity and tired of the vague desire, longs for worldly images in which a view of the supernatural seems to linger. [...] This notion of the eternal in the visual senses is the Romantic. (Uhland 8)[7]

The most famous and influential phrasing goes back to Joseph von Eichendorff's poem "Wünschelrute" in which he refers to a poetic "song" that sleeps in the surrounding world, a song that can be awoken by the magic word ("Zauberwort") of the poet:

> Sleeps a song in things abounding
> That keep dreaming to be heard:
> And the world shall start resounding
> If you find the magic word.[8]
> (Eichendorff 121, translation by Walter Aue)

I have commented on Eichendorff's poem in another paper:

> The world is to be brought to sing, a metaphor that points out that the magical poetic word stands in the centre of the Romanticist view of art and the world. It contains the hope of the changing power of poetry and with that the longing of Romanticist artistic work, to be able to disclose the secret of prosaic reality by way of the principle of romanticising and so to come to the aesthetic, i.e. the true core of things. (Eilmann, "Sleeps" 167)

Thus the Romanticists aim at transcending the prosaic world by means of their artistic work and endeavour to reveal another layer of reality that in everyday life can only be glimpsed by sensitive individuals. In former times this hidden and yet essential aspect of reality was identified with the Divine and in Christian societies called "God", whose presence is manifest in the surrounding world. It is interesting to notice that although the Romantic movement was heavily influenced by Christianity, and many of the Romanticists were practising Christians, the transcendent quality of reality stressed by them is not always referred to as "Christian". This is all the more astonishing since there has been a

---

[7] "Das Unendliche umgibt den Menschen, das Geheimnis der Gottheit und der Welt. Was er selbst war, ist und sein wird, ist ihm verhüllt. Süß und fruchtbar sind diese Geheimnisse. [...] Der Geist des Menschen aber, wohl fühlend, daß er nie das Unendliche in voller Klarheit in sich auffassen wird und müde des unbestimmten Verlangens, knüpft bald seine Sehnsucht an irdische Bilder, in denen ihm doch ein Blick des Überirdischen aufzudämmern scheint. [...] Dies Ahnen des Unendlichen in den Anschauungen ist das Romantische." (Uhland 8)

[8] "Schläft ein Lied in allen Dingen,/ Die da träumen fort und fort,/ Und die Welt hebt an zu singen,/ Triffst du nur das Zauberwort." (Eichendorff 121)

strong Christian influence throughout the centuries, so that it would be natural to discuss and classify the transcendent and the miraculous in Christian terms.

Some poets such as Eichendorff or Novalis centred entire verse anthologies (e.g. "Hymnen an die Nacht") around traditional Christian topics such as the Resurrection or the veneration of the Virgin Mary, yet other contemporary authors were far more reluctant to make use of traditional Christian ideas and symbolism. It would go beyond the scope of this paper to attempt an adequate discussion of the complex historical and philosophical context, but I want to point out one aspect that influenced the apparent diversity of Romantic terminology.

Because the Romanticists were eager to create new and fresh symbols and images to illustrate their poetological and philosophical notions, many of them were reluctant to use explicit Christian iconography in their literary texts. As a consequence, we have a deliberate vagueness in the depiction of the numinous and the Romantic individual's experience of the transcendence always retains an element of the unexplained.

Since Romantic artists no longer used an exclusively Christian framework, they felt free to explore other historical mythologies or belief systems, which they included or referred to in their artistic production. Thus Northern (Scandinavian and Icelandic) mythology, as found for example in the *Edda*, or even Indian traditions came into focus and were appreciated as exotic and "Romantic". Furthermore, Romantic scholars and philologists such as the Grimm or Schlegel brothers studied these traditions diligently and provided the scholarly foundation for the artistic work of their fellow-Romanticists. Some Romantic authors even hoped to create a new and original mythology, i.e. a set of mythological tales and myths that could work as a new mythological framework and be shared and developed by other authors of the time. This is what Friedrich Schlegel addresses in his famous speech on mythology in the year 1800:

> Especially you [the poets] have to know what I mean. All of you have been writing poetry and you must have felt the lack of a solid ground for your art, a topsoil, a heaven, a vital air.
> A modern artist has to work from what he finds in himself and many have done so brilliantly, but until now everyone has worked on his own, every work of art was like a new creation from scratch.
> Our literature is lacking, I claim, a centre, as mythology has been for the Ancients. And where modern literature is inferior to the ancient it is due to

one thing, which can be summed up in one sentence: We have no mythology. But I want to add that we are close to obtaining one, or rather it is time that we have to seriously do our part in creating one.

The ancient mythology was the first fruit of the young imagination, immediately connecting to the liveliness of the sensual world. The new mythology, by contrast, has to erupt from the deepest depths of the mind. It has to be the most artificial of all works of art, because it should cover everything, providing a new bed and vessel for the old and eternal wellspring of poetry. [...] The core, the centre of poetry is to be found in mythology and in the mysteries of the Ancients. (Schlegel 528)[9]

Schlegel points out how "artificial" and yet connective such a new mythology could be, a complex of stories that would enable modern artists of the time to find a highly attractive common ground on which to base their poetic writings (cf. Schanze 381, 430). The dream was – metaphorically speaking – to build a new wellspring for the endless stream of poetry that runs through the cosmos.

To sum up, it is the intention of Romantic art in all its forms to enable the recipient to experience the poetic quality of life, which is nothing less than transcendence. It is of secondary importance whether one calls this metaphysical layer underlying the material world poetical, magical or divine. The choice of terminology merely reflects the personal predilections of the respective author or recipient. Furthermore it should have become clear that the prominence of the fantastic in Romantic art is due to the fact that "fantasy" is the most suitable vehicle to transport the relevant philosophical ideas, awake a sense of wonder and evoke the typical Romantic longing for transcendence.

---

9 "Ihr müßt vor allem wissen, was ich meine. Ihr habt selbst gedichtet, und ihr müßt es oft im Dichten gefühlt haben, daß es euch an einem festen Halt für euer Wirken gebracht, an einem mütterlichen Boden, einem Himmel, einer lebendigen Luft. Aus dem Innern herausarbeiten das alles muß der moderne Dichter, und viele haben es herrlich getan, aber bis jetzt nur jeder allein, jedes Werk wie eine neue Schöpfung von vorn an aus nichts. Es fehlt, behaupte ich, unsrer Poesie an einem Mittelpunkt, wie es die Mythologie für die der Alten war, und alles Wesentliche, worin die moderne Dichtkunst der antiken nachsteht, läßt sich in die Worte zusammenfassen: Wir haben keine Mythologie. Aber, setze ich hinzu, wir sind nahe daran, eine zu erhalten, oder vielmehr es wird Zeit, daß wir ernsthaft dazu mitwirken sollen, eine hervorzubringen. Denn auf dem ganz entgegengesetzten Wege wird sie uns kommen wie die alte ehemalige, überall die erste Blüte der jugendlichen Phantasie, sich unmittelbar anschließend und anbildend an das Nächste, Lebendigste der sinnlichen Welt. Die neue Mythologie muß im Gegenteil aus der tiefsten Tiefe des Geistes herausgebildet werden; es muß das künstlichste aller Kunstwerke sein, denn es soll alle andern umfassen, ein neues Bette und Gefäß für den alten ewigen Urquell der Poesie [...] Der Kern, das Zentrum der Poesie ist in der Mythologie zu finden und in den Mysterien der Alten." (Schlegel 528)

Tolkien's poetology and the Romantic spirit

Tolkien's literary and poetological work, then, shows some obvious analogies to the Romantic ideology outlined before. Among Tolkien's texts, his lecture "On Fairy-stories" is probably of greatest importance in this context. It discusses the origin and purpose of fairy-stories and fantastic literature in general and, in my view, it mounts a strong Romantic defence of imagination against the accusation of escapism, childishness and irrelevance. Tolkien's attempt to vehemently defend imaginative writing or "fantasy" in times when – in Tolkien's view – a materialistic worldview dominated, can be understood as another chapter in the fight that the Romanticists fought to promote imagination and Romantic – i.e. fantastic – art against philistinism. When Tolkien claims that "Fantasy is a natural human activity" (OFS 55) and concludes his lecture with the fundamental assertion that "Fantasy remains a human right" (OFS 56) he seems to echo the Romantic axiom that imagination has to be understood as a *conditio humana*. Tolkien devotes a great part of his lecture to explore the reasons why imaginative fantasy is so important for human beings and defines four main benefits of fantasy as a literary art form: Fantasy, Recovery, Escape, and Consolation (cf. OFS 46). First of all he talks about imagination and complains that imagination is far too often reduced to "the mental power of image-making" (OFS 47). He argues that the term "imagination" also implies the ability to use "Sub-creative Art" (OFS 47) in order to give these mental images concretization and realization, which is only "a difference of degree in Imagination, not a difference in kind" (OFS 47). Tolkien furthermore introduces the term "Fantasy" to refer to this form of image-making and artistic creation. Since he knows that imagination does not have the best of reputations in post-enlightenment times, he immediately criticizes the "depreciating tone" with which fantasy is associated "with mental disorders, in which there is not even control: with delusion and hallucination" (OFS 48). Tolkien argues that the opposite is true:

> Fantasy (in this sense) is, I think, not a lower but a higher form of Art, indeed the most nearly pure form, and so (when achieved) the most potent. (OFS 48)

We have to pause for a moment and consider the meaning of Tolkien's words. We are confronted with a philologist and author of the 20th century who self-confidently states that fantasy is "the most nearly pure form" of art with the highest artistic potential. Taking into account our preceding discussion of the Romantic concept of art it is easy to see the parallels between Tolkien and the poetological notions of Romanticism. As the Romanticists not only praised imagination as the most appropriate artistic mode but also as an essential form of human perception, one could argue that Tolkien is to be counted among the Romantic philosophers and writers. Tolkien and the Romanticists both understand artistic imagination/fantasy not as something that merely entertains or something that is primarily aimed at children with their – from a depreciatingly adult point of view – immature tastes. On the contrary, fantasy is seen – poetologically and philosophically speaking – as a very serious form of art and perception that enables human beings to see things in a new light and gain a fresh perspective on the so-called "Primary World" (OFS 48) and its often overlooked wonders.

This is what Tolkien calls Recovery: Fantasy has the unique quality of making us consider anew all those things surrounding us in the real world that have been taken for granted for too long:

> We should look at green again, and be startled anew (but not blinded) by blue and yellow and red. We should meet the centaur and the dragon, and then perhaps suddenly behold, like the ancient shepherds, sheep, and dogs, and horses – and wolves. This recovery fairy-stories help us to make. In that sense only a taste for them may make us, or keep us, childish. Recovery (which includes return and renewal of health) is a re-gaining – regaining of a clear view. (OFS 57)

Tolkien goes on to explain that although he does not claim that this new perspective on things enables us to see them "as they are" (OFS 58), we as human beings "need, in any case, to clean our windows; so that the things seen clearly may be freed from the drab blur triteness or familiarity – from possessiveness" (OFS 58). This idea is very similar to the philosophical concept of "Noumenon", as used by Kant and Fichte. Fantasy enables us to overcome the blurred look of everyday life, which gives us the false security of knowing everything that we interact with. It is illuminating that Tolkien uses the term "possessiveness" to illustrate the human intention to subdue things even verbally, as in Tolkien's mythology possessiveness is a major sin and associated with the corrupting force of evil (as seen in Smaug, Gollum, Sauron, and others):

> Of all faces those of our *familiares* are the [...] most difficult really to see with fresh attention, perceiving their likeness and unlikeness: that they are faces, and yet unique faces. This triteness is really the penalty of "appropriation": the things that are trite, or (in a bad sense) familiar, are the things that we have appropriated, legally or mentally. We say we know them. They have become like the things which once attracted us by their glitter, or their colour, or their shape, and we laid hands on them, and then locked them in our hoard, acquired them, and acquiring ceased to look at them. (OFS 58)

So making things or beings too familiar means that the very same things that once were wondrous and beautiful to human beings in their own right have now lost the power to enchant us. I will discuss the role of enchantment in this context in greater detail below. For the moment it is important to notice that Tolkien's idea that Fantasy evokes the desire to see familiar things with fresh attention leads us directly to one of the most famous statements of Romanticism, i.e. Novalis's definition of how Romantic art should work:

> The world must be romanticized. Only in that way can one understand its original significance. Romanticization is nothing other than qualitative potentialization [...] By giving a lofty sense to what is vulgar, a mysterious aspect to what is commonplace, the dignity of the unknown to what is familiar, an infinite extension to what is finite, I romanticize them. (Novalis, *Schriften* 545)[10]

The parallels between Tolkien's poetic notion of "imagination" and Novalis's project are obvious. Novalis sees the central mission of Romantic art in the attempt to re-establish the "dignity of the unknown to what is familiar", i.e. to give back to all those things that have become so familiar to us their original mysterious quality – a concept that closely agrees with Tolkien's view. Romanticism uses and promotes imagination and fantastic elements in Romantic art not so much as to blunt our perception of the so-called "real world", but as a means to penetrate to the true core of things (cf. Schanze 98f). Tolkien found an apt metaphor for the transcending beneficial effect that fantasy – or rather Romantic art – has on human perception:

---

10 "Die Welt muß romantisirt werden. So findet man den urspr[ünglichen] Sinn wieder. Romantisiren ist nichts als eine qualit[ative] Potenzirung. Das niedre Selbst wird mit einem bessern Selbst in dieser Operation identificirt. [...] Indem ich dem Gemeinen einen hohen Sinn, dem Gewöhnlichen ein geheimnißvolles Ansehn, dem Bekannten die Würde des Unbekannten, dem Endlichen einen unendlichen Schein gebe, so romantisire ich es." (Novalis, *Schriften* 545)

> Creative fantasy [...] may open your hoard and let all the locked things fly away like cage-birds. The gems all turn into flowers or flames, and you will be warned that all you had (or knew) was dangerous and potent, not really effectively chained, free and wild; no more yours than they were you. (OFS 59)

Although Tolkien argued that fantastic elements in other forms of literature or art can help to highlight the "dignity of the unknown to what is familiar", human beings need fairy-stories because only here do we have Fantasy as the primary source for the transcending eye-opening effect of Romantic art:

> It was in fairy-stories that I first divined the potency of the words, and the wonder of the things, such as stone, and wood, and iron; tree and grass; house and fire; bread and wine. (OFS 60)

It therefore comes as no surprise that Tolkien's appreciation of the fairy-story and its enchanting power goes back directly to Romanticism. It was the Romanticists at the turn of the 19th century who promoted the fairy-story as a genuinely Romantic literary genre (cf. Schanze 257ff). They praised the fairy-story as the ideal literary form to transport their ideas. As Novalis asserts: "The fairy-tale is in fact the canon of poetry, everything poetic has to be fairy-tale-like" (Novalis, quoted in Korff 278).[11] Or, to paraphrase Korff's argument: for the Romantic poet fairy-story and Romantic art are the same.[12] The reason why fairy-stories were so popular in the age of Romanticism becomes clear when we bear in mind what Romantic art is aiming at: to give us a glimpse of "the wonder of the things" (OFS 60), the magic, the poetry or whichever way one wants to classify the transcendental element inherent in the cosmos. It is thus the intention of the Romantic artist to transform the (all too) familiar everyday world into its original state: a poetic fairy-story.

> What Romantic art aims at is the transformation of the natural world into a fairy-story. This is the true nature of the world, though the human mind is able to explain it in all its technical connections. It *is* a fairy-story! And literature is the

---

11 "Das Märchen ist gleichsam der Kanon der Poesie, alles Poetische muß märchenhaft sein." (Novalis quoted in Korff 278)
12 "[Novalis] sagt damit nichts anderes, als daß alle wahre Dichtung romantisch sein muß. Denn märchenhaft und romantisch sind dasselbe." (Korff 278)

more independent the freer it is from the boundaries of the "natural world-view". (Korff 279)[13]

So, while the fairy-story is the perfect literary vehicle to transport Romantic ideas, it is the magical Realm of "*Faërie*" (OFS 9) that comes to life in fairy-stories and that can have a special effect on the open-minded reader, an effect Tolkien calls "enchantment". For Tolkien the nature of *Faërie* is an essential element of a fairy-story:

> *Faërie* contains many things besides elves and fays, and besides dwarfs, witches, trolls, giants, or dragons; it holds the seas, the sun, the moon, the sky; and the earth, and all things that are in it: tree and bird, water and stone, wine and bread, and ourselves, mortal men, *when we are enchanted*. (OFS 9, my emphasis)

In the fictional context of fairy-stories the power to enchant individuals is frequently wielded by non-human beings and fantastic creatures such as fairies or elves. Humans often lack the necessary understanding and expertise to differentiate enchantment from supernatural "magic" (OFS 49). But we learn that for him it is important to distinguish this "elvish craft" (OFS 49) with its purely artistic qualities "from the greed for self-centred power which is the mark of the mere magician" (OFS 50) (cf. Eilmann, "Sängerkrieg" 73ff). I have discussed elsewhere how in his Middle-earth mythology Tolkien designed many scenes where mortal characters are enchanted by the presence of elves and other superhuman creatures such as the Maiar Goldberry (cf. Eilmann, "I am the song" 103-107). The ability of characters such as Tom Bombadil, Goldberry and the elves to evoke living images and ideas in the listener's mind is thus a literary manifestation of what Tolkien says about the power of Faërie. The power to enchant an audience by means of art thus functions as a text-inherent equivalent to Tolkien's poetological concept of sub-creation (cf. Eilmann, "I am the song" 104). The best example for the enchanting quality of elvish art is a scene in *The Lord of the Rings* where Frodo, during his stay at Rivendell, spends an evening in the Hall of Fire and becomes completely enthralled by the elvish music and song:

---

13 "Was erstrebt sie [die romantische Kunst] anders, als die natürliche Welt in das Märchen zu verwandeln, das sie nach ihrem letzten Wesen ist – mag der Verstand ihren technischen Zusammenhang auch noch so sehr im einzelnen erklären? Sie *ist* ein Märchen! Und eine Dichtung ist umso wahrer je unabhängiger sie sich von den Schranken des 'natürlichen Weltbildes' macht." (Korff 279)

> At first the beauty of the melodies and the interwoven words in elven-tongues, even though he understood them little, held him in a spell, as soon as he began to attend to them. Almost it seemed that the words took shape, and visions of far lands and bright things that he had never yet imagined opened out before him; and the firelit hall became like a golden mist above seas of foam that sighed upon the margins of the world. Then the enchantment became more dreamlike, until he felt that an endless river of swelling gold and silver was flowing over him, too multitudinous for its pattern to be comprehended; it became part of the throbbing air about him, and it drenched and drowned him. Swiftly he sank under its shining weight into a deep realm of sleep.
>
> There he wandered long in a dream of music that turned into running water, and then suddenly into a voice. It seemed to be the voice of Bilbo chanting verses. (*LotR* 227)

This is an example of a character being "held in a spell" (Eilmann, "I am the song" 104) by an enchantment that enables him to undergo a visionary and wondrous experience (cf. Eilmann, "I am the song" 105). There are many other scenes in *The Lord of the Rings* and *The Silmarillion* that illustrate this form of poetic enchantment and, as mentioned above, the mere encounter with elves may cast the spell of enchantment on mortal beings.[14]

Comparing the central concept of Romantic poetology with the concept of enchantment in Middle-earth, Frodo's reaction to nature in the elven realm of Lothlórien can be seen as the one scene that illustrates the close parallels perfectly. Frodo is, of course, not alone in perceiving the "magical" atmosphere of the elvish haven, yet he is the one most sensitive to what he sees, hears and feels. It can be argued that he approaches elvish reality in a romantic spirit and experiences thus a state of enchantment. This is in keeping with the way he has been introduced as Bilbo's nephew and heir, i.e. as an intellectual who, in contrast to the often philistine hobbits, is fascinated by the elves, who stand for the realm of wonder and transcendence. It therefore comes as no surprise

---

14 Another example illustrating the visionary power of elvish enchantment is the first encounter between an elf and a group of mortal men as told in *The Silmarillion*. The elf-lord Finrod Felagund uses music and song to communicate with the humans and thus enchants them by the "wonder of the song": "[Felagund] took up a rude harp which Beor had laid aside, and he played music upon it such as the ears of Men had not heard [...] Now men awoke and listened to Felagund as he harped and sang, and each thought that he was in some fair dream until he saw that his fellows were awake also beside him; but they did not speak or stir while Felagund still played, because of the beauty of the music and the wonder of the song. Wisdom was in the words of the Elven-king; and the hearts grew wiser that hearkened to him; for the things of which he sang, of the making of Arda, and the bliss of Aman beyond the shadows of the sea, came as clear visions before their eyes, and his Elvish speech was interpreted in each mind according to its measure." (*S* 163)

that he later on becomes a poet himself. Frodo can thus be seen as a Romantic protagonist with a deep longing for the wide world and its wonders (cf. Eilmann, "Sleeps a song" 172-175). When Frodo's eyes are uncovered in Lothlórien, Tolkien describes in detail how he reacts to the beauty of the surrounding trees. It becomes clear that this is not the typical reaction of a wanderer to a beautiful landscape:

> The others cast themselves down upon the fragrant grass, but Frodo stood awhile still *lost in wonder*. It seemed to him that he had stepped through a high window that looked on a vanished world. A light was upon it for which *his language had no name*. All that he saw was *shapely*, but the shapes seemed at once clear cut, as if they had been *first conceived* and drawn at the uncovering of his eyes, and ancient as if they had endured for ever. He saw no colour but those he knew, gold and white and blue and green, but *they were fresh and poignant, as if he had at that moment first perceived them and made for them names new and wonderful*. In winter here no heart could mourn for summer or for spring. No blemish or sickness or deformity could be seen in anything that grew upon the earth. On the land of Lórien, there was no stain. (*LotR* 341, my emphasis)

In this frequently quoted passage Tolkien describes a quasi-magical experience of a mortal being in the realm of Faërie. For my analysis of Tolkien's work within the context of Romantic poetology this description is highly relevant since it illustrates in many ways the effect the Romanticists were so eager to achieve within and by means of their literary work. First of all we are informed that the experience of Lothlórien has indeed an effect one normally would call "magical" since Frodo "stood awhile still lost in wonder" (*LotR* 341). The narrator explains this feeling of awe and wonder as resulting not primarily from the picturesque scenery itself but from the unique and new way Frodo perceives his surroundings. In the eyes of the hobbit everything looks "shapely" (*LotR* 341) and like something that has come into existence the very moment he looked at it. The novelty of his heightened perception is emphasised by the narrator who points out that "his language had no name" (*LotR* 341) for the things he encounters. This, of course, reminds us of Adam in the Garden of Eden and the original process of naming. Yet in contrast to the biblical account, Frodo sees only things that are (basically) well-known to him[15] with new eyes:

---

15 Of course, as a hobbit from the Shire Frodo has never before seen Mallorn trees, but in this particular scene it is not primarily the strangeness of unknown trees that is important but the way Frodo perceives them.

"He saw no colour but those he knew, gold and white and blue and green, but they were fresh and poignant" (*LotR* 341). This description of the eye-opening quality of elvish enchantment coincides with Tolkien's definition of fantasy's ability to "clear" the reader's view:

> We should look at green again, and be startled anew (but not blinded) by blue and yellow and red. [...] Recovery [...] is a re-gaining – regaining of a clear view. (OFS 57)

It is interesting to see how Tolkien created a scene like this to illustrate one of his highest poetological and literary ideals. At the same time, the awe and wonder of Frodo's experience must be seen as a characteristic of the principle of Romanticization which aims at giving back "the dignity of the unknown to what is familiar" (Novalis, *Schriften* 545) – which is exactly what Frodo experiences in Lothlórien. For Frodo the original state of wonder has been renewed – at least as long as he stays in Lothlórien. Interestingly enough it is Sam, who starts out as a rustic hobbit, who undergoes a profound personal spiritual change during the journey, and who comments on the "magic" experienced in Lothlórien:

> "If there's any magic about, it's right down deep, where I can't lay my hands on it, in a manner of speaking" "You can see and feel it everywhere," said Frodo. (*LotR* 351)

You cannot directly lay your hands on it, but the wonder is everywhere, "down deep" in the material world itself. A Romanticist like Eichendorff would say it is the magical "song" that sleeps "in things abounding" and that in an enchanted place like Lothlórien one is able to awake the sleeping tune so that "the world shall start resounding" (Eichendorff 121, translation by Walter Aue).

The state of enchantment cannot be experienced constantly and everywhere, even in a sub-created world like Middle-earth which, though containing strange beings and elements of magic, is identified by Tolkien as our world during an unspecified pre-historic age. Experiences of magic or transcendence are therefore rare. In fact Frodo's state of enchantment in Lothlórien is a delightful exception for a character who is sufficiently sensitive to perceive the "magic" that pervades everything. Setting foot on the leaf-covered ground of Lothlórien, the Fellowship has entered a place where the wonder inherent in the world has the chance to reveal itself. This step from the ordinary world into a realm of magic and transcendence – Faërie – is another characteristic that can be found in many Romantic novels and stories. The protagonists of these novels become aware of another layer of reality they have always been longing for; thus the fantastic (temporarily) becomes part of the ordinary world. Of course, in Romantic novels we are most often confronted with characters who live in a modern 18th or 19th century society, meaning that at first glance their confrontation with the fantastic seems to be completely different from the experience in Middle-earth which itself is a fantastic world. But if we consider that in the Third Age of Middle-earth elves and the transcendent marvel they stand for are seen by other races as representing otherworldliness[16] we understand that the encounter between an "ordinary" mortal like Frodo and the Faëry Realm of Lothlórien can in fact be compared with the impact of "fantasy" in a Romantic novel like those by E.T.A. Hoffmann.

As we have seen enchantment is a central concern of fantasy as Tolkien understands it and in the Lothlórien chapter he has created a sequence where we can follow the characters into "Other Time" (OFS 32), into Faërie, and accompany them as they are "regaining [...] a clear view" (OFS 57). Tolkien's intention was, of course, that while reading a novel such as *The Lord of the Rings* the reader him- or herself could undergo such an experience:

> Such stories [fairy-stories] have now a mythical or total (unanalysable) effect, an effect quite independent of the findings of Comparative Folk-lore, and one which it cannot spoil or explain; they open a door on Other Time, and if we pass through, though only for a moment, we stand outside our own time, outside Time itself, maybe. (OFS 32)

Taken seriously – and we can be sure that Tolkien took his poetological notions and his own fantastic writings very seriously – this approach to Fantasy is a genuinely Romantic conception. Most importantly, as we have seen, Tolkien's poetology can be understood as one of the strongest defenses of imagination

---

16 E.g. Faramir comments on the estrangement between men and elves in the Third Age: "But in Middle-earth Men and Elves became estranged in the days of darkness, by the arts of the Enemy, and by the slow changes of time in which each kind walked further down their sundered roads. Men now fear and misdoubt the Elves, and yet know little of them. And we of Gondor grow like other Men, [...] shun the Elves and speak of the Golden Wood with dread. [...] For I deem it perilous now for mortal man wilfully to seek out the Elder People. Yet I envy you that have spoken with the White Lady" (*LotR* 664).

and fantastic art in the first half of the 20th century and in this way Tolkien is also one of the most influential successors of the Romantic movement.

About the author

JULIAN EILMANN studied History, German Philology, and History of Arts in Aachen and Nottingham and is working as a grammar school teacher for German and History at the Inda-Gymnasium Aachen. Before following his vocation to teach he worked as an author for a film production company and is winner of the German Youth Video Award. In addition, he is conservator for an artists' foundation. His main research is in Tolkien's poetry, a topic on which he has published several papers. Contact: julianeilmann@web.de

Bibliography

Beil, Ulrich. "Phantasie." *Historisches Wörterbuch der Rhetorik*. Vol. 6. Ed. Gert Ueding. Tübingen: Max Niemeyer, 2003. 927-943.

Eichendorff, Joseph von. *Sämtliche Werke des Freiherrn Joseph von Eichendorff. Historisch-kritische Ausgabe*. Vol. 1. Eds. Wilhelm Kosch, August Sauer, Hermann Kunisch, Helmut Koopmann et al. Stuttgart: Max Niemeyer, 1993.

"Wünschelrute." Transl. Walter A. Aue. Available online at http://myweb.dal. ca/waue/Trans/Eichendorff-Wuenschelrute.html, accessed 22 September 2013.

Eilmann, Julian. "J.R.R. Tolkien und die romantische Nostalgie." *Hither Shore* 7 (2010): 94-109.

"Sleeps a song in things abounding. J.R.R. Tolkien and the German Romantic Tradition." *Music in Middle-earth*. Eds. Heidi Steimel and Friedhelm Schneidewind. Zurich and Jena: Walking Tree Publishers, 2011. 167-184.

"I am the song. Music, Poetry and the Transcendent in J.R.R. Tolkien's Middle-earth." *Light Beyond all Shadow: Religious Experience in Tolkien's Work*. Eds. Paul Kerry and Sandra Miesel. Madison New Jersey: Fairleigh Dickson University Press, 2011. 99-117.

"Romantische Sehnsucht im Werk J.R.R. Tolkiens" *Hither Shore* 8 (2012): 245-261.

Korff, Hermann August. *Geist der Goethezeit: Versuch einer ideellen Entwicklung der klassisch-romantischen Literaturgeschichte*. Vol. 3. Leipzig: Koehler & Amelang, 1959.

Novalis. *Schriften. Die Werke Friedrich von Hardenbergs*. Vol. 2. Eds. Paul Kluckhohn and Richard Samuel. Stuttgart: Kohlhammer, 1960.

Werke in zwei Bänden. Vol. 1. Ed. Rolf Toman. Köln: Könemann, 1996.

Reilly, R.J. *Romantic Religion: A Study of Owen Barfield, C.S. Lewis, Charles Williams, J.R.R. Tolkien*. Great Barrington: Lindisfarne Books, 1971.

Schanze, Helmut. *Romantik-Handbuch*. Stuttgart: Alfred Kröner, 1994.

Schlegel, Friedrich. "Die neue Mythologie." *Die deutschen Romantiker. Vol. 1: Werke*. Ed. Gerhard Stenzel. Salzburg: Das Bergland Verlag, 1986. 526-529.

Simon, Ralf. "Phantasie." *Reallexikon der deutschen Literaturwissenschaft. Neubearbeitung des Reallexikons der deutschen Literaturgeschichte*. Vol. 3. Eds. Jan-Dirk Müller et al. Berlin, New York: Walter de Gruyter, 2003. 64-68.

Tolkien, J.R.R. "On Fairy-stories." *Tree and Leaf*. London: Unwin, 1964. 1-81.

The Lord of the Rings. London: HarperCollins, 1995.

The Silmarillion. Ed. Christopher Tolkien. London: HarperCollins, 1999.

UHLAND, Ludwig. "Über das Romantische." *Ludwig Uhland Werke*. Vol. 2. Ed. Hans-Rüdiger Schwab. Frankfurt, 1983.

WEINREICH, Frank. *Fantasy – Einführung*. Essen: Oldib Verlag, 2007.

ZELTNER, Hermann. "Johann Gottlieb Fichte." *Neue deutsche Biographie*. Vol. 5. Ed. Historische Kommission bei der Bayerischen Akademie der Wissenschaften. Berlin: Duncker & Humblot, 1971. 122-125.

Tom A. Shippey

Jack Vance: il ottimo fabbro

Abstract

Jack Vance has been generally hailed as a stylist, and a case has been made for the underlying seriousness of his recurrent themes. This essay, however, tries to demonstrate his unmatched ability as a creator of different worlds, exemplifying this by consideration of three of Vance's many series: the "Dying Earth" tetralogy, the "Planet of Adventure tetralogy", and the "Lyonesse" trilogy, which between them cover Vance's sixty-year long writing career almost from start to finish. All three sequences show Vance's greatest quality, his copiousness of invention, and do so in different modes, which one could describe as, respectively, the febrile gaiety of age, a sense of epic struggle, and a blending of fairy-tale with historic chronicle. It is the world's loss that Vance has not been granted the popularity of Tolkien, but has remained within the smaller orbit of "fandom".

Jack Vance, who died on May 26th 2013 aged 96, was in the opinion of many the greatest creator of imaginary worlds of the 20th century, which may well mean, of all time. His genius was recognised within the science fiction and fantasy community by every award in its power to give: three Hugos, a Nebula, a World Fantasy Award, a World Fantasy Award for Lifetime Achievement (granted rather prematurely in 1984), and several others; as also by the care taken by many fans to collect and reprint even his earliest stories from scattered and now-defunct magazines.[1] But outside that community, unlike J.K. Rowling, George R.R. Martin or J.R.R. Tolkien, Vance has remained all but unknown. None of his works has been filmed, still less become a TV series, and the sales of all his books together probably do not match those of any of the writers just mentioned. If, however, he has remained within the "ghetto" of genre fiction, the loss is the world's, not the ghetto's.

---

1 See three recent volumes of *The Early Jack Vance*: *Hard Luck Diggings* (Vol. 1, 2010), *Dream Castles* (Vol. 2, 2012), and *Magic Highways* (Vol. 3, 2013); all edited by Terry Dowling and Jonathan Strahan.

Vance's writing career spanned seven decades, from his first story "The World Thinker", published in *Thrilling Wonder Stories*, Summer 1945, to his last novel, *Lurulu*, 2004. In between he created one secondary world after another. The list given here cannot be comprehensive,[2] although listing is made easier by Vance's habit of writing connected stories within the same universe. Thus, on the science fiction side, we have the five novels of the "Demon Kings" series, set within the multi-planet "Oikumene", or in the lawless "Beyond" outside of it, and united by their theme of revenge (1964-81); the three novels of the "Alastor" series, each of them set on a different world with markedly different customs, if subject to the loose over-government of "the Connatic" (1973-78); the "Durdane" trilogy, set on one world, which is however divided into sixty-four separate cantons, all with their own laws, these latter never over-ridden and only rarely enforced by the even looser over-government of "the Faceless Man" (1973-74); and the late "Cadwal Chronicles" trilogy (1988-92), also set on a single world, which nevertheless consists of the descendants of a scientific research establishment set in a vast unpoliced hinterland.[3]

It can be seen already that Vance was one of the many writers of science fiction's "Golden Age" who hoped that expansion into space would create ever more scope for human diversity, thus reversing the 20th-century trend towards centralisation and state control. Other repeated themes include the world with no accessible iron, seen in *The Blue World* (1966), where the descendants of a crashed convict-ship live on floating pads in a waterworld, threatened externally by the native "kragens", and internally by their own priesthood. The priests draw their power from kragen-control but seed their own doom by feeding and sacrificing to "King Kragen", who grows ever bigger, impossible to kill with weapons of bone and hardened withe. An earlier iron-deficient world was *Big Planet* (1957), with its later sequel *Showboat World* (1975). One of the delights of the latter was the extended sub-plot, in which the owner of the showboat "Miraldra's Enchantment" puts on performances of Shakespeare's *Macbeth*, with ever-increasing roles for the witches, a nude scene for Lady Macbeth, and turns for fire-eaters, jugglers and dancers scripted in to the banquet interrupted by

---

2 A.E. Cunningham's "Jack Vance: A Bibliography", is complete up to the year 2000.
3 The "Cadwal Chronicles" appear to be set within the larger framework of "the Gaean Reach", which forms a kind of super-set including a number of otherwise not-connected novels and novellas.

Banquo's ghost – all against the furious protest of the purist who had unearthed this ancient and apparently unplayable text.

But each of Vance's many novellas has its own delights. Three particular favourites are "The Dragon Masters" (1962), "The Last Castle" (1966), and "The Miracle Workers" (1958). The first, which won Vance a Hugo in 1963, is set on a forgotten-colony world where the inhabitants war among themselves and intermittently against alien raiders, the raiders using specially-bred humans, the humans using their "dragons", specially-bred aliens. The tale shows Vance's love of detail, with the different types of war-dragon and war-human carefully listed,[4] and his astonishing skill at onomastics, or the invention of place-names: Starbreak Fell, High Jambles, the Skanse, Barch Spike, all giving a sense of the world's rocky and marginal geography. "The Last Castle" (Hugo and Nebula in 1967) is again remarkable for its detail, with many footnotes outlining the elaborate etiquette of a thoroughly decadent society, almost too self-absorbed (another recurrent Vance theme) to save itself. "The Miracle Workers" (1958) adds to its forgotten-colony scenario and alien-conflict plot the serious theme of belief-structures and scientific paradigms. On this isolated world magic (which we rapidly recognise as formalised ESP) is the ruling orthodoxy, and it rules because (so far) it has worked. New circumstances, however, seem to dictate a return to the superstitions of the ancestors (which we rapidly recognise as scientific method).

Even what little I have so far been able to say perhaps gives a hint of the variety of Vance's *oeuvre*.[5] It is even harder to indicate the qualities which have led to his general acceptance as one of the great "stylists" of science fiction – his love of colour, the formality with which his characters speak even in the most distressing of circumstances, the irony with which the formality is often mixed.[6] When it comes to theme, I have tried to make the case elsewhere that far from being a mere "stylist" or "entertainer", all through his career Vance has engaged with arguably the most important issues of modern anthropology and indeed modern politics: how far "human nature" is natural or innate, how far it is

---

4 In the original magazine publication, *Galaxy* August 1962, they were also carefully illustrated.
5 The list given furthermore omits mention of remarkable or distinguished novels like *The Languages of Pao* (1958) and *Emphyrio* (1969), as well as many early novels and collections of short stories.
6 He is praised for these qualities in the entry on him in John Clute and Peter Nicholls, *The Encyclopedia of Science Fiction*, 2nd ed., esp. col. 2, 1265.

culturally generated, and whether there are any absolute standards by which cultural behaviour, and so morality, may be judged.[7] The way Vance does this is characteristically to indicate human "plasticity" – both cultural, as with the sixty-four cantons of Durdane, and genetic, as with the purpose-bred humans of Coralyne – and then to indicate the disastrous results once that plasticity, so to speak, sets hard. Vance has clearly absorbed the lessons of American structural anthropology; tested them in a way that discipline has shied away from, along with its mass-market descendants; and in his way foreseen the kind of conclusions drawn by now-famous books like Jared Diamond's *Collapse* (2005).

Vance should accordingly be seen as a great writer (generally accepted, within SF and fantasy), and a serious thinker (a claim much more rarely advanced). It is the aim of this essay, however, to focus on his ability as a world-creator. And having tried above to indicate some fraction of his life's work, and having looked elsewhere in some detail at smaller fractions of it, I hope to achieve that aim here by concentrating on three sequences not so far mentioned. Two are fantasy sequences. The first is the "Dying Earth" series of four books (1950-84). Each consists of separate stories, or episodes, usually first published separately, but linked by setting or by central character. The second is the "Lyonesse" trilogy of three longer novels (1983-90) forming one continuous narrative. The third sequence returns us to science fiction: the "Planet of Adventure" series of four novels (1968-70) centred on Adam Reith, a spaceman wrecked on a world inhabited by many varieties of human, and by at least four other intelligent and mutually-hostile species.

The most startling of these must be the "Dying Earth" sequence. It certainly startled me. I still remember the day, more than fifty years ago, when I came across a copy of the first collection in the series, *The Dying Earth* itself, and sat reading it on a bench all afternoon on my one day off from my job as a barman in the Scottish Central Highlands. That was in 1962, but twelve years earlier, when the book first came out, the shock must have been even greater for his readers. Up till then Vance had been publishing stories in pulp magazines like *Thrilling Wonder* or *Startling Stories*, one extended sequence being the ten stories centred on Magnus Ridolph, a kind of cultural detective. These were well

---

7 See Tom Shippey, "People are Plastic: Jack Vance and the Dilemma of Cultural Relativism."

worth the reprinting, ingenious, funny, often mocking the kind of two-fisted, rock-jawed hero normally found in the pulps, but they were straightforward: puzzles with a twist, like "The Unspeakable McInch" (1948) or "The Howling Bounders" (1949).[8]

The contrast with the sheer lushness and inventive superfluity of the "Dying Earth" stories is immense. Their scenario was unexpected, though not quite unique: a very far future, so far that the sun flickers and lurches like a dying fluorescent tube, and will one day soon go out. Humanity has also progressed very far, so far that most of its acquired knowledge has been forgotten again, or dwindled to ancient lore, to magic spells. In the first story, "Turjan of Miir", the enchanter Turjan is trying like Dr Frankenstein to create life, with limited success. To go further, he knows he has to visit a more powerful enchanter, Pandelume, in the land of Embelyon. A spell takes him there, but Pandelume's price for the knowledge is that Turjan must steal an amulet from round the neck of Prince Khandive the Golden, in his city of Khaiin. The theft becomes a contest of spells, for one of Vance's ground rules is that the wizardly spells are so difficult to retain that no mind can contain more than three or four. Phandaal's Mantle of Stealth gets Turjan into Khandive's presence, to be dissolved by a guard spell. Khandive's protecting Omnipotent Sphere is penetrated by Laccodel's Rune, and Khandive himself is threatened by Turjan's last spell, the Excellent Prismatic Spray; Khandive lets the amulet be taken from round his neck – Turjan has to guard his sight from it, for even a glimpse through closed fingers sets off "a murmur of avid [and probably demonic] voices".[9] Khandive's last threat is mechanical: a trapdoor which will drop Turjan instantly into a dungeon. Which it does. Only Turjan holds a magic crystal given by Pandelume, and breaking this returns him, even as he is falling, to Pandelume: there to use the amulet to save Pandelume from another unseen demonic attack. Turjan uses the knowledge he gains to create a twin to a beautiful but insane girl who attacked him on his way to Pandelume, one of Pandelume's failures – which will lead on to further stories.

---

8 Six of the ten "Magnus Ridolph" stories appeared in *The Many Worlds of Magnus Ridolph*. Seven were reprinted in *Magic Highways*, including four found also in *Many Worlds*. The tenth was reprinted (with the remaining two from *Many Worlds*) in *Hard Luck Diggings*. Vance's bibliography baffles even his fans.
9 The four "Dying Earth" volumes were collected as *The Compleat Dying Earth*, New York: SFBC, 1998. The quotations here are from page 10.

The summary above reads like a complex Stone-Paper-Scissors game. It leaves out the constant hints of further knowledge, of worlds and creatures only hinted at, which give the story its (at that time) unprecedented depth. Merely approaching Khandive, Turjan sees "a garlanded courtesan of the Kauchique littoral danc[ing] the Dance of the Fourteen Silken Movements to the music of flutes"; "a sunken pool where a pair of captured Deodands, their skins like oiled jet, paddled and glared"; a game where spectators "tossed darts at the spread-eagled body of a Cobalt Mountain witch" (*Compleat Dying Earth* 9). Deodands appear often in the Dying Earth tetralogy, man-eaters, always hungry, curiously polite: "Mazirian, you roam the woods far from home [...] Are you with powerful spells today?" (25) They seem to be some kind of hybrid creature, like erbs ("creatures mixed of beasts, man and demon", 39), gids, visps, mermelants, grues, and the flying pelgrane. But like the magicians' spell-book, Vance's bestiarium seems inexhaustible. All this in fourteen pages.

The succeeding five stories in *The Dying Earth* all have their charming moments. "Mazirian the Magician" has Mazirian controlling a lesser wizard with a bronze gong and a silver hammer: "'Stay the strokes, Mazirian! [...] Strike no more on the gong of my life!'"(19) It also introduces Thrang the ghoul-bear; the Twk-men, who ride dragon-flies, see everything in the forest, and cannot be trusted for a moment; vampire grass; and Mazirian's ingenious ideas of torment by shrinkage, far in advance of anything in Richard Matheson's almost-contemporary, and far inferior screenplay, *The Incredible Shrinking Man* (1957). The story I chose, however, for my collection *The Oxford Book of Fantasy Stories*, was the fourth in the sequence, "Liane the Wayfarer," which introduces Liane, a new kind of anti-hero: quick, deadly, self-satisfied, fatally thoughtless, and golden-eyed. Liane has found a circlet which, so a Twk-man tells him, makes him vanish when he steps into it, apparently into some other dimension. The Twk-man also tells him that "a golden witch called Lith has come to live on Thamber Meadow. She is quiet and very beautiful" (56). The witch is unresponsive to Liane's approaches, and her hut has defences he cannot breach. Like Pandelume, she demands a service; the remaining half of her tapestry, stolen by Chun the Unavoidable. Liane sets off, confident that he has a new magical escape route in his circlet. Undeterred by the fear aroused by any mention of Chun's name, Liane finds the hall, seizes the tapestry; "behind was Chun the Unavoidable", wearing his robe of eyeballs threaded on silk (64). Liane flees, at last resort steps into his circlet. Behind him a voice says, "I am Chun the Unavoidable" (64). In the short coda Lith sits in the dark on Thamber Meadow, door barred, windows shuttered. She hears a creak as the lock is tested. Chun has brought her two long threads from her tapestry, "[t]wo because the eyes were so great. So large, so golden [...]" Once it is safe she emerges, retrieves the threads, fits them into her half of the golden tapestry of the land of Ariventa. She tells herself, "[t]he cloth grows slowly wider [...] One day it will be done, and I will come home" (64).

Clearly there is a story behind the story, one never told. But Vance was to tell many more stories set within the same world and time. *The Eyes of the Overworld* (1966) introduced a Liane-successor, Cugel the Clever, a thief, cheat and confidence-trickster. His attempt to rob the manse of Iucounu the Laughing Magician goes wrong, and he is despatched to a far and dreary northern shore, to recover a pair of "the eyes of the overworld": purple cusps which create in those who wear them a completely satisfying illusion, so that sordid surroundings become palaces filled with every luxury. The running joke is that while Cugel is extremely resourceful in stealing the cusps, setting out for home, and exploiting everyone he meets, his exploitations frequently backfire. Thus, he returns to Almery, imprisons Iucounu in a bottle, and prepares to send him to the northern wastes, where he can repeat Cugel's own journey, if he survives. But Cugel, never good at magic, gets one "pervulsion" wrong, and is instead seized himself by the summoned demon. The story ends with him once more on the desolate beach where his journey home began.

He was not allowed to rest there, for his second journey home, with a renewed sequence of adventures, formed the narrative of *Cugel's Saga* (1983). Even before that an admirer, Michael Shea, himself author of Vance-rivalling fantasies, had received permission to continue Cugel's story from the end of *Eyes of the Overworld*. This appeared as *A Quest for Simbilis* (1974). A further tribute to Vance's invention is *Songs of the Dying Earth*, a collection of twenty-two stories set in the "Dying Earth" imaginary world, and written by most of the leading names in American fantasy.[10] Vance rounded off his own sequence with *Rhialto the Marvellous* (1984), a further set of three novellas centred on a different group of 21st Aeon magicians.

Once again the bare list given in the last couple of paragraphs gives no idea of the variety of characters and incidents which surround Cugel in particular, such as the beautiful Derwe Corome, in her boat-shaped car which runs on six swan-feet. In the village of Vull Cugel is lured into accepting the post of Watchman against Magnatz, a post he is assured is a sinecure with many privileges, only to find that the tower from which he keeps his watch has no exit. Cugel escapes nevertheless, neglecting his watch – which turns out not to have been a sinecure, as the long-vanished giant Magnatz appears from the centre of the lake to which the previous watchers had confined him. In another adventure Cugel comes upon a gang of men of all shapes and sizes constructing a sculpture with meticulous care, as they have been for five hundred years. Its purpose was to attract a creature called TOTALITY, and it succeeds. Unfortunately Cugel, not yet employed and with no rations, immediately toasts and eats it while the workers are taking their own lunch, with consequences which lead him far afield.

In *Cugel's Saga* he acquires a valuable demon-scale called "Spatterlight", which devours anything living which it touches, so that Cugel keeps it carefully wrapped. It saves him when he finds himself visited by a pelgrane as he travels in the flying bedstead he has acquired. "Today I shall breakfast in bed [...] Not often do I so indulge myself", remarks the pelgrane, civil like most of Vance's man-eaters (*Compleat Dying Earth* 442). His adventures as a seagoing worminger, and as a caravan-guard are also remarkable: though it was unwise to set Cugel alone for ten successive nights to guard seventeen virgins, all of them aware that their position in a future rite of sacrifice depended on their virginity. On being interrogated, cries the enraged high priest to the caravan master, the girls "merely raise their eyes to the ceiling and whistle between their teeth" (516). One might sum up by saying that the "Dying Earth" sequence has the variety and invention of *Grimms' Fairy Tales*, with the controlling shape, depth, and hints of power in reserve of Tolkien's Middle-earth.

---

10 *Songs of the Dying Earth: Stories in Honour of Jack Vance*, edited by George R.R. Martin and Gardner Dozois. One of them, Mike Resnick's "Inescapable", gives us the "backstory" of Lith and Chun the Unavoidable (105-121).

"The Planet of Adventure" is something else again.[11] Its hero, Adam Reith, is an honest man, unlike Cugel. He has no magical powers, unlike Turjan. And he operates under the laws of science fiction, not fantasy. He is the only survivor of a crashed space-boat, sent to investigate a mysterious radio call, and shot down without warning. Reith finds himself marooned on a steppe, the slave of a nomad tribe, with no more than a small kit of possessions. His space-boat has been salvaged by one of the three intelligent races (Chasch, Wankh and Dirdir) who maintain bases on the planet of Tschai (there is a fourth indigenous race, the Pnume, rarely seen, living underground). Can Reith retrieve and repair his space-boat from the devious and malevolent Blue Chasch? Even to reach them he has to cross the steppe, assisted by two companions he acquires en route. They slowly educate him in the facts of life on Tschai, facts which are also myths: for all four of the alien races maintain themselves by modifying humans to their own purposes, and reinforcing their control by myth. Chaschmen are told that when they die they will be reincarnated as Chasch imps, and advance to a higher stage. Dirdirmen are told that both they and Dirdir hatched long ago from the same egg, one into Sun, one into Shadow. The children of Shadow can only emulate those of Sun, though they alter themselves surgically to make the resemblance closer. The Pnume drug their humans into permanent pre-pubescence. The Wankhmen, by contrast, have exploited their position as translators and communicators to keep their masters uninformed about the real situation on Tschai, thus perpetuating their own power. All inhabitants of Tschai believe that the many other varieties of human have been created by the mutation and cross-breeding of runaways from their own alien-human group. Reith's insistence that there is a world of men – from which the spacefaring races must have kidnapped their breeding stock long ago – is dismissed by all as a myth. Humans have proved once again to be fatally "plastic".

As with Cugel, Reith endures many adventures: he survives the Blue Chasch, launches the Green Chasch against them, breaks through the language barrier policed by the Wankhmen, fixes on the Dirdir as the likeliest, because least organised and most individualistic race to steal a working space-boat from, and controls the Pnume, from whom he has escaped, by threatening to make public to Chasch and Dirdir alike their great manual of hidden exits and entrances to

---

11 The four volumes were collected as *Planet of Adventure* (1985).

the underground world. To gain the sequins which are the currency of Tschai, and which come to the surface in nodes in one area alone, he has to enter that area: but it is the hunting preserve of the Dirdir, which they in effect challenge humans to enter. The Dirdir hunt humans. But no one has thought to hunt the Dirdir. Reith succeeds, assisted by his two companions, Anche at Afram Anacho, a Dirdirman who seems to have been exiled for wearing "Blue and Pink" without undergoing the surgical procedures necessary to reach that rank; and Traz, a steppe-boy who also shelters the much more adult and dominant personality of Onmale, his Emblem. In a later scene Reith rescues Anche from the Glass Box, a giant structure which duplicates the ecology of the Dirdir homeworld of Sibol, and which the Dirdir use to exercise themselves while hunting human rebels and criminals. Ecology and xenology are carefully worked up. The padding, bounding Dirdir, like bipedal pack-hunting leopards, outclass even Crichton's velociraptors as the stuff of nightmare.

By the time Vance received his World Fantasy Award for Lifetime Achievement in 1984, aged 68, one might have been forgiven for thinking the award was what is often called a "gold-watch" presentation, a sign one's career is thought to be over. Yet Vance had what may be his greatest achievement still in him, the creation of the "Lyonesse" trilogy. Volume 1 appeared in 1983 as *Lyonesse: Suldrun's Garden*, volume 2 in 1985 as *The Green Pearl*, and volume 3 in 1989 as *Madouc*. In my judgement, the "Lyonesse" trilogy is the only work of fantasy to match *The Lord of the Rings* as an achievement: the latter is superior in structure and philosophical depth, the former in variety, charm, and sheer unpredictability. I'd add that it is certainly true that every top-class romance needs a top-class forest: Broceliande, Sherwood, the Forest of Arden, the Forest Sauvage, Mythago Wood, and in Tolkien's case Fangorn, Mirkwood, the Old Forest. Vance matches them all, however, with his Forest of Tantrevalles.

This has even entered my dreams. When I was younger I sometimes had the good fortune to have "Jack Vance dreams" – dreams from which I woke sure that I had found the seed of a story which would have the quality of the great man's. Naturally, all faded or disintegrated with consciousness. Yet I remember one which was set in "Drumdramdrigill Wood". When I woke up, I even remembered the spelling. As a name it derives, I suppose, from the Gaelic prefix Drum-, a bridge, which I knew from place names like Drumnadrochit, crossed with my memory of the Great Caledonian Wood, which John Buchan once identified, in his novel *Witchwood* (1927), as "Melon Udrigill". I am sure, though, that the dream and the word were stimulated by Tantrevalles: even superior to Lith the witch's "golden Ariventa" as a place of longing.

What is there in Tantrevalles? It is the place where they hold the Goblin Fair, at Twittens Corner, with its inn, the House of the Laughing Sun and the Crying Moon. There the fairies come to trade with humans, and not only fairies, but also the lower-ranked falloys, goblins, imps and skaks. Giants, ogres and trolls form a different category of halflings, while a third class – rarely if ever encountered – includes five grades from merrihews down to darklings. The most powerful of the magic breeds are sandestins, in a class by themselves (and encountered also in the "Dying Earth" series). Human magicians are capable of controlling even sandestins, to some extent and with due precaution, but magical activity is limited in Lyonesse by the Edict of Murgen, the most powerful of the magicians, who prohibits involvement in temporal affairs.

The main struggle on the temporal plane in Lyonesse is between the kingdoms of Lyonesse itself, whose king is Casmir, and the sea-power Troicinet, to whose throne Aillas succeeds towards the end of the first volume. Casmir is perturbed by the prophecy of the magic mirror Persilian, that one day the son of his daughter Suldrun will sit on the throne Cairbra an Meadhan, and reunite the Elder Isles (which lay, before they drowned, south of Ireland, west of France). Suldrun's only child, Casmir thinks, is the girl Madouc. He does not know that she is a changeling, that Suldrun had a son Dhrun by Aillas, now King of Troicinet, then a mere wanderer and soon a forgotten prisoner, thought to be dead. But Aillas escaped, and Dhrun has since been reared by the fairies of King Throbius in Thripsey Shee – where he grows at nine times the rate of a normal child. The age-difference impedes Casmir's search for him once he realises that Suldrun's son exists.

This central theme, however, gives Vance the opportunity to spiral off in many directions. Aillas, escaped from Casmir's dungeon, is captured by the Ska, a people in many ways admirable, but implacably opposed to all other forms of human, whom they regard as degenerate hybrids with the extinct Neanderthals. He escapes from slavery; is captured once again by the Ska, and condemned to a tunnel-digging gang who will be executed as soon as their work is done; he escapes again and leads his companions through many adventures in Tantrevalles in the attempt to find and rescue his son. Dhrun, meanwhile, has been given by the fairies a magic sword which comes to his call, an inexhaustible purse, a pebble which banishes fear – but also a curse or mordet of seven years bad luck. He uses his sword, and even more, his wits, to rescue a band of children from the child-eating ogre Arbogast; but his bad luck means he is blinded by angry fairies. His only companion is the girl Glyneth, until both of them are befriended by the magician Shimrod.

Shimrod, meanwhile, is an avatar or scion of Murgen who has slowly developed an independent personality. The main clash on the magical plane (of course restricted by the Edict) is between Shimrod and Murgen's enemy Tamurello, who for the most part works through the creations of his witch-lover Desmei. She has somehow dissolved herself into three parts: the male Faude Carfilhiot, the female Melancthe, and the green pearl which incorporates all the worst parts of Desmei, and brings destruction on whoever wins it. Shimrod links with Dhrun, Aillas with Carfilhiot.

But the charm of "Lyonesse" lies not in the plotting, which even more than Tolkien recapitulates the old mode of "interlacement", by which one narrative strand weaves into another. It lies in the many adventures, escapades, enchantments and strange creatures which waylay all the main characters. To name only a half-dozen favourites, there are:

- Shimrod's friend, the completely unclassifiable Grofinet, with the personality of a talkative spaniel, who is tortured to death during the robbery of Shimrod's manse Trilda, but avenged by Shimrod, masquerading as "Dr Fidelius", curer of sore knees;
- Aillas's folktale journey to consult Murgen, where he encounters in succession a raven who waits to drop a feather on a boulder which will at once topple on whoever goes through Binkings Gap; an old woman with a fox's head and chicken legs who should on no account be carried over the river; bearded gryphs who have to be paid off with honey. All of whom have to be circumvented again, and in a different way on the return;

- Aillas's recapture of the Ulflands from the Ska, by superior tactics and by the short shrift he shows to Sir Hune, most intransigent of the Ulfland robber barons;
- his journey across the "brakes" of North Ulfland with the Ska girl Tatzel, each brake beset by a different enchantment, some hostile, some friendly;
- the history of the green pearl, which parallels classic narratives such as Chaucer's "Pardoner's Tale" and Kipling's "The King's Ankus", as also Neil Gaiman's much more recent retelling in *The Graveyard Book* (2008);
- and the three adventurers in *Madouc*, the Princess herself, her squire whom she calls "Sir Pom-Pom", and Travante the Sage, who set out in search of, respectively, the name of her father (can he be Sir Pellinore?), the Holy Grail, and the Sage's lost youth. The Holy Grail at least is retrieved from Throop, the three-headed troll, with the aid of a magic vessel capable of pouring both elixirs and poisons, as selected.

Even such a list necessarily leaves out Aillas's recapture of Fair Aprillion, Glyneth's dealings with King Rhodion, supreme king of the fairies, the failed and then the successful siege of Carfilhiot's castle Tintzin Fyral, Shimrod's encounter with the philosophical mountains, Visbhume's capture of Glyneth and removal of her to the unknown world of Tanjecterly, from which she is rescued by an Aillas-avatar, or perhaps Aillas-feroce hybrid (the details are as often only suggested): and others beyond tabulation.

Each of the three imagined worlds highlighted here furthermore has its own atmosphere. The dominant mode of the "Dying Earth" series is, naturally, age. Every breath of air has already passed through a million lungs. One of the cults Cugel encounters has calculated that the entire surface of the Earth now consists of human remains, so that, out of respect, they never set foot on it. Ghosts are everywhere. One result is a mix of gaiety and gloom: "They were gay, these people of waning Earth, feverishly merry, for infinite night was close at hand, when the red sun would finally flicker and go black" (*Compleat Dying Earth* 9). Along with this goes a certain lack of ambition. Cugel repeatedly emerges from deodand-haunted wasteland to find some comfortable village or community, where the inhabitants live in rustic peace and plenty – marred by the observance of some custom whose purpose (like the watch against Magnatz) has been forgotten, or dwindled into myth. The hero of the last *Dying Earth* story, "Guyal of Sfere", is a freak, for he continually asks questions. In the end his irritated father despatches him to the Curator of the Museum of Man, said to be in the Land of the Falling Wall. Protected by the blessing his father lays on the trail, Guyal almost reaches the Museum, until he is decoyed off the trail in the village of the Saponids. They insist on making him judge a beauty contest, the winner of which is sent off with Guyal to the Museum itself. The Saponids do this because they always have. No young man or woman so sent off has ever returned.

This is because the Museum is now home to a malignant ghost, the sending of an even more malignant demon. But it also contains the Curator, immensely old, barely aware of his surroundings, still wondering why the Nocturnal Keykeeper has not come to terminate his shift, and telling Guyal and Shierl they are out of Museum hours. Guyal manages to trick him into self-cure, though this also dissolves the Curator's magical longevity. The demon is (literally) unwound, Guyal becomes Curator. Even he, however, has no plan to use his new power. The story, and the book, end with the words, "What shall we do …" (130).[12] One suspects nothing. There is no mention of Guyal or the Museum in any of the three sequels.

By contrast, the phrase which occurs to me on reading "Planet of Adventure" is the line "Far on the ringing plains of windy Troy", from Tennyson's poem "Ulysses", a poem which ends with the line "To strive, to seek, to find, and not to yield". Much of the action is set on the steppelands of Tschai, inhabited by warlike nomads, crossed by heavily-guarded caravans. Vance has a liking for settings on the steppe. In the "Star Kings" series we hear several times of the venefices, or master-poisoners, of the world Sarkovy. A Sarkoy venefice can infect someone with the poison "cluthe" by passing him a paper napkin: as Kirth Gersen does to the Sarkoy venefice Skop Suthiro, for he also has studied on Sarkovy. As Suthiro lies dying, Gersen says to him, "Godogma, the long-legged walker with wheels on his feet […] has wheeled across the path of your life, and you will never drive your wagon across the Gorobundur" (*Star King* 144). The Sarkoy idea of happiness is freedom (and sufficient wealth earned by assassinations elsewhere) to ride a wagon across the prairies of their

---

12 The words are repeated, first with a question mark, finally without.

home planet. The attraction of the steppes of Tschai, however, seems to be a sense of the limitless. And where there are frequent episodes of cosiness in the "Dying Earth" books – who would not want a manse like Iucounu's on the River Scaum? – "Planet of Adventure", like Tennyson's "Ulysses", projects a sense of constant struggle, towards a clearly-defined goal: reclaim the space-boat, find or build a space-boat, release the alien-controlled humans from their unnatural servitude.

As for "Lyonesse", like Tolkien's Middle-earth, it is to some extent a trilogy controlled by a map, and like Middle-earth again, it is remarkable for its many different environments. Tangled Tantrevalles in the centre; many islands including Troicinet to the south and Skaghane to the west, where Ska and Troice fight their sea-war; the bare moors of Ulfland, which King Aillas aims to reconquer from the Ska; Celtic Godelia to the north, where the Druids rule; and in the centre, Casmir's Lyonesse, rich, powerful, outdone in decadence only by Pomperol, where Mad King Deuel believes himself to be a bird, and decrees bird-costumes for all at the Avian Grand Gala, if necessary surgically inserted. Vance also leads his readers out of the human world into the fairyland of Thripsey Shee, with further glimpses of the worlds entered by the sandestins.

Vance's characteristic copiousness in *Lyonesse* seems to have outrun even his own powers. In the "Epilogue" to volume 1 he looks forward in nine paragraphs to what shall appear in later volumes (*Lyonesse* 429-430). Some of what is promised there does indeed appear in *The Green Pearl* and *Madouc*, but a good half does not. We hear no more of the wizard Shaun Farway, nor of the name "Joald", mention of which makes Casmir and Tamurello fall silent, like the name of Chun the Unavoidable. The boy Traven, who saves himself by teaching the ogre Osmin chess? A no-show, like "the Knight of the Empty Helmet", and his adventure at Castle Rhack. The last paragraph admits that Murgen himself "must presently tire, and in great sorrow concede defeat" – to an adversary never named, but surely one more powerful than Tamurello. Perhaps this is why Lyonesse no longer exists. One more incident we are sorry to have lost is the reappearance of Falael, the malevolent fairy who set upon Dhrun the mordet of bad luck. "From motives of sheer perversity", we are told, "Falael provokes the trolls of Komin Beg to war, in which they are led by a ferocious imp named Dardelloy."

Enough in that page-and-a-half to keep many writers of fantasy occupied for volumes, but to Vance, mere discards. He has in superior measure to any other writer the one gift which is impossible to develop, and stands outside criticism: copiousness of invention. Although the American fantasy tradition, which pre-existed Tolkien and owed nothing to him, produced many fine writers (Avram Davidson, Poul Anderson, Lyon Sprague de Camp, Fritz Leiber), Vance stands on its very pinnacle. It is astonishing that he and his American colleagues have not found more honour from the general reading public in their own country, which has preferred imports like Tolkien, C.S. Lewis, Pullman, Rowling. But once again, the loss is borne by the general reading public: not by those of us who discovered Vance long ago in the prestige-less pages of *Astounding, Galaxy, Fantastic* or *The Magazine of Fantasy and Science Fiction*, ignored by critics, loved by the discerning.

About the author

TOM SHIPPEY has written widely on Old English, Old Norse, and other medieval topics, but is best known for his three books on Tolkien, *The Road to Middle-earth* (4th ed., 2004), *J.R.R. Tolkien: Author of the Century* (2000), and *Roots and Branches: Selected Papers on Tolkien* (2007). He is currently a regular reviewer of fantasy and science fiction for *The Wall Street Journal*.

Bibliography

CLUTE, John, and Peter NICHOLLS (eds.). *The Encyclopedia of Science Fiction*, 2nd ed. London: Orbit, 1993.

CUNNINGHAM, A.E. "Jack Vance: A Bibliography." *Jack Vance. Critical Appreciations and a Bibliography*. ed. A.E. Cunningham. Boston Spa and London: The British Library, 2000. 153-213.

DOWLING, Terry and Jonathan STRAHAN (eds.). *The Early Jack Vance Vol. 1: Hard Luck Diggings*. Burton, MI: Subterranean Press, 2010.

(eds.). *The Early Jack Vance Vol. 2: Dream Castles*. Burton, MI: Subterranean Press, 2012.

(eds.). *The Early Jack Vance Vol. 3: Magic Highways*. Burton, MI: Subterranean Press. 2013.

MARTIN, George R.R. and Gardner DOZOIS (eds.). *Songs of the Dying Earth: Stories in Honour of Jack Vance*. London: HarperVoyager, 2009.

SHIPPEY, Tom. "People are Plastic: Jack Vance and the Dilemma of Cultural Relativism." *Critical Appreciations*, ed. A.E. Cunningham, 67-84.

VANCE, Jack (John HOLBROOK). *Star King*. [1966] London: Panther Books, 1968.

Lyonesse. Suldrun's Garden. [1983] London: Panther Books, 1984.

Planet of Adventure. London: Grafton, 1985.

The Compleat Dying Earth. New York: SFBC, 1998.

Doreen Triebel

Stories That Last: Storytelling in Terry Pratchett's *The Amazing Maurice and His Educated Rodents*

Abstract

Terry Pratchett's *The Amazing Maurice and His Educated Rodents* is a story about stories and the impact they can have on our lives. The most significant tale that is told in the novel is that of a group of sentient rats, who attempt to find a peaceful solution for the problems arising from their troubled relationship with humans and the struggle for limited resources. With the inclusion of these topics, Pratchett gives the otherwise very humorous novel an important ecocritical dimension and he, furthermore, points out the importance of establishing a sustainable coexistence within and between different species. Many characters in this novel, be they human or animal, turn to different kinds of stories in search for guidance and the text shows how these books can instil questionable ideas in their minds, if these fictional texts are taken too literally. However, it also suggests that stories can serve as good sources from which people can derive principles or courses of action that may help them to navigate the real world.

Terry Pratchett's 2001 novel *The Amazing Maurice and His Educated Rodents* is part of the author's extensive Discworld series and one of the few stories associated with this fictional universe that has been marketed specifically as a work for young audiences.[1] The novel has been awarded The Carnegie Medal as an "outstanding book for children" ("Carnegie Medal" n.p.) and elements like the talking animal protagonists, the children characters, the fairy tale allusions or the light, humorous tone render the book particularly suitable for this age group. Nevertheless, the novel, just like Pratchett's other stories, deals with serious topics, which makes it possible for the text to be read on different levels, some of which may pass children and young adults by on first reading but can be fully appreciated by adult audiences. One of the most pervasive and implicitly self-reflexive themes that lie at the very heart of the book is the act of storytelling and the potentially transforming effects that different kinds

---

1 The other children or young adult oriented Discworld novels are the four Tiffany Aching books: *The Wee Free Men* (2003), *A Hat Full of Sky* (2004), *Wintersmith* (2006) and *I Shall Wear Midnight* (2010).

of narratives can have on human beings (and educated rodents). The novel's characters repeatedly refer to and quote from other stories. Some of these are entirely fictional and do not exist outside of Pratchett's book, whereas others are well-known fairy tales, which have, however, been frequently given a modern twist. Of all the stories that are told in the book, however, one is particularly significant. As the narrator asserts, "the thing about stories is that you have to pick the ones that last" (Pratchett, *Maurice* 269) and in this novel that applies to the overshadowing tale that deals with the way in which humans and animals co-exist in the world, making the text a notable contribution to ecocritical literature.

The novel is based on *The Pied Piper of Hamelin*, a German folk tale that goes back to the fourteenth century (Krogmann 67) and that has made its way into the works of many authors, among which are the Brothers Grimm, Johann Wolfgang von Goethe, Berthold Brecht, Robert Browning and China Miéville. When Pratchett started to write the story, it was merely supposed to be a witty and modern rewriting of the original tale but, as he has remarked himself, it soon developed into something more meaningful and profound:

> I came up with the book title a long time ago, and it became just a one-line gag in an adult Discworld book. Then one day I just sat down and thought hard about it and, being me, got hold of every book about rats I could find. I thought it was going to be a simple little fun story that'd take me a couple of months to write. Boy, was I wrong… (Pratchett, "Interview" n.p.)

The story's protagonist is a streetwise, talking cat called Maurice, who has teamed up with a young human rat piper, named Keith, and a group of sentient rodents. After having eaten enchanted garbage disposed of by a university for wizards, the changelings, as the rats call themselves, developed self-consciousness and the ability to talk, and Maurice's capacity for language emerged after he devoured one of the sentient rats. Together they move from one place to the other in order to trick villagers into thinking they have a rat infestation and to offer them chargeable services. Keith then eliminates the alleged problem by pretending to lure the rats out of the village and after their work is done, the group shares the profits. When Maurice and his companions arrive at the town of Bad Blintz in Überwald, the rats agree that this is going to be their last job, because they have moral qualms about practicing trickery and deceit in order to enrich themselves. However, there is something strange about this allegedly rat-afflicted place, in which, despite obvious attempts to eradicate rats wherever they might do damage,[2] no rodents are actually visible. Another group of rat catchers, who has arrived in Bad Blintz long before Maurice and the talking rodents, are seemingly fighting the rats in the town rigorously but they are quite dubious and, as the group discovers, are passing off bootlaces as tails of dead rats. Furthermore, it turns out that the rat catchers have been breeding rats for coursing[3] and that they have created a powerful rat king,[4] which calls itself Spider, by tying together the tails of eight rats. Spider, whose main goal it is to take revenge on humankind, is a superorganism that has only a single mind, with which he can gain access to the consciousness of other individuals and exert power over them. With the help of Malicia, the daughter of Bad Blintz' mayor, the group around Maurice successfully fights the rat king and the rat catchers who have brought it into being. What is more, in the end the talking rats and Keith manage to strike a deal with the inhabitants of the town that guarantees a peaceful co-existence between rodents and man.

The two characters or groups of characters that are particularly connected with storytelling are Malicia[5] and the educated rats. While the first is a somewhat quixotic character who has internalised the folk tales she has read and perpetually refers to different problem solving strategies that were successfully employed by the protagonists of these stories, the latter seek spiritual guidance in what they regard as a sacred book, *Mr Bunnsy Has an Adventure*. Shortly after the rodents gain consciousness, they discover this book among others in a shop and take it with them, because its content seems to be particularly intriguing to them. The rats start to ask philosophical questions and create a code of ethics that is based on the book. The story about an anthropomorphised rabbit and his friends calms them down in dangerous situations and gives them hope for

---

[2] There is a very generous reward for everyone who kills a rat.
[3] Coursing is a method of hunting game or other animals that involves dogs trained to chase the quarry by sight instead of scent.
[4] Rat kings are rare but actually existing phenomena, which assumedly occur when a group of rats are tied together at their tails or intertwined, because excrements, ice or other substances cause them to stick together. For more information regarding rats and the formation of rat kings, see Hart (66ff).
[5] The fact that the girl's name is evocative of the Latin adjective *malus* – meaning bad, ugly or unlucky – is a somewhat ironic joke by Pratchett. He uses a story to suggest that a character that reads and tells narratives carries negatively connoted characteristics.

a world they regard as better, a world in which different species are not hostile towards each other and lead a friendly co-existence:

> There was a rabbit who walked on its hind legs and wore a blue suit. There was a rat in a hat, and he wore a sword and a big red waistcoat, complete with a watch on a chain. Even the snake had a collar and tie. And all of them talked and none of them ate any of the others and – and this was the unbelievable part – they all talked to humans, who treated them like, well, smaller humans. There were no traps, no poisons. (Pratchett, *Maurice* 48)

This utopian vision of a future in which individuals belonging to different species have reached a stage of mutual respect and harmonious co-operation is evoked again and again in the text and it is a particularly desirable one for the rodents.[6] Through the incorporation of this story within the story and the associated topic of the relationship between humans and animals Pratchett adds an important ecocritical dimension to the book.

Ecocriticism has only recently begun to pay more attention to literature for children and young adults.[7] One of the main reasons for that may be that fiction for this specific age group is an "often trivialized genre" (Sigler 148), but ecologically conscious stories written for a young target audience are particularly significant, because they have the potential to help promote an awareness of environmental problems among future generations. As Reynolds points out, stories for juvenile audiences are often highly subversive, because authors are aware of "the fact that children will not just inherit the future, but need to participate in shaping it" (14). Furthermore, studies have shown that "younger people tend to be more concerned about environmental quality than older people" (Van Liere and Dunlap 182), from which it follows that children and young adults could be more susceptible to environmental problems expressed in stories and more willing to influence and transform the social discourse about our relationship with the natural world. The propensity of young adult literature to give expression to non-conformist ideas and to question the current status quo makes this kind of fiction very suitable for the purpose of pointing out certain problems in our environmental policy and the often problematic

---

6 In this respect, the story bears some resemblance with *Animal Farm* but, in contrast to Orwell's allegorical story, the rat characters in *Maurice* do not clearly stand for human beings only.
7 See Pavlik or Dobrin & Kidd, who point out in their "Introduction" to *Wild Things: Children's Culture and Ecocriticism*, published in 2004, that "[t]hus far, children's culture studies and ecocriticism have been largely separate undertakings" (3).

manner in which humans treat their natural surroundings. If ecologically conscious stories question the dominant cultural ideology, according to which humans have the right to control nature and to exploit natural resources in order to further their development goals, they can favour a shift in environmental thinking. These narratives can emphasize the interrelatedness of humans and non-human species, rather than placing the former at the centre of the story and marginalizing animal characters or portraying predominantly domesticated animals in an anthropomorphic manner. In addition to calling attention to certain issues concerning our relationship to the natural world, stories may even suggest potential solutions for problems like environmental degradation, climate change, pollution or the disconnectedness between human individuals and nature. All this suggests that these texts can indeed offer a contribution to the environmental socialization of children and young adults and cause them to reconsider the ways in which humanity interferes with the non-human environment.[8]

The theme of the interconnectedness of all individuals on Earth and the questioning of the way in which humans, as the dominant species, treat their natural surroundings are among the more serious aspects in *Maurice*. They are introduced to the novel by means of the aforementioned story within the story. The book *Mr Bunnsy Has an Adventure*, which the sentient rats carry with them at all times, is reminiscent of many children's tales featuring highly anthropomorphised animal characters that speak, dress and act like human individuals, stories like Beatrix Potter's Peter Rabbit stories or Kenneth Grahame's *The Wind in the Willows*. The tale Pratchett embeds in his narrative is also in many ways the kind of story that ecocritics have frequently found fault with, because it presents an anthropocentric world view. However, names such as *Furry Bottom*, which refers to the place where Mr Bunnsy, Ratty Rupert and Olly the Snake have to solve different kinds of more or less trifling problems, suggests that the story is also an exaggeration of these popular children's tales and a parody of books that show humanity not as part of the ecosystem but as being above it.

---

[8] For a more detailed discussion of eco-critical stories for children and young adults, see for example Henderson, Kennedy and Chamberlin.

Pratchett's novel contains short excerpts of the *Mr Bunnsy* tale in the form of epigraphs and the rats are frequently shown to read from the story. What is significant with regard to the intelligent rodents and this book is the approach that they take to it. When they first found it in the bookshop, their initial response was an attempt to imitate the characters, for instance in clothing: "They'd tried wearing waistcoats, but it had been very difficult to bite out the pattern, they couldn't make the buttons work and, frankly, the things got caught on every splinter and were very hard to run in. Hats just fell off" (Pratchett, *Maurice* 48). As this mildly humorous passage suggests, trying to ape the characters and their human actions or appearances is not a successful strategy in dealing with the story. Although *Mr Bunnsy* incorporates characters that seem to resemble the rats in many ways and gives them something to aspire to, several aspects of the tale and its characters' lives are not directly applicable to the clan's reality. Only later do they realize that trying to mimic Mr Bunnsy and his friends is not a practical and helpful way of responding to the book.

The adoption of more abstract propositions from the tale in other areas of life, however, results in substantial and positive changes in the rats' behaviour. After experiencing some disappointments with imitating Mr Bunnsy's actions, the younger members of the clan realize – much more than Hamnpork,[9] their leader – the potential of stories as well as writing to gather vital information and transfer knowledge to future generations. With this awareness they initiate an attempt to record guidelines for action, which they derive from the tale. Peaches, the official carrier of the book, translates the human letters into a sign system that is understandable for rats and Dangerous Beans, the near-blind brain of the group, has made it his task to convince the other rats to follow these principles. The "Thoughts" they put down in writing concern different aspects of their lives and they read as follows: 1. "In the Clan is Strength", 2. "We co-operate, or we die", 3. "Not to Widdle where you Eat", 4. "No Rat to Kill Another Rat" and 5. "We Are The Changelings. We Are Not Like Other Rats" (Pratchett, *Maurice* 56-61).

---

9 The names of the individual rats are derived from the labels of tin cans that they found on the garbage heap.

Most of these imperatives reflect the rats' growing awareness that they are part of the ecosystem, just like normal rats, which are referred to as "Keekees", humans or other individuals. Moreover, they show that the rats have realized the necessity of collaborating closely within their group and of forming alliances and partnerships with other individuals in order to achieve a sustainable co-existence. The members of the clan are prepared to risk their lives to help each other in dangerous situations. When, for example, one of them is in danger of being killed by one the rat catchers' trained dogs, the others do everything in their power to save him, even if that involves considerable risks for themselves. This sense of fellowship among the rats is, furthermore, emphasised through their unwavering trust in the support of the others and the manner in which they solve all problems that stand in their way as a group. They allocate tasks according to the specific talents of each rat – one rat is a daunting fighter, whereas another is more on the intellectual side and a third is a skilful tap dancer, which comes in handy when they need to distract some humans – and it is this form of collaboration that enables them to eliminate the rat king in the end. This notion of having to work together does, as Thought no. 2 suggests, also extend to individuals from other species, which has led them to team up with one of their most perilous enemies, a cat, and even to trust him with their lives. The co-operation with Maurice proves to be in many ways highly advantageous for all sides. In the beginning of the story, it helps them to surreptitiously obtain money that they could not have gotten on their own, Maurice plays a decisive role in the elimination of the rat king and in the end he even assists in bringing about peace between the educated rats and the human inhabitants of Bad Blintz. The collaborations with Keith and later also Malicia are similarly important for the clan.

Right from the beginning, the novel shows not only the problematic relationship that humans have with rats, but also the fact that the different life forms in a village are necessarily closely interconnected. The first is exemplified by Malicia's initial remark that "the only good rat is a *dead* rat!" (Pratchett, *Maurice* 71). This is, however, an opinion that she almost immediately revises after she gets to know the changelings and learns more about their way of life. In order to illustrate the latter point, the text shows how the actions performed by one group affects the living environment and the resources that it shares with fellow inhabitants of the same space. The story about the rats' transformation, for instance, portrays how the waste that the human academics have disposed of rather thoughtlessly on a nearby dump provides food for rodents and it furthermore shows that this interchange of resources results in mutual influence between the different living beings co-existing in a certain environment. In this way, the story does, as Oziewicz (88) points out, implicitly promote ecological literacy, i.e. an understanding of the basic ecological principles that enable life on earth to flourish. He demonstrates that the novel deals with and educates about five of the six principles that Fritjof Capra considers to be essential for life: "networks, cycles, [...] partnership, diversity and dynamic balance"[10] (*Connections* 230). The pervasion of these topics in *Maurice* marks the book as an ecologically conscious tale, but what is also significant is that most of these aspects already find expression in *Mr Bunnsy* or in the rats' reaction to the book.

The tales in which the talking rabbit and his friends experience various adventures strongly emphasize the importance of networks and partnerships among different kinds of animals and the necessity of working together in order to solve more or less existential problems. The rats pick up these ideas and make them part of their guiding principles. As a consequence of their becoming aware of the importance of these interrelations they do not only work closer together within their group but also resolve to co-operate with individuals that are usually considered to be their mortal enemies if that helps them to survive. Although the stories Peaches repeatedly reads out to the other rats do not paint a realistic picture of interspecies communication or collaboration, and neither does Pratchett's novel, they all serve to draw the readers' attention to the intricate ways in which the different life forms are interconnected and to emphasize that no species can exist outside of this natural order. In so doing the stories reject the Human Exemptionalism Paradigm (HEP), according to which "human beings, by virtue of culture and human ingenuity, will overcome all social and environmental problems" (McDonald and Patterson 170), i.e. the notion that humankind is not dependent on their natural surroundings.

The insight that individuals who possess a higher level of intelligence should not necessarily regard themselves as hierarchically above other beings and treat

---

10 The sixth principle that Capra names is solar energy.

them in a careless manner is reflected in the rats' opinion of Keekees. Not unlike human beings, who are derived from less-developed animals, the changelings initially regard themselves as superior to those rats who have not undergone the transformation. This idea finds expression in Thought no. 5[11] and Dangerous Beans adds that they are now "more than that [i.e. normal rats]" (Pratchett, *Maurice* 59). The sentient rats believe that they can control their basal instincts with the help of their newly acquired intelligence, but later on in the novel the voice of Spider, which gets inside their heads in an almost telepathic manner and which is capable of arousing deadly terror in the changelings, turning them back into Keekees, teaches them otherwise.

Moreover, shortly after their transformation the sentient rats deem it their right to kill especially non-sentient rats whenever they see fit, but in the course of the novel they experience a change of mind, which is already suggested by Thought no. 4. At the beginning, however, they do not take this to include Keekees. Dangerous Bean's narrative-induced ethical reasoning brings about this altered attitude in the near-blind rodent, and he starts to see, more clearly than the others, that their treatment of Keekees is only slightly less condemnable than the way in which humans have been dealing with rats in the past. If it is the clan's goal to establish a friendly co-existence with humans and other species, in which all are accepted as equal, they must learn that, despite the notion of their own supremacy, normal rats have an equally inalienable right to life. Later in the story, they even assist non-sentient animals to escape the rat-catchers' traps and cages, because they realize that "[they] can think about what [they] do. [They] can pity the innocent one who means [them] no harm" (Pratchett, *Maurice* 103). As a consequence, they begin to treat Keekees not as inferior beings but as individuals who deserve as much respect as any of their clan members.

In addition to these ideas, which stress the significance of communication and co-operation within and between species, Pratchett's novel and, albeit far less clearly, the story within the story deal with the other ecological principles identified by Capra. They show, for instance, how resources "cycl[e] continually through

---

11 This Thought, "We Are The Changelings. We Are Not Like Other Rats," is somewhat reminiscent of one of the pigs' commandments in Orwell's *Animal Farm*, "ALL ANIMALS ARE EQUAL. BUT SOME ANIMALS ARE MORE EQUAL THAN OTHERS" (Orwell 118).

the web of life" (Capra, "Challenge" 49), which is to be seen in the way the rats obtain their food from a "dump they called 'home' and also called 'lunch'" (Pratchett, *Maurice* 23) and in Maurice's preying on smaller animals such as rats or receiving food from humans who are well-disposed towards him. *Maurice* also demonstrates that "diversity increases resilience" (Capra, "Challenge" 49). As Oziewicz points out, this idea of biodiversity as something that is valuable and worthy of protection is promoted especially "in episodes in which the human and animal protagonists are able to come up with solutions to problems only because they are so different from one another and have to engage in dialogue" (88). An example for this kind of fruitful co-operation is the way the group handles the problem concerning the real rat piper who is due to arrive in Bad Blintz. The plan that is devised by Keith, Malicia, the rats and also Maurice is successful just because it incorporates their individual experiences. When the former three first propose their ideas of shaming the piper and thereby causing him to leave the town to the cat, the latter immediately rejects their scheme remarking, "You don't know anything about people, do you?" and he adds, "Cats know about people. We have to. No-one else can open cupboards. Look, even the rat king had a better plan than that. A good plan isn't one where someone wins, it's where nobody thinks they've lost. Understand?" (Pratchett, *Maurice* 223-224) Together they think of a better course for action that includes the initial plan but also takes Maurice's suggestions into consideration and, being prepared for all contingencies, Malicia can provide the cotton-wool they need to block the rats' ears, so that they will not be charmed by the sounds of the famous piper's magic flute. Keith challenges the man to a piping duel during which he strikes a deal with the stranger:

> "We'll do it together, and the rats will *follow* us, really follow us into the river. Don't bother about the trick note, this will be even better. It'll be... it'll be a great ... story," said Keith. "And you'll get your money. Three hundred dollars, wasn't it? But you'll settle for half, because I'm helping you." (Pratchett, *Maurice* 243)

Together they lead the Keekees out of the village and everyone, including the inhabitants of Bad Blintz, is satisfied with the outcome of this agreement. The story makes clear that this plan could not have been thought up by humans, rats or Maurice alone but only by an act that Alan Palmer (218-230) has referred to as "intermental thought". This concept describes a form of shared thought in which two or more individuals are aware of each other's ideas and mental workings and can come up with the solution to a problem for which not one of them can take credit but which emerges in the interaction with one another and the exchange of thoughts and opinions. In depicting this form of interaction between different species and showing that obstacles can only be overcome if all of them contribute ideas that lead to a solution, the story makes a strong point for the value of biodiversity.

An issue that *Mr Bunnsy*, however, fails to address but that is illustrated quite clearly in Pratchett's story about the sentient rats is that human interaction with and manipulation of the ecosystem can become problematic for the natural environment. This is also the major point of critique for Malicia, who refers to the book as "stupid stuff for ickle kids" with animals that "all go around wearing clothes and talking to humans and everyone's so nice and cosy it makes you absolutely sick" (Pratchett, *Maurice* 161). Moreover, she criticises that "there's no sub-texts, no social commentary" (Pratchett, *Maurice* 161). *Mr Bunnsy* presents an idealised and overly harmonious world, in which animals can speak with humans and are treated as equals by them. The text excludes any reference to ecological problems, violence, predation or killing of rats and other individuals, whereas Pratchett's novel, in contrast, describes quite extensively how humans attempt to free their villages from the rats that feed on their provisions by using poison, traps or other means. In so doing, the novel shows a certain degree of self-referentiality. This divergence between the story world presented in the main narrative and that of the *Mr Bunnsy* tale, especially with regard to problems concerning interspecies interactions, can be seen as an indirect comment on and critique of a certain kind of stories, namely those that present animal characters in the same way as the embedded children's tale. Despite its shortcomings, however, the book about the anthropomorphised rabbit and his friends has the potential of giving the rats a set of principles that they use as a basis to establish moral rules and something they can aspire to – a future in which they are not at war with humans but have learned to co-operate with them.

The negative way in which humans influence the environment is connected to the last of Capra's principles, dynamic balance. As Oziewicz argues, the novel shows the flexibility of ecosystems, which are perpetually subject to change, "as life-affirming by contrasting it with the dominance-based stasis envisioned by the rat catchers or the Rat King" (88). Living environments that show an element of change and natural development, as we see it in Bad Blintz, where many smaller animals, including rats, have slowly adapted to sharing a living space with humans, are depicted as positive and so is the final agreement between the clan and the inhabitants of the village. At the same time, the rat catchers' aim of artificially breeding particularly sturdy rodents that could earn them plenty of money in coursing but that are no longer subject to a natural evolution, is clearly criticised. Spider, on the other hand, represents a hostile way of dealing with the negative manner in which humans influence the ecosystem. He responds particularly to the living conditions of rodents and plans to wreak vengeance on humans for having poisoned and killed his fellow rats for centuries. As he points out to Dangerous Beans trying to win him as an ally,

> But we, we are RATS! And my rats will swim, believe me. Big rats, different rats, rats who survive, rats with part of my mind in them. And they will spread from town to town and then there will be destruction such as people cannot imagine! We will pay them back a thousandfold for every trap! Humans have tortured and poisoned and killed and all of that is now given form in me and there will be REVENGE. (Pratchett, *Maurice* 206)

Realizing that the rat king's plans would not only mean interspecies war and destruction but also result in the death of many rats, mostly the weaker ones, Dangerous Beans refuses to join Spider's cause. Moreover, the rat king's vision would probably also result in a certain developmental stasis. If his plans were realized, both species would actively oppose changes in their living conditions, which would go hand in hand with evolutionary stagnation. The rat king refuses to accept the developments that led humans and rats to share a living space. The battle he wants to incite would ensure that both species continue to live quite isolated from one another instead of adapting to the changed circumstances and trying to lead a peaceful co-existence. As the white rat points out to the man-made creature,

> Once we were just another squeaking thing in the forest [...] and then men built barns and pantries full of food. Of course we took what we could. And so they called us vermin, and they have trapped us and covered us in poison and, somehow, out of that wretchedness, you have come. But you are no answer. You are just another bad thing humans made. You offer rats nothing except more pain. (Pratchett, *Maurice* 211)

Dangerous Beans is very vehement in his opposition to the ideas of Spider. He has another future in mind, not just for the changelings but for all rats, a future that does not mimic but is inspired by the tales he had been cherishing for a long time and that is characterized by solidarity and co-operation. The effectiveness of this approach is shown in the annihilation of the rat king, which is brought about by the joint efforts of Maurice and the rats to unknot the creature's tails. The value of comradeship is, furthermore, demonstrated when Maurice performs a selfless act in giving up one of his remaining cat lives to death in order to save Dangerous Beans, who would otherwise have been taken by the Bone Rat.

For the changelings, the myth of the Bone Rat exists separately, but alongside the *Mr Bunnsy* stories. It is another narrative that they use to explain death and to make it less frightening. After Darktan, who is something like the military leader of the rat clan and fills Hamnpork's shoes after his death, gets caught in a trap and has a near-death experience, he feels as if he has stared the Big Rat in the face, which for him is a quite formative but much less daunting occurrence than he had anticipated. The myth helps him to get through this situation and survive, although it is Nourishing, a young rat, who saves his life by gnawing through the spring of the trap. Later, Darktan, the "rat who wears the teeth-marks of the Bone Rat like a belt" (Pratchett, *Maurice* 192), tells others about this encounter and the vision it has inspired in him:

> When I was in that … place, I … saw the shape of an idea. There's been a war between humans and rats for ever! It's got to end. And here, now, in this place, with these rats… I can see that it can. This might be the only time and the only place where it can. I can see the shape of an idea in my head but I can't think of the words for it, do you understand? So we need the white rat [Dangerous Beans], because he knows the map for thinking. We've got to think our way out of this. Running around and squeaking won't work any more! (Pratchett, *Maurice* 193)

These words, which are reminiscent of Martin Luther King's famous "I Have A Dream" speech, suggest that the myth, together with this experience leads him to reject the idea of an isolated place just for rats and makes him realize that the future lies in a mutually beneficial and sustainable co-existence with the humans. As Darktan points out, only the changelings may be capable of bringing about peace between rats and humans, because they can serve as mediator and bridge the gap between the two species by convincing the latter that the difference between rodents and human beings is not as fundamental as it is assumed. This realisation of similarities could then lead to more friendly contacts and eventually even to a transformed attitude towards the other, which may enable animals and humans to establish a symbiotic relationship that would benefit all sides.

What is more, Darktan is aware of the fact that Hamnpork, their preceding leader with his somewhat outdated principles and view of life, could not have brought about this necessary change, whereas Dangerous Beans, whose thinking has been strongly affected by storytelling, may be able to fulfil this vision. In view of narratives such as the one about the "Grim Squeaker" (Pratchett, *Maurice* 220), it becomes clear that myths and stories provide a basis for the changelings to philosophise about important events or entities and that they help them to make sense of the world around them. To this end, these stories are notably more significant than the old axioms that they followed before they started to tell each other narratives or read stories like *Mr Bunnsy*. One of these older principles is the advice that Hamnpork gives Darktan just before he dies and that he obviously regards as the most important message to pass on to the new leader and future generations: "Don't eat the green wobbly bit [of dead rats]!"[12] (Pratchett, *Maurice* 264) This may, as Darktan asserts, still be a useful recommendation but, given the changed circumstances, it is no longer sufficient as a sole guideline for their behaviour. It does not lead to the establishment of moral or ethical rules, which have become necessary for the sentient rodents, and it does not help to create mutually beneficial and balanced co-operations between different species. Furthermore, this piece of advice is closely associated with violent behaviour like mutual killing, which the rats attempt to overcome. This is why Darktan comments on Hamnpork's advice with the words, "but all he had to do was be big and tough and fight all the other rats that wanted to be leader" (Pratchett, *Maurice* 264). The new leader, however, has to face problems of a very different nature. After the rats gained self-consciousness and started to ask questions about the meaning of their existence or appropri-

---

12 Although the story never makes quite clear what part exactly "the green wobbly bit" is, this phrase is kind of a running joke in the story. It is mentioned several times and the sentient rats but also Maurice seem to be aware that they should always avoid eating that particular piece of a dead rat.

ate ways to interact with other individuals, stories have proved to be a more practical basis for guidelines than the rigid and simple axioms that they used to follow in the past.

Towards the end of the novel, when rats and humans have come to a mutually satisfactory agreement, the rodents move beyond the mere possession of knowledge about the principles that govern the natural processes in an ecosystem. As Oziewicz points out, the "ecoliterate protagonists apply their knowledge and experience to create an ecologically sustainable community based on sustainable co-existence between the rats and the humans" (88). At this point they start using these insights in order to establish a peaceful way of living together with individuals from other species and to find practices for interacting with others in a manner that benefits all parties involved. With this final agreement between allegedly irreconcilable species, the text also offers environmentally aware readers a "map" (Pratchett, *Maurice* 257) for a potential solution to some of the ecological problems they experience in their reality. While the text makes clear that this solution will not suit everyone, it again stresses the importance of stories in general and their significance for the achieved rapprochement in particular:

> And there are lectures about the Rat Tax and how the whole system works, and how the rats have a town of their own under the human town, and get free use of the library, and even sometimes send their young rats to the school. And everyone says: How perfect, how well organized, how *amazing*! And then most of them go back to their own towns and set their traps and put down their poisons, because some minds you couldn't change with a hatchet. But a few see the world as a different place. It's not perfect, but it works. The thing about stories is that you have to pick the ones that last. (Pratchett, *Maurice* 269)

Although *Mr Bunnsy* paints a highly romanticised and unrealistic picture of nature, and does not try to raise awareness of the finite nature of natural resources or anthropogenic impacts on the environment, some of the story's implied moral axioms or rather the more abstract conclusions that the sentient rats draw from these are highly significant and become part of the final pact between talking rats and humans. The most important of these is certainly the awareness of the importance of co-operation.

After Darktan and the Mayor of Bad Blintz had a talk in which they found surprisingly many commonalities, which, in turn, enables them to establish some kind of bond between the groups they represent, everyone seems to accept the changes quite naturally. In a self-referential comment, however, the narrator of the novel makes clear that this is by no means a fairy tale happy ending:

> If it was a story, and not real life, then humans and rats would have shaken hands and gone on into a bright new future. But since it was real life, there had to be a contract. A war that had been going on since people first lived in houses could not end with just a happy smile. And there had to be a committee. (Pratchett, *Maurice* 257)

This again makes quite clear that the story of Darktan and the other changelings, which is ironically referred to as "real life," is not necessarily consistent with narratives like *Mr Bunnsy*. The latter draws a romanticised picture of co-existence between species, which is far removed from reality, but it can, nevertheless, inspire readers to seek a solution, although it might diverge quite clearly from the ones presented in stories and involve numerous hardships. The approach taken by the rats and the inhabitants of Bad Blintz is much less idealized than the harmonious idyll depicted in many other stories but these narratives prove useful in the process of bringing about an understanding between the two opposing parties. Dangerous Beans and the others realize that, rather than giving concrete instructions, stories can serve as thought-provoking impulses or show possible outcomes of certain courses of action, they can illustrate various options and allow the reader simulate future situations. The rats learn not to adhere strictly to ideas or alleged instructions that are to be found in *Mr Bunnsy*, as they did earlier when they put on human-like clothing, but to accept the story as a source for rough guidelines, which they can use in order to establish a moral code or possibly even to help them find solutions to problems.

The other character, with whom the novel emphasizes the significance of stories but also the importance of a critical distance to them, is Malicia. She has internalised numerous stories and prides herself upon being a relative of the famous Sisters Agoniza and Eviscera[13] Grim. As this and other references to authors, characters or plot details of well-known narratives show, Pratchett frequently takes up elements from well-known fairy tales, myths or legends, adapts them and comically reworks them into his novel[14] and particularly the subplot of the Mayor's daughter. In contrast to the rodents, Malicia clearly distinguishes between "*real* fairy-tales" and "stories about little people with wings going tinkle-tinkle"[15] (Pratchett, *Maurice* 77). With this character Pratchett introduces an element of self-reflexiveness into the text. He uses the fantastic story to ask what characteristics a fairy tale should or can possess and whether certain elements, character types or the lack of social commentary can make a story irrelevant, trivial or simply too fantastic. When she tells the rats about *Mr Bunnsy* and discloses to them that it is merely a fictional story and not, as they believed up to this point, a true account, she makes clear that in her opinion the first kind of stories is worthy of serious attention, whereas the latter is not. This is, as she remarks, because fairy tales like the ones written by her grandmothers are suspenseful, contain "a bit of interesting violence" (Pratchett, *Maurice* 161) and express some social criticism. Although it seems at first sight as if the novel supports this distinction by poking fun at whimsical and anthropocentric stories, in which animals dress and behave like humans, Pratchett's book self-consciously shows that tales like this can still bring readers to question certain ideologies or social practices. What is heartily ridiculed in *Maurice* is that Malicia, not unlike the rats in the beginning, also makes the mistake of taking the narratives she has read quite literally. At the same time, however, the novel suggests that her reading of the tales enables her and the rodents to overcome some challenges, before the rat clan can eliminate Spider and come to an agreement with the inhabitants of Bad Blintz.

---

13 Similar to Malicia's name, the names of the sisters, Agoniza – derived from the Anglo-Norman noun *agonie* meaning agony – and Eviscera – derived from the Latin verb *ēviscerāre* meaning to eviscerate –, are ironical comments on storytelling.
14 There are, among others, references to "Puss in Boots", "Bluebeard" and Washington Irving's "The Legend of Sleepy Hollow".
15 This comment might allude to the character Tinker Bell in J.M. Barrie's *Peter Pan*, whose fairy language sounds like the tinkling of bells, or similarly diminutive and butterfly-like creatures in comparable fairy stories.

When Malicia sees the talking cat for the first time, her tendency to interpret everything in terms of fairy tales and prototypical characters becomes quite obvious. She is immediately reminded of the tales she is so familiar with and even small deviations from her expectations irritate her immensely. In this respect she resembles literary characters like Cervantes' Don Quixote or Twain's Tom Sawyer, who have read romances about chivalry or stories about pirates and robbers, respectively, and who imagine themselves in the roles of the protagonists of these stories. Moreover, just like these two fictional adventurers, she has a companion, Keith, who serves as a less imaginative foil character and the tension between the two and their different world views is a continual source of humour in the book. Right from the beginning, the other characters poke fun at the Mayor's daughter for her bookish nature and her strong belief in and strict adherence to stories. At one point, for instance, Maurice teases her by claiming that the witch he allegedly belongs to, Griselda, lives in a crisp bread cottage instead of a gingerbread house, "cos she was slimming. Very healthy witch, Griselda" (Pratchett, *Maurice* 64). Malicia expects Keith to be a prince of sorts, because he seems to fit the cliché of the abandoned orphan boy who has a secret past that is to be revealed by the end of the tale. Later on in the story, when the rat catchers discover the group in their den, Malicia expects the young piper to develop supernatural strength and to fight the villains, thus enabling her group to escape. Although Malicia even succeeds in convincing Maurice of her point of view, Keith does not turn out to be a fairy tale hero who fulfils their narrative-inspired hopes:

> Here it comes, thought Maurice. He's going to leap forward with superhuman strength because he's so angry and they're going to wish he'd never been born ... Keith leapt forward with ordinary human strength, landed one punch on Rat-catcher 1 and was smacked to the floor again by a big, brutal, sledgehammer blow. (Pratchett, *Maurice* 125)

Just like in this case, many of Malicia's expectations regarding the characters she meets prove to be comically inaccurate. Furthermore, there are situations in which her profound knowledge of narratives cannot help her and she is left at a loss of what to do. When she has to face the rat king and his rodents, for instance, she – feeling unprepared – complains that "there's never been a book about having an adventure in a rat-catcher's cellar!" (Pratchett, *Maurice* 213) What this example suggests is that she lacks the capacity or willingness to draw abstract conclusions from the tales. Unlike the sentient rats, who learn from their experiences, Malicia consistently uses the stories first and foremost as manuals that should give her direct instructions rather than as rough ideas. This often flawed approach to stories taken by the character could serve to undermine the notion that narratives are useful sources of information, and that they have the potential to suggest courses of action, which may help readers to cope with diverse situations. Yet, even if Malicia's way of reading some stories on a rather literal level and of taking the characters therein as direct role models is humorously criticised, her narrative-induced assumptions and actions are not in all cases wrong.

The story makes clear that her knowledge of stories and the comically precise and detailed application of these narrative elements onto the present situation is in many cases exactly what allows her to see through many a secret and it is also what enables Maurice, Keith and the rats to overcome certain difficulties. After she gets to know the sentient rats, she immediately senses a fairy tale like story behind their supernatural abilities and she also rightly assumes that the newcomers to Bad Blintz plan to hoax the humans in the village in order to get money. Later, when the group attempts to get inside the rat catchers' house, it is Malicia who opens the door with a hair pin, because, as she asserts, "hair pins always work in the books I've read. You just push it into the keyhole and twiddle. I have a selection of pre-bent ones" (Pratchett, *Maurice* 98).[16] She carries a bag with her in which she has all utensils that she could possibly use in case she ever comes into one of the situations she has read about in stories and, although she is frequently ridiculed for her behaviour, some of these items do indeed help the group around Maurice to free the village from the insidious rat catchers. She can also give invaluable advice regarding the detection of secret passages or the treatment of villains who need to be kept in check.[17]

---

16 Passages like this one are again reminiscent of the character of Tom Sawyer, who tries to follow the books he has read as closely as possible. When he and his friends, for instance, decide to found a band of robbers, he wants them to sign an oath with their blood and hold people to ransom. Being asked what the latter means, he answers: "I don't know. But that's what they do. I've seen it in books; and so of course that's what we've got to do" and he adds, "Do you want to go to doing different from what's in the books, and get things all muddled up?" (Twain 11-12)

17 Her "weapon of choice" in this case is a laxative, but she tricks the rat catchers into believing that they have swallowed a deadly poison.

It is, however, significant that her advice is often most effective when she allows herself a bit more creativity in her treatment of stories and that is also what she advises Keith to do while they are both caught in the rat catchers' den and he attempts to make her understand that life is not a story:

> "I used to get beaten when I was small for telling stories," Malicia went on.
> "Beaten?" said Keith.
> "All right, then, smacked," said Malicia. "On the leg. But it *did* hurt. My father says you can't run a city on stories. He says you have to be practical."
> "Oh." [...]
> The calm voice infuriated Malicia. "Well, I'll *tell* you something," she said. "If you don't turn your life into a story, you just become a part of someone else's story."
> "And what if your story doesn't work?"
> "You keep changing it until you find one that does."
> (Pratchett, *Maurice* 148)

Malicia also shows some creativity with regard to storytelling when she starts to make up narratives in order to solve certain problems. When she has to explain the broken crockery caused by Sardines[18] to her father, she tells him a story about having had to escape from a giant rat and, as she asserts, "[i]t was a good one, too. It was much more true than the truth would sound. A tap-dancing rat?" (Pratchett, *Maurice* 86) Malicia's storytelling is essential to the plot of the novel and its happy ending and it is certainly no coincidence that, after the rat king has perished, it is the bookish daughter of the Mayor who successfully urges her father to enter into negotiations with the rodents, thereby facilitating the process of rapprochement between the two parties.

In the first chapter Pratchett introduces the novel with the help of a metanarrative element, two characters' opinions as to what the story is about: "as the amazing Maurice said, it was just a story about people and rats. And the difficult part of it was deciding who the people were, and who were the rats. But Malicia Grim said it was a story about stories" (Pratchett, *Maurice* 9). Both views prove to be correct and, as we have seen, these two topics are closely intertwined. *Maurice* is in essence a novel about storytelling and the capacity of narrative to make people see things from another perspective, to encourage them to question existing norms and possibly even to devise new ethical principles. As the novel also makes clear, however, stories should not be taken as behavioural guidelines

---

18 Early in the novel, Sardines, the tap dancing rat, breaks some crockery in the Mayor's house, while he is doing one of his dance routines. This is when Malicia sees the sentient rats for the first time.

that are to be followed closely but rather as rough maps, which show possible courses of action and explore different perspectives and outcomes. Although some of the educated rats wear pieces of clothing and all of them are capable of speech, they are notably not anthropomorphised in the same way as many animal characters in stories for children and young adults; stories such as the Peter Rabbit tales, which are simultaneously parodied and paid homage to in *Maurice*. The rats in Pratchett's novel do not construct or live in human-like dwellings, most of the time they act like rodents and not like humans in disguise and their clan does not directly represent a human society. Nevertheless, the text emphasises that rats are fellow inhabitants of this planet and that they are, together with other species, worthy of protection. It is stressed that rats are in many ways quite similar to human beings in that they show intelligence and prosocial behaviour[19] and the story, furthermore, highlights the necessity of finding a way to a sustainable co-existence. *Maurice* addresses the issue of humanity's often problematic relationship to rats and other animals considered vermin, thereby making many readers reconsider previously held attitudes towards these creatures. Thus, the most significant stories that are told in the novel –"the ones that last" (Pratchett, *Maurice* 269) – are characterized by a strong eco-awareness. This lends the text significance for environmental education that goes beyond that of "a simple little fun story" (Pratchett, "Interview" n.p.) and also exceeds that of many tales for young adults incorporating sentient animal characters.

About the author

DOREEN TRIEBEL is a Ph.D. student in British Literature at the University of Jena. While the main focus of her research lies on the field of cognitive approaches to literature, she also harbours an intense interest in fantasy literature and speculative fiction.

---

19 It may be quite interesting to know that a number of studies have actually suggested that rats show behaviour indicative of a certain degree of empathy and altruism, e.g. Langford et al. or Ben-Ami Bartal, Decety and Mason. Furthermore, rats have been found to possess a relatively high degree of intelligence and even metacognitive abilities (Foote and Crystal).

Bibliography

Ben-Ami Bartal, Inbal, Jean Decety, and Peggy Mason. "Empathy and Pro-Social Behavior in Rats." *Science* 334.6061 (2011): 1427-1430.

Capra, Fritjof, "The Challenge of the Twenty-First Century." *Tikkun* 15.1 (2000): 49.

The Hidden Connections: A Science for Sustainable Living, New York: Anchor, 2004.

"The Carnegie Medal." Available online at http://www.carnegiegreenaway.org.uk/carnegie/, accessed 7 July 2013.

Dobrin, Sidney I. and Kenneth B. Kidd. "Introduction: Into the Wild." *Wild Things: Children's Culture and Ecocriticism*. Eds. Sidney I. Dobrin and Kenneth B. Kidd. Detroit: Wayne State University Press, 2004. 1-15.

Foote, Allison L. and Jonathon D. Crystal. "Metacognition in the Rat." *Current Biology* 17 (2007): 551-555.

Hart, Martin. *Rats*. London: Allison & Busby, 1982.

Henderson, Bob, Merle Kennedy and Chuck Chamberlin. "Playing Seriously with Dr. Seuss: A Pedagogical Response to *The Lorax*." *Wild Things: Children's Culture and Ecocriticism*. Eds. Sidney I. Dobrin and Kenneth B. Kidd. Detroit: Wayne State University Press, 2004. 128-148.

Krogmann Willy. *Der Rattenfänger von Hameln. Eine Untersuchung über das Werden der Sage*. Berlin: E. Ebering, 1934.

Langford, Dale J., Sara E. Crager, Zarrar Shehzad, Shad B. Smith, Susana G. Sotocinal, Jeremy S. Levenstadt, Mona Lisa Chanda, Daniel J. Levitin and Jeffrey S. Mogil. "Social Modulation of Pain as Evidence for Empathy in Mice." *Science* 312.5782 (2006): 1967-1970.

McDonald, Garry W. and Murray G. Patterson. "Bridging the Divide in Urban Sustainability: From Human Exemptionalism to the New Ecological Paradigm." *Urban Ecosystems* 10.2 (2007): 169-192.

Orwell, George. *Animal Farm*. New York, San Diego and London: Harcourt Brace, 1990.

Oziewicz, Marek. "'We Co-operate, or We Die': Sustainable Co-existence in Terry Pratchett's *The Amazing Maurice and His Educated Rodents*." *Children's Literature in Education* 40.2 (2009): 85-94.

Palmer, Alan. *Fictional Minds*. Lincoln and London: University of Nebraska Press, 2004.

Pavlik, Anthony. "Children's Literature and the Ecocritics." *The Future of Ecocriticism: New Horizons*. Eds. Serpil Oppermann, Ufuk Özdağ, Nevin Özkan and Scott Slovic. Newcastle upon Tyne: Cambridge Scholars Publishing, 2011. 420-435.

Pratchett, Terry. *The Amazing Maurice and His Educated Rodents*. London: Corgi, 2002.

"Interview with Terry Pratchett about *The Amazing Maurice*." Available online at http://www.fantasticfiction.co.uk/p/terry-pratchett/amazing-mauriceand-his-educated-rodents.htm, accessed 5 June 2013.

Reynolds, Kimberley. *Radical Children's Literature: Future Visions and Aesthetic Transformations in Juvenile Fiction*. New York: Palgrave Macmillan, 2007.

Sigler, Carolyn. "Wonderland to Wasteland: Toward Historicizing Environmental Activism in Children's Literature." *Children's Literature Association Quarterly* 19.4 (1994): 148-153.

Twain, Mark. *The Adventures of Huckleberry Finn (Tom Sawyer's Comrade)*. New York: Harper & Brothers, 1912.

Van Liere, Kent D. and Riley E. Dunlap. "The Social Bases of Environmental Concern: A Review of Hypotheses, Explanations and Empirical Evidence." *Public Opinion Quarterly* 44.2 (1980): 181-197.

James Fanning

Thursday Next, or: Metalepsis Galore – and More

Abstract

The relationships between the various fictional levels in the first and sixth novels of Jasper Fforde's "Thursday Next" series, *The Eyre Affair* (2001) and *One of Our Thursdays is Missing* (2011), are examined mainly with the help of Gérard Genette's narrative model. This shows how the major comic device of the series is renewed by means of additional diegetic complexity, adumbrated in the fifth novel but making the sixth one very different from the early ones.

In a brief review of Jasper Fforde's third Thursday Next novel, *The Well of Lost Plots* (2003), John Sutherland stated: "It is as hard to come up with a new fictional gimmick (a really "novel" novel) as a new vice. There is only so much the human imagination can do with those seven orifices and eight archetypal plotlines. Jasper Fforde has gone where no fictioneer has gone before." In the spirit of the novel, we should perhaps not take this hyperbole too seriously. However, he identifies two plot devices used by Fforde: on the one hand "the 'Alternative Universe' scenario, pioneered by Philip K. Dick in the 1950s", and on the other hand the fact that "the world of fiction and the real world ("outland") run into each other". In this essay I shall consider these two features in the first novel of the series, *The Eyre Affair* (2001),[1] also glancing at other specific features of the text, before discussing how Fforde modified his fictional world(s) in the sixth, *One of Our Thursdays is Missing* (2011).[2]

---

[1] Hereafter cited as *TN-1*, using Fforde's own convention on his website <<http://www.jasperfforde.com/>>
[2] Similarly: *TN-6*

The cover of *TN-1*[3] gives what may be recognized as a clear generic signal (Fowler 88-105[4]). The title, *The Eyre Affair*, is borrowed from Primary World[5] history, where it refers to the closest equivalent to the Dreyfus Affair in the UK, the controversy following the brutal suppression of the 1865 Morant Bay Rebellion in Jamaica by Governor Eyre (Morse 81; Sedley; Wilson 269-72). However, any possible relevance of this is immediately belied by the picture of a car painted with irregular red, blue and green stripes bursting out through the grass into a landscape, with the torn edges of the paper bearing the painting-by-numbers-like landscape curling away from the hole; the car is, significantly, depicted with a slightly – but not much – greater degree of realism, perhaps suggesting a different level of diegesis. We are clearly approaching the realm of comic fantasy, and when we start reading we soon notice that, as with the title of the novel,[6] we cannot expect the allusive names we are constantly confronted with to reveal meaning. The heroine and autodiegetic narrator is Thursday Next; the man she loves and eventually marries is Landen Park-Laine;[7] among her colleagues are Victor Analogy and Bowden Cable: these and others are merely funny, and even when Bowden Cable interacts with Sturmey Archer,[8] it remains a superficial pun, not even relevant to the fictional situation. On the other hand, classic "telling names" are to be found denoting sinister people and organizations: the main villain Acheron Hades, and Goliath Corporation[9] together with its repulsive operative Jack Schitt.

At the bottom of the page bearing the dedication to the author's deceased father we find something analogous to a "paper durability statement" (*Chicago* 15, §1.35):

---

3 At least that of the first edition.
4 In my copy page 88 is printed between 105 and 107, with page 106 between 87 and 89, as if someone in one of Thursday Next's worlds had been playing around with it.
5 I bow to Tolkien in using his term to refer to the world in which we live and in which this volume is being published, where others might say something like "the empirical world". At this point I confess openly that I have never read a book by Tolkien. The recipient of this volume knows this, nevertheless he seems to accept me as fully human.
6 Of course, the other association of "Eyre", presumably more familiar to most readers, i.e. *Jane Eyre*, does turn out to be relevant, but is not mentioned until Chapter 4 (38).
7 London Park Lane, especially if said with a Cockney pronunciation.
8 Hyphenated*, the most famous brand of bicycle hub gears in the UK (*Wikipedia*). (*Nothing to do with "hyphenated" in Fforde's Book World, which is the equivalent of drunk in the RealWorld.)
9 Partly reminiscent of Tyrell Corporation in *Blade Runner*, but above all satirically prophetic of the nature and role of Serco in the present-day Primary World UK (Harris).

> The typography and binding of this book conform to accepted Goliath Corporation standards
> Goliath©
> For all you'll ever need.™

This would normally be on the copyright page; the fact that it is not suggests that it is fictional, which is confirmed by the threat in almost illegibly small type: "Warning: Misuse of the Goliath Corporation's products or services may interfere with you and your family's continued rights to health, liberty and the pursuit of happiness" (*TN-1* vii). At least retrospectively, this and the cover picture may be seen as hints that the novel is going to employ *metalepsis* as one of its main devices (Genette, "Discours du récit" 243-45; *Nouveau discours* 234-36; *Métalepse*).

The play with diegetic levels has been treated by various authors (e.g. Lutas; Martínez-Dueñas Espejo; Mikkonen; Seibel), and Fforde's basic conceit is by now quite well known: we are introduced on the first pages to the fictional world in which the main characters live and which is similar to our world in many ways but different in many others. Physical geography is apparently mainly similar, but political geography is very different: the main polity is not the UK but the Republic of England; Scotland is not mentioned, but the People's Republic of Wales is important for the plot; the only other country mentioned, as the home of a visiting character, is Japan. Various places, objects and brand names in the text make this fictional England (potentially) familiar to the reading public: a Revox tape recorder (*TN-1* 35), Tesco's (*TN-1* 196), Hobnobs (*TN-1* 198), a Barbour jacket (*TN-1* 248). On the other hand, Thursday has a regenerated pet dodo (*TN-1* 2), goes to her home town of Swindon by airship (*TN-1* 77) and studied there in 1968 (*TN-1* 25), also the tentacular Goliath Corp. is ubiquitous (see above). The biggest discrepancy is that this England's history is in major respects different from that in our world: Wellington died at Waterloo (*TN-1* 4; ch. 1), in 1985 the Crimean war is still continuing (*TN-1* 6f). Above all, history is not fixed and may be changed retrospectively by "ChronoGuards", of which Thursday's father is an outlawed ex-one, "eradicated" in the present world and now (?) "a lonely itinerate in time, belonging to not one age but to all of them and having no home other than the chronoclastic ether" (*TN-1* 2):

"I was in '78 recently,' he announced. "I brought you this."
He handed me a single by the Beatles. I didn't recognise the title.
"Didn't they split in '70?"
"Not always." (*TN-1* 3)

This time-travel topos is basically Science Fiction. The other, less familiar, one is a variant of the alternative-universe topos cited above from Sutherland, pulling the story into a related genre we might call Literary Theory Fiction, a variant of Metafiction.[10]

As a Literary Detective or "LiteraTec", Thursday deals with forgery, illegal trading, copyright infringements and fraud (*TN-1* 2). That is, until the original manuscript of *Martin Chuzzlewit* is stolen under extremely mysterious circumstances. This introduces the main plot of the novel, which would be a straightforward detective thriller were it not for the fact that the purpose of the theft is to enact a rehearsal for entering the *intradiegetic* world[11] of *Jane Eyre*, in order to remove Jane from all copies of the book in the world by kidnapping her from the manuscript into the RealWorld.[12] This is done by means of a "Prose Portal"[13] stolen from Thursday's uncle Mycroft, who has invented it.

As Lutas points out (59), the first instance of metalepsis to be presented in the narrative (*TN-1* 62) is in fact an *antimetalepsis* (cf. Genette, *Métalepse* 27): Rochester emerges from the Book World to save the life of the unconscious Thursday. How this transition is achieved remains a mystery, although Seibel (91f) credibly suggests that it might be contingent on a bullet having penetrated the copy of *Jane Eyre* in Thursday's breast pocket that saved her life in the first place (*TN-1* 55). In an *analepsis* (*TN-1* 66ff; ch. 6) Thursday then recounts how

---

10 My own first acquaintance with such literature was John Fowles's *Mantissa* (1982). Other well known examples are Italo Calvino's *Se una notte d'inverno un viaggiatore* (1979) and Woody Allen's "The Kugelmass Episode" (1980). Genette draws attention to the latter in his 1983 thoughts on metalepsis (59), and on a technical level it partly resembles Fforde's use of metalepsis as discussed in the following.
11 From our point of view, *metadiegetic*. I retain Genette's original term, which some authors prefer to replace with Shlomith Rimmon-Kenan's alternative, "hypodiegetic" (Herman & Vervaeck 83).
12 Also called the Outworld in the novels. This is at first confusing, but it becomes clear that the denotation is the same. For some unfathomable reason, in the novels "Book World" is written as two words, "RealWorld" as one, with a capital in the middle. (I have not checked thoroughly to see whether this is consistent.)
13 Perhaps only pedants like myself might be disconcerted by the fact that the first and last uses of the Prose Portal are for entering Wordsworth's "I wandered lonely as a cloud" (*TN-1* 126ff) and Poe's "The Raven" (*TN-1* 370f), respectively.

as a child in the Brontës' home in Haworth she had entered the manuscript of *Jane Eyre* and made Rochester's horse slip on the ice when Jane first met him (cf. *Jane Eyre Vol. 1* 143; ch. 12). It is this episode that introduces us to the diegetic rules of the Book World:

> From subsequent readings of the book I was later to realise that the dog Pilot had never had the opportunity to fetch a stick, so he was obviously keen to take the opportunity when it presented itself. He must have known, almost instinctively, that the little girl who had momentarily appeared at the bottom of page 81 was unfettered by the rigidity of the narrative. He knew that he could stretch the boundaries of the story a small amount, sniffing along one side of the lane or the other since it wasn't specified; but if the text stated that he had to bark or run around or jump up, then he was obliged to comply. It was a long and repetitive existence, which made the rare appearances of people like me that much more enjoyable. (*TN-1* 67)

Thursday tried but never managed to enter *Jane Eyre* again after that, and now assumes that it was because "my mind had closed too much by the time I was twelve, already a young woman" (*TN-1* 69). This corresponds to *Alice in Wonderland* and *Peter Pan*, where it is clear that only children can enter the Wonderland or the Land of Make Believe. She told only her Uncle Mycroft about the experience, who believed her. We may assume that this planted the seed of the Prose Portal in his inventor's mind.

The Prose Portal is, of course, functionally analogous to the wardrobe in Lewis's Narnia novels or the subtle knife in Pullman's *His Dark Materials* series. A narratological comparison between these two series and the Thursday Next novels is instructive. Narnia and the fictional "real" world are on the same diegetic level according to Genette's model. Within the diegesis the two worlds even seem to have the same ontological status.[14] Also, in narratological terms they are in the same "realm of existence"[15] according to Stanzel's model: indeed it is precisely in order to cope with such cases – as well as interplanetary and interstellar SF – that he coined the terms "Identität/Nicht-Identität der Seinsbereiche" rather than using the ambiguous term "worlds" to define the categorial opposition of "person" (*Theorie* 109-48; ch. 4; *Theory* 110). The same is true of the various

---

14 Admittedly, one could argue that Narnia is merely a dream world like Carroll's Wonderland or Barrie's Land of Make Believe, but I find it at least less obvious than in those cases.
15 I retain the translation used in the CUP edition for "Seinsbereich[e]", although I would have rendered it as "ontological sphere[s]".

worlds in Pullman's books, where it is even clearer that they all have the same ontological status. Will's world is obviously a fictional representation of our Primary World, but in the text it has no priority, especially as it is not presented until the second novel of the trilogy. From a strictly rational, narratological point of view, the Thursday Next novels conform to this analysis: the Book World and the fictional RealWorld are diegetically and ontologically identical for us as Primary World readers. However, the difference is that *within* the diegesis of our Thursday Next novels, the diegesis of fiction[16] must be assumed to have a different fictional ontological status from the point of view of characters in the RealWorld, although from our point of view the distinction becomes problematic. By comparison, this highlights the fact that the ontological distinction between an authorial narrator and the characters in a story, posited by Stanzel and so essential for his narratological model, is in fact itself fictional. This is not to deny the usefulness of Stanzel's theory, after all I have been told that legal fictions do sterling service in jurisprudence.

In Chapter 32 we learn that the Book World observes a strict logic of narrative perspective (*TN-1* 320), so that since Jane as a homodiegetic narrator did not notice Thursday, the latter does not appear in the book. Similarly, the Japanese tourists "touch nothing and never speak to Miss Eyre" (*TN-1* 325). However, in the above-quoted passage from chapter 6 we have an early intimation that Thursday herself, rather like Proust's narrator, is not so constrained. She first says of the dog "he must have known", but then slips into "he knew". This might be taken as mere linguistic economy, however there are other, more egregious deviations from Thursday's point of view. In Chapter 11, when Aunt Polly enters "I wandered lonely as a cloud" through the Prose Portal (*TN-1* 126ff), the narration changes to a clearly authorial point of view: the episode is heterodiegetic, as are the episode where the ChronoGuard watch Thursday and Bowden approach the spacetime fault to repair it (*TN-1* 275f; ch.27) and Chapter 29, in which Acheron Hades's henchman Hobbes enters *Jane Eyre* to kidnap the heroine (*TN-1* 293-96). Fforde follows Proust in occasionally positing an *intermediary narrative* (Genette, *Narrative Discourse* 241; "récit intermédiaire", "Discours du récit" 249), e.g.: "As Mycroft told me later, Hades had been furi-

---

16 This is, however, from our point of view not strictly intradiegetic, as it is not narrated but assumed to have been narrated.

ous" (*TN-1* 233; ch. 24), but as with Proust this does not satisfactorily explain the multiple examples of *pseudo-diegetic narrative* (Genette "Discours du récit" 246ff; *Narrative Discourse* 236ff).

What is missing from accounts of novels in Fforde's Book Worlds is any equivalent of an authorial narrator: the texts that play a major part are mostly 1st-person narratives, plays and poems. When Polly enters "I wandered, lonely as a cloud", she meets the author Wordsworth, presumably the "I" of the text;[17] otherwise authors do not appear, either, although they are frequently referred to. An inconsistency is that at the end of *TN-1* Thursday's father comes up with a wittily original solution to the Shakespearean authorship controversy: "'They don't exist. They were never written. Not by him, not by anyone.'" So he went back to 1592 and gave a copy of the complete works to the actor Shakespeare. (*TN-1* 368; ch. 36) Of course this does not explain how the plays came to exist at all, and in later novels Shakespeare definitely is the author: in *Something Rotten* (*TN-4*), the plot of which centres on *Hamlet*, the author William Shgakespeafe [*sic*], the only surviving clone of Shakespeare, appears.

In *First Among Sequels* (*TN-5*, 2007) the fictional diegetic complexity is taken to a new level, further elaborated in *TN-6*. Thursday Next is not only the name of a RealWorld character who can enter the Book World: there is also a Book World character called 'Thursday Next',[18] in novels that correspond roughly to the first four Thursday Next novels of our world. Roughly is important: Chapter 2 opens with a passage which is almost, but not quite identical with the opening of *TN-1* (17f). At the end of this it is also confirmed that the narrator is not Thursday, but 'Thursday':[19] "'– hang on,' said Dad, or rather the character *playing* my book-father" (*TN-1* 18). So instead of a RealWorld

---

17 Curiously, he is presented as "a man aged about eighty", whereas in the Primary World, Wordsworth wrote this poem between the ages of 34 and 37 (note by Gill in Wordsworth 714)
18 I shall try to avoid confusion by placing the Book World 'Thursday Next' in single inverted commas to distinguish her from the RealWorld Thursday Next. In Fforde's text, where the distinction is made, the former is called by herself and others "the written Thursday Next" as opposed to "the real Thursday Next".
19 The first hint of this is given in Chapter 1, when the narrator recounts the remaking of the Book World (see below for a consideration of this topic), saying "the only world that I knew started to disassemble in front of my eyes" (*TN-6* 10).

autodiegetic narrator who can also enter the Book World,[20] we have one who is a denizen of the Book World.[21]

Already in *TN-1* it was implied that the Book World characters are like actors. Rochester tells Thursday: "'We will be quite alone as Jane takes the narrative with her to Moor House and those fatuous cousins. I am not featured again in the book,[22] so we may do as we please, [...]'" (*TN-1* 319f; ch. 32), but this liberty must not affect the plot:

> [Thursday:] "With all that is going on here, do you think it is wise?"
> Mrs. Fairfax looked at me as though I were an infant.
> "You don't understand, do you? After the fire Mr Rochester goes away for a week. That's how it happens." (*TN-1* 323)

We are given enough information to realize that the two series of novels are in fact quite different in many ways. Apart from Thursday not having "slept her way around the Book World" like 'Thursday 1-4', her husband Landen and her children by him do not feature in the 'TN' novels:

> Despite the real Thursday's wishes that Landen should be included in the series after I took over, he wasn't – and neither were any of the children. Thursday was overridden by a senator named Jobsworth at the council of Genres. So they reverted to the previous plan and had Landen continue to die in a house fire in the first chapter of *The Eyre Affair* [...] (*TN-6* 77f; ch. 7)

On the other hand the RealWorld of this novel is not the same as that in Jasper Fforde's first four novels: here Jack Schitt is only called that in the Book World, but is Adrian Dorset in the RealWorld (*TN-6* 243; ch. 24). With this new situation Jasper Fforde has combined the metalepses of his earlier novels with a *mise en abyme*, for it must be assumed that the 'Thursday Next' novels have their own BookWorld. However, this does not (yet) include equivalents of those Thursday Next novels that include the 'Thursday Next' novels.

In *TN-6* the histrionic nature of the Book World characters becomes central to the plot. Just as a character in a play may be recast, there was one 'Thursday'[23]

---

20 By now Thursday is a famous member of Jurisfiction, an interworld police force to enforce fictional law and order.
21 She is merely a member of JAID, the Jurisfiction Accident Investigation Department.
22 This is before Thursday changes the plot to yield the ending that we know!
23 Sometimes referred to as "Thursday 1-4".

in the first four 'Thursday Next' novels, "who slept her way around the Book World and caused no end of murder, misery and despair," and was therefore replaced by the 'Thursday'[24] who is the narrator of *TN-6*: "I was committed to promoting the type of Thursday the *real* Thursday wanted to see in the series" (*TN-6* 18).

The plot of *TN-6* revolves around the "real" Thursday having disappeared just before fulfilling an important diplomatic function in a dispute between two fictional genres. 'Thursday' is put on the case, which involves her being catapulted into the RealWorld by means of a Large Textual Sieve Array.[25] In both worlds she is taken for Thursday, notably by Landen, so that she spends some time discussing with him whether she might not actually be Thursday (*TN-6* 209-17; ch. 21; 249-55; ch. 26). This hypothesis is supported by the fact that she can actually see and hear Jenny, the "mindworm" placed in Thursday's mind by Aornis Hades, the daughter of her late adversary, Achilles Hades, in *TN-5* to make he think she has a second daughter (*TN-6* 281ff; ch. 21f). However, Jenny draws two logical conclusions: 'Thursday' must be fictional because she can see the "spooks", people's imaginary childhood friends, which she has so far taken for ghosts (*TN-6* 223; ch. 22); and Thursday must still be alive: "*I'm still here.* Unlike you, who are the figment of a ghost writer and are now carved into a textual matrix, a part of Thursday is all I am. If she were dead, I wouldn't be around to be thought of" (*TN-6* 224). This still leaves a residual confusion, which may well be shared by the reader, over 'Thursday'/Thursday's identity. This is finally resolved at the end of an adventure, when 'Thursday' with the intrepid support of her faithful mechanical butler, Sprockett, finds the injured Thursday within the Book World (*TN-6* 377; ch. 40).

Before she goes there, 'Thursday' is told how disorderly the RealWorld is, with no coincidences and a lot of redundancy in speaking and acting. She cannot grasp the concept of "unintended consequences" (*TN-6* 192f; ch. 19). When she arrives there, she is faced with the laws of physics (*TN-6* 195ff; ch. 20), which do not apply in the Book World (*TN-6* 185; ch. 19). These points adapt

---

24 Sometimes referred to as "Thursday 5", because in the fifth Thursday Next novel, First Among Sequels, she features in the fifth 'Thursday Next' novel, which is (fictionally) pulped and appears as "The Great Samuel Pepys Fiasco" [sic] under "Also by Jasper Fforde" at the front of *TN-6*.
25 The Prose Portal was destroyed earlier.

the technique well known from more political works such as *Lettres Persanes*, *L'ingénu*, *Letters from Earth* and many others of their ilk, to give a very gently satirical look at our world from an outsider's point of view, while actually inverting the tradition and directing the satire more strongly towards the conventions of narrative which make the Book World so different from the RealWorld. It is ironic that this disorderly RealWorld, so different from the narrated Book World, is being represented in a novel for readers in the Primary World. We might also ask whether everything that Book World characters do when they are not acting their book parts is really so orderly and purposeful. Additionally, the whole topic is tongue-in-cheek on an extra level, for the physical laws to which the Book World is not subject are just what in fact make the RealWorld orderly, even if the order is too complex for all aspects of it to be comprehended on a common-sense level (assuming that the RealWorld is meant to be a fictional representation of the Primary World).

The real innovation in the Secondary World(s) of *TN-6* compared with earlier works in the series is the "remaking of the Book World" several years earlier, which is the topic of Chapter 1. Whereas the Book World had been previously housed in the "Great Library", with each book constituting a discrete unit, the result was that it is now a geographical world in which Fiction is an island with different genres (e.g. "Adventure", "Crime", "Horror", "Dogma" etc.) represented by different regions. At various points near its coast lie the smaller islands of "School Essay", "M.P.s' Expenses", "Gimcrack Religion" etc. (frontispiece map). As it is on the *inside* of a sphere, one can see all over the world:

> About ten degrees upslope of Fiction, I could see our nearest neighbour: Artistic Criticism. It was an exceptionally beautiful island, yet deeply troubled, confused and suffused with a blanketing layer of almost impenetrable bullshit. Beyond that were Psychology, Philately, and Software Manuals. But the brightest and biggest archipelago I could see upon the closed sea was the scattered group of genres that made up Nonfiction. They were positioned right on the other side of the inner globe and so were almost directly overhead. (*TN-6* 13)

It is interesting that Psychology, Philately, and Software Manuals are not included in Nonfiction, but it would perhaps be churlishly pedantic to complain about such a minor blemish in a comic text like this.

This geographical redesigning of the Book World gives rise to the main conflict on which the plot depends, between Comedy and Racy Novel, as well as travels in various regions, including a steamboat trip full of clichés on the Metaphoric River, leading to the dénouement.

Lutas (61) is not wrong when he says, "*The Eyre Affair* is [...] primarily a popular detective novel. The detection aspect remains central to the novel despite the various excursions into the fantastic," and this is equally true of *One of Our Thursdays is Missing*. Nevertheless, the playful use of metafictional elements including various forms of metalepsis is an essential part of the fun of these immensely enjoyable novels.

About the author

JAMES FANNING was born in Jamaica, attended schools in the UK and studied German and French in Durham. He received his PhD for a thesis on the poetry of A.C. Swinburne from the University of Greifswald, where he teaches English Language, English Literature, British Cultural Studies and Phonetics & Phonlology.

Bibliography

Brontë, Charlotte. *Jane Eyre: An Autobiography.* Vol. 1-2. Eds. T. J. Wise and J. A. Symington, Oxford: Blackwell, 1931. (The Shakespeare Head Brontë cited from *Die Digitale Bibliothek*, vol. 59: *English and American Literature*, CD-ROM).

Chicago Manual of Style. 15th ed. Chicago: Chicago University Press, 2003.

Fforde, Jasper. *The Eyre Affair.* (*TN-1*) London: Hodder, 2001.

One of Our Thursdays is Missing. (*TN-6*) London: Hodder 2011.

Fowler, Alastair. *Kinds of Literature: An Introduction to the Theory of Genres and Modes.* [1982] Oxford: Clarendon, 1987.

Genette, Gérard. "Discours du récit." *Figures III.* Paris: Seuil 1972. 67-282.

Narrative Discourse: An Essay in Method [English Edition of "Discours du récit". Transl. Jane E. Lewin.] Ithaca: Cornell University Press, 1983.

Nouveau discours du récit. Paris: Seuil, 1983.

Métalepse. Paris: Seuil, 2004.

Harris, John. "Serco: the company that is running Britain." *The Guardian* 29 July 2013. Available online at http://www.theguardian.com/business/2013/jul/29/serco-biggest-company-never-heard-of, accessed 30 July 2013.

Herman, Luc and Bart Vervaeck. *Handbook of Narrative Analysis.* Lincoln & London: Nebraska University Press, 2005.

Lutas, Liviu. "Narrative Metalepsis in Detective Fiction." *Metalepsis in Popular Culture.* Eds. Karin Kukkonen and Sonja Klimek. Berlin & New York: de Gruyter, 2011. 41-64.

Martínez-Dueñas Espejo, José Luis. "The Language of Metatextual Fiction: The Narrative Discourse of Jasper Fforde." Available online at http://dialnet.unirioja.es/descarga/articulo/3867435.pdf, accessed 30 July 2013.

Mikkonen, Kai. "'There is no such thing as pure fiction': Impossible Worlds and the Principle of Minimal Departure Reconsidered." *Journal of Literary Semantics* 40 (2011): 111-131.

Morse, Deborah Denenholz. "'Some girls who come from the tropics': Gender, Race and Imperialism in Anthony Trollope's *He Knew He Was Right*." *The Politics of Gender in Anthony Trollope's Novels. New Readings for the Twenty-First Century.* Eds. Margaret Markwick, Deborah Denenholz Morse and Regenia A. Gagnier. Ashgate, 2009. 77-98.

SEDLEY, Stephen. "No Law at All." *London Review of Books* 28:21 (2 November 2006) Available online at http://www.lrb.co.uk/v28/n21/stephen-sedley/no-law-at-all, accessed 30 July 2013.

SEIBEL, Klaudia. "Literatecs, Nursery Crimes, and Dragonslayers: The Fantastic Fictional Universes of Jasper Fforde." *Inklings: Jahrbuch für Literatur und Ästhetik* 30 (2012): 87-95.

STANZEL, Franz. *Theorie des Erzählens*. [1979] Göttingen: Vandenhoeck, 1989.

A Theory of Narrative. [*Theorie des Erzählens*. Transl. Charlotte Goedsche.] Cambridge: Cambridge University Press, 1984.

SUTHERLAND, John. "If it's Thursday it must be the valley of death." *The Guardian* 26 July 2003. Available online at http://www.guardian.co.uk/books/2003/jul/26/featuresreviews.guardianreview15, accessed 30 July 2013.

Wikipedia, s.v. "Sturmey-Archer." Available online at http://en.wikipedia.org/wiki/Main_Page, accessed 30 July 2013.

WILSON, A.N. *The Victorians*. London: Arrow, 2003.

WORDSWORTH, William. *William Wordsworth*. (The Oxford Authors). Ed. Stephen Gill. Oxford: Oxford University Press, 1984.

Thomas Honegger

From Faëry to Madness
The Facts in the Case of Howard Phillips Lovecraft

Abstract

H.P. Lovecraft's "Cthulhu Mythos" is often hailed as the scientific, post-enlightenment answer to the traditional metaphysical tales of horror. Yet such a view is, as I argue, one-sided since it ignores both the actual reception and further development of Lovecraft's "Mythos" as well as its inherent contradictions. As a consequence, the highly heterogeneous body of Lovecraftian texts is too often put into the Procrustean bed of his ideological framework instead of being appreciated as literature with a dynamic aesthetic dimension.

Were we to write the history of secondary worlds and their concomitant mythologies, the year 1926 would be given special mention since it proved crucial in the development of two important sub-creative mythologies of the twentieth century: J.R.R. Tolkien's "legendarium" and H.P. Lovecraft's "Cthulhu Mythos".[1] In that year, Tolkien wrote – with his "Sketch of the Mythology"[2] – the first coherent text outlining and explaining the full mythological and historical dimension of his "legendarium". On the other side, we have with Lovecraft's short story "The Call of Cthulhu"[3] the first significant

---

1 The term "legendarium" is used to refer to the entire body of (un-)published texts, manuscripts, sketches, fragments etc. charting the development of Middle-earth. "Cthulhu Mythos" is used as a convenient (though somewhat inaccurate) label to refer to the collaborative effort of H.P. Lovecraft and his contemporaries and successors to create a "mythology" centred around the assumption that the earth had been home to pre-historic and pre-human civilisations originating in outer space. On the problems of terminology concerning Lovecraft's "mythology", see fn. 4 below.

2 "Tolkien writes a prose manuscript of twenty-eight pages entitled "Sketch of the Mythology with especial reference to "The Children of Húrin" [...] to explain the background of the poem to R.W. Reynolds. This is the first text to cover the whole of Tolkien's mythology from the rebellion of Morgoth to the age of Men and "the last end of the tales"." (Scull and Hammond 134).

3 "[T]his period – from the summer of 1926 to the spring of 1927 – represents the most remarkable outburst of fiction-writing in Lovecraft's entire career [...] [and] "The Call of Cthulhu", written probably in August or September [1926] [is] the first significant contribution to what came to be called the "Cthulhu Mythos"" (Joshi, *A Dreamer* 242-43).

contribution to what is now widely (though somewhat inaccurately) known as the "Cthulhu Mythos".[4]

The two authors, although contemporaries,[5] are not likely to have known their respective work and any parallels[6] real or imaginary are accidental or due to the fact that almost any writer of the fantastic draws from a larger reservoir of common motifs and themes. Nor are their theoretical and pseudo-historical frameworks comparable: Tolkien, as the "Sketch of the Mythology" indicates, set out to create a cycle of loosely linked tales within a clearly delineated framework depicting the (mythical) "pre-history" of our world in general and of the lands that would become England in particular. Lovecraft, by contrast, never formulated such a master plan and the "Cthulhu Mythos" just happened. Its elaboration, codification, and to some extent falsification, was largely the work of August Derleth who acted as Lovecraft literary executor and had thus privileged access to his unpublished manuscripts and notebooks.[7] What unites the two "mythologies", however, is the power to enchant and to inspire large-scale sub-creative elaboration and imitation. The way Tolkien inscribed his work, and in particular *The Lord of the Rings*, into the tradition of sub-creation has been well researched and is the subject of several studies.[8] Lovecraft's achievements in this area are less explored and it is therefore the aim of my paper to discuss the development of the "Cthulhu Mythos" as an example of multi-authored *mythpoeia*.[9]

---

4 Joshi ("The Cthulhu Mythos") differentiates between the "Lovecraft Mythos", i.e. the form based on Lovecraft's published texts, the "Derleth Mythos", i.e. the "Manichean" interpretation of the Mythos as found in Derleth's stories, and finally the "Modern Mythos", i.e. the continuation of the Mythos in various forms and formats by contemporary authors. Adopting Joshi's usage, I will use the "Cthulhu Mythos" as the overall term and differentiate between the sub-categories only when necessary. Schultz (222) even talks about an "antimythology".
5 Tolkien lived from 1892-1973, Lovecraft from 1890-1937. It is theoretically possible that Tolkien had come across some of Lovecraft's texts since they were available in print from the 1920s onwards. The great majority of Tolkien's legendarium-texts, by contrast, were published only posthumously.
6 There are "Lovecraftian elements" in Tolkien's work. His Watcher before the Gates of Moria, the Balrog, the "nameless gnawing things" as well as Shelob and Sam's "speaking in tongues" in moments of terror would fit nicely into any "Lovecraftian" story. Yet these elements are isolated instances of horror and the basic tone and ethos of Tolkien's creation is radically different from Lovecraft's.
7 See Haefele's recent monograph *A Look Behind the Derleth Mythos: Origins of the Cthulhu Mythos* (2012) for a re-appraisal of Derleth's contribution to the "Cthulhu Mythos".
8 E.g. Kocher, Saler and, most prominently, Shippey.
9 Most recently, Vanderbeke and Turner (4-5) have commented on the relationship between Lovecraft's and Tolkien's mythopoeic creations.

mythopoeia – "The creation of myth or myths"[10]

H.P. Lovecraft is often mentioned in the same breath as other "myth-creating" authors such as William Blake, Lord Dunsany, George MacDonald, C.S. Lewis and J.R.R. Tolkien. Although there are good reasons for including him in such a roster of mythopoeic writers, it would be wrong to think that they all shared the same view of the function and value of "sub-created" mythologies. C.S. Lewis's attitude towards myths, though by no means representative for all the other mythopoetic writers, is a good example to bring out the "otherness" of Lovecraft's point of view. Before his conversion to Christianity, Lewis looked upon myths as "lies [...] "breathed through silver"" (Tolkien, "Mythopoeia" 97),[11] i.e. texts that have some artistic and aesthetic value (hence "breathed through silver"), yet which nevertheless fall short of the "gold standard" of truth. After his conversion Lewis not only began to appreciate myths as one way of expressing transcendental truths – and the life of Christ as the one myth to become historical reality – but he also started to write tales and stories in a "mythological mode", most prominently in his Narnia chronicles with their thinly disguised religious dimension. Lewis's motivation for composing his mythopoeic texts was thus not only the delight (*delectare*) of his audience, but as much (and sometimes even more so) his desire to instruct them in matters of Christian ethics and orthodoxy (*prodesse*). As a consequence, Lewis's sub-created worlds, like those of his colleague and friend Tolkien, remain firmly rooted within the Christian framework and aim at expressing in a more (Lewis) or less (Tolkien) explicit form the fundamental Christian truths. Many of their literary creations can thus be rightly called *mythopoeia* since they aim at explaining and illustrating how the world (or the worlds of their fictional universe) came into being and what the function and place of the created beings is, i.e. they strive to present the "bigger picture" and to provide (transcendental) meaning to human existence – just as real myths do.

Lovecraft's take on myth is radically different. His stories and tales of the "Cthulhu Mythos" may make use of the traditional paraphernalia and trappings of myths, yet the underlying reality and the frame of reference is not the

---

10 *OED* online.
11 The poem "Mythopoeia" was composed by J.R.R. Tolkien in September 1931 and dedicated to C.S. Lewis. On the importance of the "mythopoeic concept" for the conversion of Lewis, see the account in Carpenter (33-45).

Christian (or any other) religion, but natural scientific materialism or cosmic indifferentism.[12] Myths are to him "lies breathed through lead" and therefore, to adapt Max Müller's dictum, "a disease of truth". Such a stance seems incompatible with the practice of *mythopoeia*, and some critics therefore consider Lovecraft's version of the "Cthulhu Mythos" an "antimythology" (Schultz 222) rather than a "mythology proper". However, it would be a serious mistake to focus solely on the theoretical framework and to neglect the equally – or even more – important evidence in the form of Lovecraft's actual literary texts. He did not write his stories primarily as illustrations for his philosophical views, but as independent literary-aesthetic products, which often flout the "rules" of the theoretical framework. As a consequence, and in spite of Lovecraft's theoretical misgivings, the "Cthulhu Mythos" has established itself in some circles as a mythology proper. This discrepancy between the nihilistic indifferentism of the theoretical stance and the "mythic" supernaturalism in many of the stories has given rise to a dynamic tension that makes the "Cthulhu Mythos" so attractive to readers and authors alike. As a result, the Mythos has inspired dozens of authors who add and contribute to an ever-growing corpus of texts, films, radio-plays, artwork etc., which by 1999, comprised some 2631 works (Joshi, "The Cthulhu Mythos" 98). It is this interplay between the different elements that turns the "Cthulhu Mythos" into a powerful mythopoeic force and the following chapters venture to explore its genesis, development and, to some extent, critical reception.

Foreshadowings and Prequels

The beginnings of Lovecraft's career as a writer fall into the second decade of the twentieth century. His first published short story, "A Reminiscence of Dr. Samuel Johnson",[13] appeared in 1917, and his first two fantastic horror

---

12 Lovecraft defined himself as an "indifferentist" who does not "make the mistake of thinking that the resultant of the natural forces surrounding and governing organic life will have any connexion with the wishes or tastes of any part of that organic life-process. [...] [the] cosmos gives a damn [...] about the especial wants and ultimate welfare of mosquitoes, rats, lice, dogs, men, horses, pterodactyls, trees, fungi, dodos, or other forms of biological energy" (*Selected Letters* 3.39, quoted in Joshi, "The Cthulhu Mythos" 109-110).
13 This short piece presents a narrator who claims to be born in 1690 and not, as his acquaintances believe, in 1890, which would make him some 227 years old. This, however, is the only potentially "fantastic" element in the story which otherwise is a whimsical and entertaining piece.

stories in 1919, namely "Beyond the Wall of Sleep" in October and "Dagon" in November.[14] From that time onwards until his premature death in March 1937, Lovecraft wrote and published about four dozen short stories and a handful of novellas.[15] We have therefore a body of publicly available texts which allowed the study of the development of Lovecraft's work even before his demise. This stands in contrast to Tolkien, who, apart from *The Lord of the Rings*, published hardly any *legendarium*-related writings during his lifetime. The difference is important since the existence of a corpus of published texts clearly pre-dating the "invention" of the "Cthulhu Mythos" proper has led some of the most prominent critics to interpret Lovecraft's writing career as a gradual unfolding of his grand concept of "cosmic horror". This "teleological view" has been championed most prominently by the eminent Lovecraft-scholar S.T. Joshi and, in an interesting variation, also by David E. Schultz.[16] The implications of such an approach will be discussed in a later chapter, but the point of departure for this paper will be a brief look at two of Lovecraft's earliest tales ("Beyond the Wall of Sleep" and "Dagon") as illustrative examples for the development of his sub-creative project.

In "Beyond the Wall of Sleep" the first-person narrator tells the tragic story of Joe Slater, a native of the Catskill Mountain region who killed one of his neighbours in a fit of madness. Slater is apprehended by the police and delivered to an asylum where the narrator is working as an intern. Over the following weeks he witnesses and becomes acquainted with the "visions" Slater experiences while asleep – visions of cosmic conflict and suggestive of a higher intelligence "imprisoned" within the body of the degenerate mountaineer. The first-person narrator, with the help of a self-made technical apparatus, is able to share partially the visionary experiences and upon Slater's death he even manages briefly to communicate telepathically with the "cosmic entity" who had been confined to this "animal body" and who is now finally released.

"Beyond the Wall of Sleep" unites two of Lovecraft's areas of interest: first, his fascination with the classical era, which most likely provided him with the motif of the liberation of the "soul" from physical bondage and imprisonment

---

14 "Beyond the Wall of Sleep" was written in 1919, "Dagon" in 1917.
15 See Joshi (*Bibliography*) for a comprehensive list of Lovecraft's writings.
16 See especially Joshi ("The Cthulhu Mythos") and Schultz.

in "matter", as found in texts such as the *Somnium Scipionis* or the teachings of the Gnostics. Second, his fascination with the universe at large – be this by linking his interest in astronomy with the final part of the story or by postulating the existence of highly developed intelligent cosmic entities. The news about the discovery of a new star on February 22, 1901, which comprises the climax of the tale, is a real-world incident and illustrates Lovecraft's technique of incorporating actual events in his fantastic stories. "Beyond the Wall of Sleep" is thus an example of an early "cosmic" narrative, although we still have a clearly anthropocentric point of view and Lovecraft's famous "cosmic indifferentism" is not yet perceptible.

The second story of interest is "Dagon" since it contains numerous elements and motifs that will recur almost a decade later in "The Call of Cthulhu". We have once more a first-person narrator, who provides an account of his traumatic experiences somewhere in the Pacific Ocean after having made his escape from a German warship in a small boat. After an unspecified time at sea, he finds himself stranded on an island that has risen from the watery depths. Exploring the strange island, he comes across a cyclopean monolith covered with unknown hieroglyphics and strange pictorial carvings. The shocking climax is reached when he witnesses a gigantic monstrous sea-creature paying obeisance to the monolith – an experience that unhinges the narrator's mind and plunges him into (temporary?) insanity. The final "climax" consists in the creature from the depths having followed and apprehending the narrator. The ending in the traditional mode is more of an "anticlimax" than a successful conclusion – although a case could be made for regarding it as due to the hallucinations of an obviously unhinged mind suffering from the effects of drug-deprivation. It deducts in either case from the "cosmic" or general implications for all mankind by unduly focusing on the fate of the narrator – the potentially "universal cosmic horror" is still perceived primarily on an individual level and lacks the "objective" quality of many of the later stories. On the other hand, it already skilfully interweaves elements from real-existing (historical) myths and cults into an implied larger and as yet little explored tapestry providing an alternative view of the development of life on earth. The strange bas-reliefs on the monolith suggest the existence of pre-historical (and pre-human) civilizations – hinted at obliquely in some of the human myths and archaeological artefacts. As a consequence, the reader experiences the "mooreeffoc" effect[17] that evokes a feeling of horror much subtler and more disturbing than the actual appearance of the gigantic sea-creature or the final "haunting" that silences the narrator's voice. This "mooreeffoc" experience causes the reader to look at the old myths with new eyes, so that he senses as yet hidden but therefore all the more disturbing depths of (pre-) human history and begins to realize that this very earth is "an utterly alien land".

It is Lovecraft's trademark that he does not banish his monstrous beings to the depths of outer space or the seas but that he sets many of his stories[18] in New England. As Janicker has shown in her recent discussion of Lovecraft's use of landscape and space, he skilfully uses "local colour" to root his "cosmic horror" in a domestic setting. The intrusion of the utterly alien is thus set off by means of the familiar background and "mooreeffocs" the homely New England places.

Lovecraft is neither the first nor the only author of horror fiction to achieve such an effect. William Hope Hodgson[19] (1877-1918) and Arthur Machen (1863-1947) are just two (near-) contemporary writers whose works Lovecraft knew and appreciated and who, to some extent, strove towards (and at least partially achieved) a similar aim. The main difference between Lovecraft's tales of the "Cthulhu Mythos" and the work of other horror-writers lies in the former's claim to an explicit and comprehensive framework. This theoretical superstructure is, on the one hand, compatible with a natural scientific and materialistic view of the universe and, on the other, able to evoke a feeling of "cosmic horror" which is significantly more unhinging than any other forms. Lovecraft provides a sketch of his approach in a letter to Donald Wandrei in 1927:

---

17 The term itself was coined by Charles Dickens. Chesterton, and later Tolkien, took it up and exploited its theoretical potential. Tolkien, in his essay "On Fairy-Stories", writes: "*Mooreeffoc* is a fantastic word, but it could be seen written up in every town in this land. It is Coffee-room, viewed from the inside through a glass door, as it was seen by Dickens on a dark London day; and it was used by Chesterton to denote the queerness of things that have become trite, when they are seen suddenly from a new angle. [...] / [...] The word *Mooreeffoc* may cause you suddenly to realise that England is an utterly alien land, lost [...] in some remote past age glimpsed by history, [...]." (Tolkien, *On Fairy-stories* 68).
18 E.g., "The Colour out of Space" (1927), "The Dunwich Horror" (1929), "The Whisperer in Darkness" (1931), or "The Shadow over Innsmouth" (1936).
19 On Hodgson as a "cosmic horror" writer, see Weinstein.

> Now all my tales are based on the fundamental premise that common human laws and interests and emotions have no validity or significance in the vast cosmos-at-large. To me there is nothing but puerility in a tale in which the human form – and the local human passions and conditions and standards – are depicted as native to other worlds or other universes. To achieve the essence of real externality, whether of time or space or dimension, one must forget that such things as organic life, good and evil, love and hate, and all such local attributes of a negligible and temporary race called mankind, have any existence at all. Only the human scenes and characters must have human qualities. *These* must be handled with unsparing *realism*, (*not* catch-penny *romanticism*) but when we cross the line to the boundless and hideous unknown – the shadow-haunted *Outside* – we must remember to leave our humanity and terrestrialism at the threshold. (*Selected Letters* 2.150, quoted in Joshi, "The Cthulhu Mythos" 103, italics in the original)

Cthulhu Rising

The earliest and probably most famous of Lovecraft's texts making explicit use of the "Cthulhu Mythos" is his short story "The Call of Cthulhu" (written 1926, first published 1928) – which eventually gave the phenomenon its name. In this short story we find three (numbers 2 to 4) out of the four central elements of the "Cthulhu Mythos" as postulated by Joshi ("The Cthulhu Mythos" 99):

> (1) a vitally realized but largely imaginary New England topography; (2) an ever-growing library of occult books, both ancient and modern […]; (3) the "gods," their human followers, and their monstrous "minions" or acolytes; and (4) a sense of the cosmic, both spatial and temporal, that often links the Mythos more firmly with science fiction than with the supernatural.

Although the home of the main narrator is Boston, the action of the multi-strand narrative stretches from Missouri to Oslo (Norway) and to an uncharted island in the Pacific Ocean somewhere off the coast of New Zealand, which means that it does not fulfil the requirements of the first category. Elements of the second category are prominent and we find mention of occult books real and imaginary, such as W. Scott-Elliott's *Atlantis and the Lost Lemuria*, James G. Frazer's *Golden Bough*, Margaret A. Murray's *Witch-Cult in Western Europe*, and, of course, the *Necronomicon* of the mad Arab Abdul Alhazred.[20] The "gods", too, and their human followers play an important role – especially

---

20 On the history of the *Necronomicon* see Lovecraft's own "History of *Necronomicon*" and the short essay by Bouchard and Lacroix.

in the tale of Inspector Legrasse where Lovecraft, in the narrative of the aged mestizo Castro, provides a concise sketch of the "Cthulhu Mythos". The reader learns that, eons before man, other beings, who came from the stars, ruled on earth and erected great cities – remnants of which can still be found on some remote Pacific islands. These "Great Old Ones" are lying in their houses in their great city of R'lyeh, awaiting their resurrection when the stars are once more in the right position. It is this moment that the secret cults are waiting for in order to revive great Cthulhu (and others) and rule with him the earth or even the universe. The "cosmic" dimension of the threat is thus spelled out clearly and though Cthulhu's monstrous appearance is terrifying enough, it must be remembered that we are not dealing with some supernatural or transcendental being in the traditional sense of the word, but with an extraterrestrial "natural" life-form. Many of Lovecraft's later works such as "At the Mountains of Madness", "The Whisperer in Darkness", "The Shadow over Innsmouth" or "The Shadow out of Time" make use of and expand the framework first sketched in "The Call of Cthulhu".

It is important to be clear about the exact nature of this framework. In his letters, Lovecraft repeatedly stresses the underlying materialistic and natural scientific world-view as the foundation of his stories and highlights the special quality of his "cosmic horror". Yet he was at the same time neither ideologically dogmatic against others, whom he motivated to contribute to and participate in the construction of the growing corpus of "mythology", nor did he consider himself slavishly bound to the "rules" in his own fiction. He continued, for example, to write "Dreamland stories"[21] such as "The Silver Key", reminiscent in style and theme of Lord Dunsany's work. These Dreamland stories are quite different in style, tone and theme from the texts comprising the "Cthulhu Mythos" proper, yet it would be wrong to see the two traditions as closed categories. Lovecraft, on the one hand, often incorporates the oneiric dimension in texts belonging to the "Mythos" tradition, while on the other hand, he also includes elements from stories belonging clearly to the "Cthulhu Mythos" in his Dreamland-fiction. Thus we find the painter Richard Upton Pickman and his ghouls from "Pickman's Model" once more in "The Dreamquest of Unknown Kadath" where he repeatedly helps the protagonist Randolph Carter

---

21 See Lippi for a discussion of Lovecraft's Dreamworld stories.

in his quest. This mutual contamination of the two otherwise distinct traditions does not alter their otherwise fundamentally different characters, yet it renders visible the open nature of each category.[22] A similar "openness", but this time towards magic and the supernatural, can be found even in tales usually seen as belonging to the "Cthulhu Mythos" canon. "The Dunwich Horror" (1928) is a good example of such a (not always fortunate) mixture.

Lovecraft's great theoretical achievement was the replacement of the metaphysical and transcendental framework by a natural scientific one. In so doing, he transformed and recast the traditional genre of the "ghost story" into a mould fit for a modern post-enlightenment era. However, it is only in some of his works, such as the novella "At the Mountains of Madness", that he succeeds in completely foregoing the use of any magical elements such as incantations, spells etc. and is able to evoke a feeling of mounting horror solely within a "cosmic" natural scientific framework. Lovecraft reflects on this technique in one of his later letters:

> Accordingly I have tried to weave them into a kind of shadowy phantasmagoria which may have the same sort of vague coherence as a cycle of traditional myth or legend – with nebulous backgrounds of Elder Forces & transgalactic entities which lurk about this infinitesimal planet ... establishing outposts thereon, & occasionally brushing aside other accidental forms of life (like human beings) in order to take up full habitation. This is essentially the sort of notion prevalent in most racial mythologies – but an artificial mythology can become subtler & more plausible than a natural one, because it can recognize & adapt itself to the information and moods of the present. (*Selected Letters* 4.70-71, quoted in Schultz 226-227)

I would like to draw special attention to the last sentence where Lovecraft stresses the fact that his stories are adapted "to the information and moods of the present," which implies the acceptance of the "modern" view of the universe as the only valid backdrop against which the horror unfolds. His readers, in order to feel the delicious frisson of terror, need not suspend any disbelief in the supernatural but can rely on the narrator[23] to have carefully analysed the evidence and excluded all "supernatural" and metaphysical ele-

---

22 See Lévy (97-108) for a competent and illuminating analysis of the relationship between the Dreamworld stories and Lovecraft's other tales.
23 All his narrator-protagonists are educated men and often pursue professions that give them additional respectability and render them unlikely to accept any explanations that run counter to rationality and received natural scientific knowledge.

ments. The seemingly "unnatural" events or things are no manifestations of a transcendental dimension in the traditional meaning of the word, but instead are simply natural phenomena not yet sufficiently explored or understood. This ties in with Lovecraft's definition of fear as "[t]he oldest and strongest emotion of mankind [...], and the oldest and strongest kind of fear is fear of the unknown" (Lovecraft, *Supernatural Horror* 25). The horror of modern man, bereft of the old certainties provided by religion and myth, is indeed that of the unknown on a cosmic, natural scientific scale. Lovecraft seems to take Blaise Pascale's famous dictum concerning mankind's position in the universe[24] as the starting point for his own radically materialistic view and considers "the existence of life on our planet [as] nothing more than an accident" (Schultz 228). The Lovecraftian "project", though only partially achieved in his stories, can be seen as nothing less than a radical and modern disenchantment of the traditional supernatural elements yet without denying their actual existence. The radicality of this paradigm shift from anthropocentrism to "cosmocentrism" is comparable to that of the Copernican Revolution.[25] However, the resultant disenchantment is superseded by a rather unlikely re-enchantment based on the reinterpretation of these very same phenomena and beings as representatives of an alien tradition that is yet compatible with the prevalent materialistic view of the universe. The *nymphae, sylvae, faunae* etc. of antiquity as well as the fairies and gnomes of folklore are simply reinterpreted as the garbled and misunderstood reminiscences of the "natural" alien and monstrous presences. Lovecraft would fully agree with a Hamletian "there are more things in heaven and earth than are dreamt of in our science – as yet" and take it as a call for the expansion of the current area of knowledge by means of scientific investigation rather than going backwards into benighted metaphysical superstition.

---

24 "I see the terrifying spaces of the universe that enclose me, and I find myself attached to a corner of this vast expanse, without knowing why I am more in this place than in another, nor why this little time that is given me to live is assigned me at this point more than another out of all the eternity that has preceded me and out of all that will follow me." Blaise Pascale, *Thoughts, Letters and Minor Works*.
25 See Leiber's aptly named essay on Lovecraft as a "literary Copernicus".

Derleth Rising

At the time of Lovecraft's death in March 1937, we have a corpus of about a dozen texts that can be seen as constituting the core of what will later be dubbed "the Cthulhu Mythos".[26] It comprises short stories and novellas and though Lovecraft has never formally or explicitly defined a "canon", the theoretical-philosophical ideas constituting the framework of the "Cthulhu Mythos" are more or less clearly recognizable in these stories as well as explicitly expressed in several of his letters. Other authors, too, have taken up elements from the nascent Mythos during Lovecraft's lifetime, used them in their own stories, and added either "gods" of their own invention to the growing cosmic pantheon[27] or new volumes to the library of forbidden knowledge.[28] This more or less random and "free for all" development of the Mythos came to an end with the foundation of Arkham House Publishers by August Derleth and Donald Wandrei in 1939. Arkham House's primary aim was to publish in hardcover the best of H.P. Lovecraft's fiction, and August Derleth became the literary executor of Lovecraft's heritage. His merits for the preservation, publication and popularisation of Lovecraft's work are undisputed and need not concern us here. Derleth's development and interpretation of the theoretical-philosophical framework, however, is highly controversial.[29] His main contribution is the re-mythologisation of the Lovecraftian "anti-mythology". Derleth rejects Lovecraft's radical materialism and relativist cosmic point of view in which mankind is nothing but a minor footnote in the history of the universe. As becomes obvious from Lovecraft's fiction as well as from the statements in his letters, the doings of man are of little importance, relevance or interest to the cosmic beings who – mostly by accident – come into contact with humans. As a consequence, the terror felt by Lovecraft's protagonists in his most "cosmic" stories[30] has its origin not so much in the concrete alien

---

26 Lovecraft merely mentioned an "Arkham cycle" (*Selected Letters* 2.246, quoted in Joshi, "The Cthulhu Mythos" 108) and never seemed to have had the intention to homogenize, unify and harmonize the sometimes disparate and contradictory elements in his published texts.
27 Tsathoggua, for example, is a creation of Clark Ashton Smith, and was "adopted" into the Lovecraftian pantheon in his "The Whisperer in Darkness" (written 1930, published 1931).
28 Thus we find Robert Howard's *Nameless Cults* (i.e. von Junzt's *Unaussprechlichen Kulten*) and Clark Ashton Smith's *Liver Ivonis* (*The Book of Eibon*) among the standard-works of forbidden knowledge in Lovecraft's stories.
29 Price ("The Lovecraft-Derleth Connection") provides a short yet concise discussion.
30 The actual stories and novellas seen as constituting the "Cthulhu Mythos" are, in spite of Lovecraft's meta-statements, too heterogeneous to allow a statement true for all texts. Many of them still contain a considerable element of traditional "metaphysical" horror.

monstrousness of these cosmic beings, but rather in the realisation of the utter unimportance of mankind and the irrelevance of any moral or religious values within the cosmic framework. Derleth, by contrast, keeps all of the outward trappings and elements of the Lovecraftian Mythos, yet redefines or, as his critics argue, falsifies its philosophical core. He puts mankind once more at the centre of a cosmic conflict between the forces of good and evil and re-interprets the Lovecraftian cosmic nihilism as a form of cosmic Manicheism. In "A Note on the Cthulhu Mythos" he explicitly refers to Lovecraft himself (cf. the quotation marks) in order to legitimize his view and writes:

> Lovecraft saw it [i.e. the "Cthulhu Mythos"] as "based on the fundamental lore or legend that this world was inhabited at one time by another race who, in practising black magic, lost their foothold and were expelled, yet live on outside ever ready to take possession of this earth again." Its similarity to the Christian mythos – as well as to other myth-patterns common to both history and fiction – will be immediately apparent to the literate reader. (Derleth, "A Note" 445)

This constitutes, as was to become clear only decades later,[31] the flawed cornerstone of the "interpretatio Derlethiana" which proved popular because it succeeded where Lovecraft had failed (in spite of his claims to the contrary): Derleth's interpretation of the Mythos provides the basis for a logically coherent and homogeneous model of the universe. Some of Lovecraft's works may have come close to doing so,[32] but on the whole we have a heterogeneous conglomeration of texts that provide as many exceptions to the "mythological" framework as there are examples in its favour. This is, of course, mainly due to the fact that Lovecraft was not a programmatic writer but first and foremost an artist striving for aesthetic effects, and as such he would not sacrifice a good story in favour of an abstract principle. Even his references to such a framework must be seen as motivated by aesthetic and narratological considerations since an alleged "cosmic" context would add depth and increase the impact of his stories. Derleth, by contrast, seems more interested in providing further textual illustrations for what he considers of prime importance: the true form of the

---

31 The quote that Derleth provides is, as has been later shown, not by Lovecraft but is based on a misremembered recollection by one of Lovecraft's correspondents. See page 129 of this paper.
32 "The Colour out of Space", "The Shadow out of Time" as well as "At the Mountains of Madness" are usually considered prime examples of "cosmic horror" untainted by "magic" and other metaphysical elements.

Mythos. The result is a collection of stories that are coherent within themselves, yet whose aesthetic quality is rather doubtful and whose plots are often repetitive and predictable: the narrator-protagonist comes into contact with an older and more experienced "tutor" figure who introduces him[33] to the dark mysteries that threaten the very survival of mankind. They are again and again able to thwart the attempts of the minions of the Old Ones to raise Cthulhu or any other eldritch entity from the growing pantheon of Ancient Horrors, which would bring about a new reign of chaos and terror. In order to achieve their missions, they rely heavily on the magic of the Elder Gods (e.g. in the form of the infamous five-pointed-star talisman)[34] and on the interstellar hitchhiker's express service given by the Byakhee, the winged servants of Hastur.[35] These creatures can be summoned by means of a simple formula[36] and the ingestion of some "magic" mead, upon which they transport the valiant ghost-busters to the safety of Celaeno, a star in the Pleiades.

Not all of Derleth stories follow this pattern, but even those that keep close to Lovecraft's texts strike the reader as programmatic and primarily vehicles to promote Derleth's view of the mythic framework. He cleans up Lovecraft's rather cluttered universe with an almost Pauline missionary zeal and in the process of doing so replaces the open, often contradictory, ambiguous and sometimes playful Lovecraftian proto-mythology by a coherent, tendentially closed and codified "mature" mythology, which, as he correctly points out, is in agreement with other common myth-patterns. Derleth, even more than Lovecraft, explicitly spells out the constituting elements of the new mythological framework in his

---

33 There are, with the exception of the shadowy presence of Kazia Mason in "Dreams in the Witch House", no women-protagonists in Lovecraft. Even Asenath Waite (in "The Thing on the Doorstep") turns out to be woman only in body since her soul-spirit has been replaced by that of her father's, Ephraim Waite.
34 See, for example, the description of the talisman and its power in Derleth's "The House on Curwen Street" (Derleth, *The Cthulhu Mythos* 277). The use of talisman-like pieces goes back to a mention of such a practice by old Zadok Allen in Lovecraft's "Shadow over Innsmouth" (Lovecraft, *Omnibus 3* 419), though the pieces mentioned did not have a five-pointed star but "somethin' on 'em like what ye call a swastika naowadays. Prob'ly them was the Old Ones' signs" (ibid.).
35 Tolkien, criticising the film-script for *The Lord of the Rings* submitted to him in 1958, warns against using the "device of the Eagles" (letter 210, Tolkien, *Letters* 273) too frequently since it would certainly "stale" the device. A similar warning could be issued for Derleth's frequent and repetitive use of the Byakhee.
36 "Beam me up, Scotty!" comes to mind.

stories – often by means of narratorial voices of authority[37] – and thus renders public and explicit what Lovecraft presented in a more implicit and ambiguous manner. In "The Return of Hastur", a story begun in 1936, Derleth has Paul Tuttle outline the "mythology" to the neophyte first-person narrator Haddon. I am quoting it in full since it is a typical example of Derleth's approach and contains all the crucial elements:

> In order to understand what follows, you should know at least a brief outline of the mythology – if indeed it *is* only mythology [...] I am tempted to say that this mythology is far older than any other – certainly in its implications it goes far beyond, being cosmic and ageless, for its beings are of two natures, and two only: the Old or Ancient Ones, the Elder Gods, of *cosmic good*, and those of *cosmic evil*, bearing many names, and themselves of different groups, as if associated with the elements and yet transcending them: for there are the Water Beings, hidden in the depths; those of Air that are the primal lurkers beyond time; those of Earth, horrible animate survivals of distant eons. Incredible ages ago, the Old Ones banished from the cosmic places all the Evil Ones, imprisoning them in many places; but in time these Evil Ones spawned hellish minions who set about preparing for their return to greatness. The Old Ones are nameless, but their power is and will apparently always be great enough to check that of the others. Now, among the Evil Ones there is apparently often conflict, as among lesser beings. [...] But through what I have learned, it is possible to know that Great Cthulhu is one of the Water Beings, even as Hastur is of the Beings that stalk the star-spaces; [...]. (Derleth, *The Cthulhu Mythos* 121-122; italics in the original)

S.T. Joshi summarized the central points of Derleth's view as follows:

> (1) that the "gods" of the Mythos are elementals; (2) that the "gods" can be differentiated between a beneficent group of "Elder Gods," who are on the side of humanity, and a group of evil and maleficent "Old Ones,"[38] who seek to destroy humanity; and (3) that the Mythos as a whole is philosophically akin to Christianity. (Joshi, "The Cthulhu Mythos" 113-114)

In the following decades, Derleth would use this framework for many of his stories, which are either based on Lovecraftian themes and elements, or so-called "collaborations". The latter have mostly a very weak and tenuous foundation in the note- and scrapbooks of the late H.P. Lovecraft which came into the possession of Derleth, whereas the former often read like re-writings of Lovecraft's

---

37 This is an important difference to Lovecraft. The Mythos-related information found in his stories is given mostly by non-authoritative (not to say mentally deranged) narrators, whereas the trustworthiness of the informants in Derleth's stories is beyond doubt.
38 Lovecraft's own use of the term varies in the different texts. Derleth, in the preceding quote, equates the "Old Ones" with the Elder Gods (a term Derleth invented), whereas Joshi uses it to designate the cosmic beings associated with the Outer God Yog-Sothoth.

stories within the new framework outlined above. Derleth takes inspiration from and re-uses many originally Lovecraftian elements, such as the books of forbidden lore, the five-pointed-star talismans, eldritch spells and incantations, or the New England setting. The supernatural elements and the magic paraphernalia are incorporated into Derleth's approach and become important elements in his stories. He furthermore systematises the unruly dark pantheon of eldritch gods, classifies them according to the four traditional elements and, following the well-known models of the Romano-Greek mythologies, provides them with family-ties and invents inter-sibling rivalries[39] which can be exploited by the undaunted human protagonists. Derleth also downplays the natural scientific dimension of the Mythos, yet without explicitly contradicting it. His strategy is rather to stress one aspect at the expense of the other. As a result, the organically grown "chaos" of Lovecraft's cosmic vision is sorted out, ordered and, not least, re-connected to the traditional mythical patterns. This stands in opposition to Lovecraft's own approach: he was happy to use these elements (sparingly) for aesthetic effect, yet would judiciously abstain from trying to fuse them with his natural scientific theoretical framework. Lovecraft's courage to leave a potentially disruptive inconsistency at the heart of his oeuvre may be one reason for its strong appeal to many readers and the ongoing fascination it exerts.

Next to losing out on the original source of cosmic horror by replacing it with more traditional ones, Derleth's stories (not surprisingly) also lack Lovecraft's sometimes blasphemous humour. As Lévy (95-96) has convincingly shown, parts of "The Dunwich Horror" can be read as a parody of the story of the Incarnation and the Passion – with an unlikely and mentally unstable albino "virgin" (Lavinia Whateley) who is impregnated by a supernatural being (Yog-Sothoth) and as a consequence gives birth to Wilbur and his invisible twin. The demise of Wilbur Whateley's monstrous brother, and especially his call on his extra-terrestrial father in his despair on the hill in the climax of the story, is more than a bit reminiscent of what happened on Golgotha with the offspring of another human-supernatural union … No danger of anything remotely like that in Derleth's work, where the Mythos is taken rather seriously.

---

39 Derleth makes Hastur the spawn of Yog-Sothoth and half-brother of Cthulhu. See Schweitzer ("Know Your Elder Gods") for a comprehensive "Who is Who" in the "Cthulhu Mythos" pantheon.

In spite (or maybe because) of its deviation from the original Lovecraftian viewpoint, the "interpretatio Derlethiana" proved popular and dominated the reception of Lovecraft's work for decades. It restored a moral and basically anthropocentric view of the universe and undid thus the "Copernican revolution" set in motion by the nihilistic-existentialist cosmic horror of the original Lovecraftian Mythos. It was only after some years that critics began to realize that Derleth's interpretation was no mere continuation, variation and recreation of the proto-Mythos but that it represented a radical deviation from Lovecraft's cosmic "nihilistic indifferentism". Later generations of scholars have therefore found Derleth culpable of attributing his own interpretation of the Mythos to Lovecraft and of spreading it by means of his introductions to the editions of Lovecraft's works, his "posthumous collaborations" and by encouraging others to write in the vein of his Mythos.[40]

Lovecraft Restored?

As we have seen, the published Lovecraftian corpus of fictional texts alone is too heterogeneous and varied as to allow the reconstruction of the author's philosophical convictions without the help of some of his explicit statements in letters or conversations with friends and colleagues. The publication of more and more of Lovecraft's letters and the growing academic interest in his work led to an ever increasing critique of Derleth's interpretation and presentation of the "Cthulhu Mythos". The authority of Derleth's version rested mainly on his "collaborations" and the "infamous Black Magic quote" (cf. p. 125 of this paper). The latter was proven to have been "obtained from a letter by a brief correspondent of Lovecraft, Harold S. Farnese, who sent this passage to Derleth and claimed that it was a paraphrase of a Lovecraft letter; in fact, Farnese had made up the passage himself" (Joshi, "The Cthulhu Mythos" 115). This motivated a new generation of scholars to re-assess Lovecraft's contribution to literature and to restore its proper framework – a project that was not without pitfalls of its own. In the following I would like to discuss the approaches of two prominent critics who provide a new, post-Derlethian reading of Lovecraft's oeuvre.

---

40 Leiber (48), for instance, attacks Derleth without naming him for trying to reduce this existentialist nihilistic horror into a traditional dichotomy of good vs. evil. See also Price ("Artificial Mythology") and Joshi ("The Cthulhu Mythos" 116) for a recent summary of the debate.

The first approach was presented by the critic David E. Schultz, who makes (unwitting) use of the typological model as developed for the interpretation of another problematic and heterogeneous corpus, namely the Old and New Testaments.[41] Within the typological interpretation, Old Testament events and persons were seen as "types", as real world prophecies foreshadowing events or persons of the New Testament ("anti-types"). Thus, for example, Abraham sacrificing Isaac was seen as a foreshadowing of the crucifixion of Christ. This way biblical exegesis connected the "pre-history" of Christianity (i.e. the time before the incarnation) with the time after the birth of Christ and tied it to the larger framework of the history of salvation.

Schultz's reading of Lovecraft's oeuvre repeats, on a textual level, this "typological pattern". Instead of the Old and the New Testaments we have "Old and New Versions" of the same stories and themes, as Schultz's (221) list shows:

---

[41] The typological interpretation is one of the two major approaches, namely allegory and typology, used by Christian interpreters faced with the problem of rendering the stories and histories in the Bible relevant for the later teachings of the Church. The New Testament poses not that much of a problem and "the Word of God" could be easily brought in line with Christian dogma. The Old Testament, by contrast, proved harder to reconcile with the new creed. Allegorical interpretation was one way of "preserving" the truth (e.g. Abraham's three wives, Sarah, Hagar, and Keturah, were interpreted as representing three of the cardinal virtues). The other major exegetical approach was the typological interpretation of Old Testament events and persons. See Paul Michel's concise and accessible summary of the various methods used for interpreting the Bible.

Lovecraft's "Cosmic" Rewrites

Old Version	New Version
"[The Picture]" (?)	"Pickman's Model"
"The Alchemist," "The Tomb," "From Beyond," "The Picture in the House," "Herbert West—Reanimator," "The Hound," "In the Vault," "Cool Air"	*The Case of Charles Dexter Ward*
"Dagon"	"The Call of Cthulhu"
"Polaris," "The Cats of Ulthar," "The Doom That Came to Sarnath," "Celephaïs," "The Other Gods," "The White Ship"	"The Silver Key," *The Dream-Quest of Unknown Kadath*
"Beyond the Wall of Sleep"	"The Dreams in the Witch House"
"Polaris," "Beyond the Wall of Sleep," "The Statement of Randolph Carter," "The Doom That Came to Sarnath," "The Nameless City"	"The Shadow out of Time"
"The Doom That Came to Sarnath"	"The Shadow over Innsmouth"
"The Terrible Old Man"	"The Shadow over Innsmouth"
"The Temple"	*At the Mountains of Madness*, "The Shadow over Innsmouth"
"Facts concerning the Late Arthur Jermyn and His Family"	"The Shadow over Innsmouth"
"From Beyond"	"The Dreams in the Witch House"
"The Picture in the House," "The Rats in the Walls"	"The Shadow over Innsmouth"
"The Nameless City," "Under the Pyramids"	"The Dunwich Horror"
"The Nameless City"	*At the Mountains of Madness*
"The Moon-Bog"	"The Haunter of the Dark"
"The Outsider"	"The Shadow out of Time"
"The Unnamable"	"Pickman's Model"
"The Horror at Red Hook"	"The Call of Cthulhu," *The Case of Charles Dexter Ward*
"Cool Air"	"The Shadow over Innsmouth"

Schultz's main argument is that from 1926 onward Lovecraft's texts reflect the fully developed mythological framework while simultaneously retaining close thematic links to his previously published texts, so that the "New Versions" could be seen as "cosmic rewrites" (to use Schultz's term) of the "Old Versions". The "cosmic" refers to the new element of "cosmic horror" since, as Schultz argues, "[i]n early stories, characters are alienated from their race; in later stories the entire race is alienated as a whole from the cosmos. The insignificance (real or perceived) of individuals is easy for us to comprehend. Lovecraft's ability to depict the insignificance of the entire population of a planet ushers us into the presence of cosmic horror" (Schultz 222). Schultz himself does not make the connection to the typological approach, yet I would argue that his interpretative project fits perfectly into the framework of the biblical typological interpretation:

Typological interpretation of Lovecraft's Work

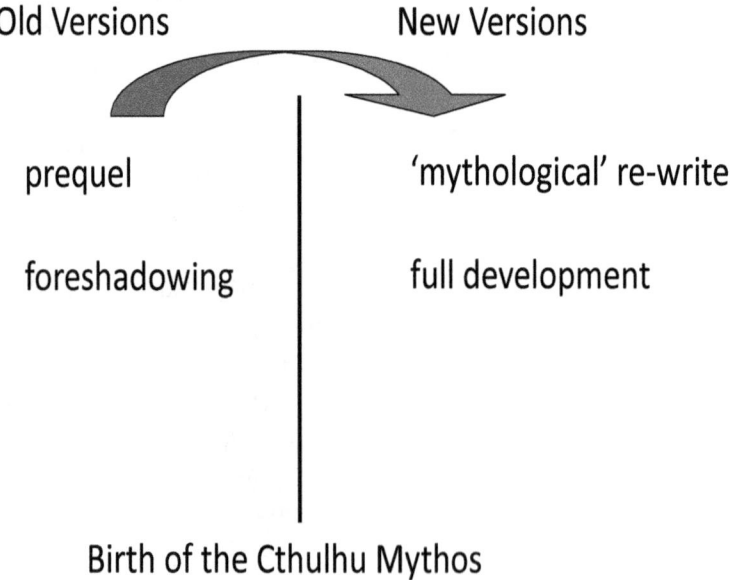

Schultz's typological "cosmic re-write" model cannot dissolve all the discrepancies and inconsistencies within the corpus and necessarily ignores many of the textual problems in the attempt to provide a new master narrative. Nevertheless, it is attractive, since it allows Schultz to stress the prominence of the cosmic indifferentism of Lovecraft's later publications on the one hand, and, on the other, to integrate his earlier texts into the larger framework without having to brand them as abortive attempts that have been superseded and replaced by the later ones.

While Schultz is (implicitly) arguing for an interpretation of the Lovecraftian corpus within the framework of a typological master narrative, S.T. Joshi ("The Cthulhu Mythos") proposes an alternative reading, which I'd like to call the "evolutionary model". Joshi accepts (with a pinch of salt) Lovecraft's statement in his 1927 letter to Donald Wandrei that "all my tales are based on the fundamental premise that common human laws and interests and emotions have no validity or significance in the vast cosmos-at-large" (quoted in Joshi, "The Cthulhu Mythos" 103) and tries to establish an "evolutionary master narrative" that runs as follows:[42] Lovecraft starts out writing stories in the vein of Poe, Dunsany, Machen, Blackwood etc., using the conventional framework of the supernatural as his point of reference. The change comes with "The Call of Cthulhu" (1926), which can be seen as the foundational text of the "Cthulhu Mythos". It unites, for the first time, "all the four subsidiary icons – topography, occult lore, gods, and cosmicism – [...] into a coherent whole" (Joshi, "The Cthulhu Mythos" 102), whereas all earlier texts lack one or more of these necessary components. Joshi specifically stresses the importance of cosmicism as the one element that raises Lovecraft's stories above all other fiction of the supernatural. A prime example for this shift from the supernatural to science fiction is "The Colour Out of Space" (1927). Then, however, "Lovecraft *unfortunately regresses* in his next major tale, 'The Dunwich Horror' (1928)" (Joshi, "The Cthulhu Mythos" 104; italics added), whose supernaturalism and frequent use of magic provided Derleth with the blueprint for his most prominent story-pattern. Luckily, "[w]ith 'The Whisperer in Darkness' (1930) things are a bit better" (Joshi, "The Cthulhu Mythos" 106), and the novella "At the Mountains of Madness" (1931) is an important milestone since it shows that

---

42 See the full account in Joshi ("The Cthulhu Mythos" 102-107).

"Lovecraft was undertaking a systematic "demythologizing" of his "gods" so that they become nothing more than extraterrestrials" (Joshi, "The Cthulhu Mythos" 110). In the contemporaneous "The Shadow over Innsmouth" (1931) the elements of cosmicism are only present "under the surface" (ibid.), and "[t]he rest of Lovecraft's fiction-writing career, marred by a lack of self-confidence and a sense of frustration with the course of his work, is somewhat uneven" (Joshi, "The Cthulhu Mythos" 111). Thus, "The Dreams in the Witch House" (1932) is "an overwritten and predictable story" (ibid.) and "The Thing on the Doorstep" (1933) "disappointing" (ibid.), but "The Shadow out of Time" (1934-35) is right on track again and "etch[es] the incalculable gulfs of time whereby all human history is merely a minuscule point amid the endless stretches of infinity" (ibid.). Lovecraft's last published story, "The Haunter of the Dark" (1935), is "a compact and satisfying tale and by no means an unfitting end to his "artificial mythology"" (Joshi, "The Cthulhu Mythos" 112).

I have quoted several passages verbatim in order to illustrate Joshi's argumentative drift, which often becomes visible only in his rhetoric. The reading implied in Joshi's analysis of Lovecraft's publication career can be summarized as follows: Lovecraft starts out as a talented writer of fiction of the supernatural in the traditional vein, with some peculiar elements that foreshadow his future achievements. The breakthrough comes with "The Call of Cthulhu" (1926) where he combines these elements into a new and coherent whole. At about the same time he explicitly formulates the ideas and concepts that constitute his philosophical conviction in several of his letters. Unfortunately, Lovecraft does not develop into a "programmatic" writer who would stick rigorously to the framework of cosmic indifferentism, but time and again lapses into the earlier mode of supernaturalism. This, and his premature death, preclude the development of the full potential and allow authors like Derleth to hijack the "Cthulhu Mythos".

As becomes clear from this summary, Joshi, as many other critics, believes that Lovecraft's main contribution to modern literature is his "natural scientific cosmic horror" and discerns in the development of his texts the reflection of an evolutionary struggle towards a form of horror fiction that adapted to the natural scientific mindset of modern man.

Ph'nglui mglw'nafh Cthulhu R'lyeh wgah'nagl fhtagn

The intense debate about the "correct" interpretation of the Lovecraftian oeuvre has been necessary to break up Derleth's virtual interpretative monopoly and to have Lovecraft's work re-enter the ongoing literary discourse. In hindsight, Derleth's interpretation of and contribution to the Mythos may no longer be considered an aberration from the "original" but rather one possible development of elements already present in Lovecraft's stories. He may not even be blamed overmuch for his desire to try and press the organically grown and therefore highly heterogeneous body of Lovecraftian texts into the Procrustean bed of his ideological framework. As we have seen in the case of Schultz and, to some extent even Joshi ("The Cthulhu Mythos"), other scholars have not been wholly immune against the temptation of imposing master narratives of their own. Although these more recent approaches reflect Lovecraft's original ideas more faithfully, the danger remains that even they ignore the heterogeneousness and diversity of his literary oeuvre. The risk of misinterpreting Lovecraft's philosophical conviction may have been minimised, yet the bigger risk of reducing his stories to mere textual illustrations of his theoretical ideas still exists.

Lovecraft's true heirs are thus not so much the literary critics, but the numerous authors, painters, film-makers, radio-play producers etc. who have composed short stories, painted pictures, produced movies and other works of art inspired by his texts, thus keeping alive and developing the "Cthulhu Mythos" as an artistic phenomenon.[43] The vigorous artistic "afterlife" in various forms testifies to the mythopoetic power inherent in the "Cthulhu Mythos", which fascinates contemporary readers and writers not only through its (not always consistent) theoretical framework but also through its aesthetic and literary qualities. It is the combination of and the resulting dynamic tension between these two aspects that gives the "Cthulhu Mythos" such a wide-reaching appeal. Some of the texts that, from a theoretical point of view, are perfect embodiments of "cosmicism", may not always attain the same literary quality and appeal as stories that are "tainted" by supernatural elements and contain (minor) theoretical

---

43 See Joshi ("The Cthulhu Mythos" 118-126) for an overview. Lovecraft actively supported (and participated in) such an approach, and his last story published during his lifetime ("The Haunter of the Dark") is part of a "literary banter" with Robert Bloch (who figures thinly disguised as the main protagonist "Robert Blake").

inconsistencies. Lovecraft seems to have known that it is sometimes advisable to sin against the rules of the theoretical framework in order to achieve the desired aesthetic and literary effects, even if he did not always succeed in striking the right balance (as he himself was all too willing to admit). I agree with Joshi's ("The Cthulhu Mythos" 99) claim that "[t]he Cthulhu Mythos, as envisioned by Lovecraft, was an expression of his deepest philosophical convictions", but want to argue that the actual literary realisation of the Mythos deviates sometimes considerably from this theoretical ideal and preserves instances of "supernatural atavisms" even in his later texts.

This, as I have pointed out, need not be an obstacle for the actual enjoyment of the texts. The cosmic indifferentism, on the one hand, allows modern readers to accept "rationally" the fictional events as potentially in agreement with the modern view of the world. They are not asked to suspend their belief in the laws of nature, but merely to accept that mankind has not yet explored or understood all the laws in the universe. The supernatural and "magical" elements, on the other hand, have not been completely eliminated, though they are (in theory) relegated to secondary rank and presented as misunderstood remnants of a more comprehensive system of cosmic communication. Lovecraft is therefore able to achieve in many of his stories a re-enchantment of the traditional myths and supernatural elements that had been discarded by the enlightenment as superstitious projections. They are rehabilitated as misunderstood and much garbled yet valid memories of an otherwise lost pre-human prehistory, and the readers are invited to look at them with new eyes. The non-rational side is attended to likewise by the very existence of the "rationalised" supernatural elements, so that readers must not forego the familiar frisson. The source for Lovecraft's ongoing fascination lies thus in the paradoxical interaction of the theoretical disenchantment by means of his "rational" cosmic indifferentism and the poetic enchantment by means of the "supernatural" and "irrational" elements in his narratives – a dichotomy that reflects modern man's inner disjunction.

I opened this essay with a brief comparison between Tolkien and Lovecraft. Both tried to "enchant" the modern reader and to bring about a "Recovery", which would allow readers to regain a clear view. The means they chose to do so, however, differ. Tolkien, on the one hand, aims at making the modern (and often disenchanted) reader see and appreciate once more the metaphysical harmony in God's creation by healing the rift that arose between man and God as a long-term result of the Enlightenment. Lovecraft, on the other hand, deepens and exploits man's estrangement from the metaphysical world while he plays at the same time with the reader's fascination with the supernatural. Tolkien's "mooreeffoc" experience opens our eyes to the inner beauty of things and reconciles us with our fallen world, while Lovecraft's "eye-opener" offers no such solace but rather the possibility to "re-enchant" a captive readership by combining the powerful *mysterium tremendum* arising from his rational indifferentism with the mesmerising fascination of the irrational in form of the supernatural elements of "magic".

About the author

THOMAS HONEGGER received his Ph.D. and later his 'habilitation' from the University of Zurich (Switzerland) where he taught Old and Middle English. He is the author of *From Phoenix to Chauntecleer: Medieval English Animal Poetry* (1996) and has edited several books with essays on medieval English language and literature as well as on the work of the late medievalist Prof. J.R.R. Tolkien. Apart from his publications on animals (real and imaginary) and Tolkien, he has written about Chaucer, Shakespeare, and medieval romance. He is, since 2002, Professor for English Medieval Studies at the Friedrich-Schiller-University, Jena (Germany). Homepage: http://www.anglistik.uni-jena.de/personen/thomas-honegger/
Contact: Tm.honegger@uni-jena.de

Bibliography

BOUCHARD, Alexandre, and Louis-Pierre Smith LACROIX. "Necronomicon: A Note." *Lovecraft Studies* 44 (2004): 107-112.

BURLESON, Donald R. *H.P. Lovecraft: A Critical Study*. Contributions to the Study of Science Fiction and Fantasy 5. Westport, CT: Greenwood Press, 1983.

CARPENTER, Humphrey. *The Inklings. C.S. Lewis. J.R.R. Tolkien, Charles Williams and their Friends*. Paperback edition 1981. London: George Allen & Unwin, 1978.

DERLETH, August. "A Note on the Cthulhu Mythos." (Originally published 1962). In August Derleth. *The Cthulhu Mythos*. Introduction by Ramsey Campbell. New York: Barnes & Noble, 1997. 445-448.

The Cthulhu Mythos. Introduction by Ramsey Campbell. New York: Barnes & Noble, 1997.

HAEFELE, John D. *A Look Behind the Derleth Mythos: Origins of the Cthulhu Mythos*. Odense: Harksen Productions, 2012.

HOUSTON, Alex. 2011. "Lovecraft and the Sublime: A Reinterpretation". *Lovecraft Annual: New Scholarship on H.P. Lovecraft* 5:160-180.

JANICKER, Rebecca. "New England Narratives: Space and Place in the Fiction of H.P. Lovecraft." *Extrapolation: A Journal of Science Fiction and Fantasy* 48 (2006): 56-72.

JOSHI, S.T. *A Dreamer and a Visionary. H.P. Lovecraft in His Time*. Liverpool: Liverpool University Press, 2001.

"The Cthulhu Mythos". *Icons of Horror and the Supernatural*. Vol. 1. Ed. S.T. Joshi. Westport, CT: Greenwood Press, 2007. 98-128.

H.P. Lovecraft. A Comprehensive Bibliography. Tampa, FL: University of Tampa Press, 2009.

KOCHER, Paul. "Middle-earth: An Imaginary World?" *Tolkien: New Critical Perspectives*. Ed. Neil D. Isaacs and Rose A. Zimbardo. Lexington, KT: The University Press of Kentucky, 1981. 117-132.

LAMPO, Hubert and Hubert VAN CALENBERGH. "A Cosmos of One's Own: Howard Phillips Lovecraft." *Lovecraft Studies* 41 (1999): 9-22.

LEIBER, Fritz Jr. "Ein literarischer Kopernikus." *Über H.P. Lovecraft*. Ed. Franz Rottensteiner. Frankfurt am Main: Suhrkamp, 1984. 44-59.

LÉVY, Maurice. *Lovecraft: A Study in the Fantastic*. Translated by S.T. Joshi. Detroit: Wayne State University Press, 1988.

Lippi, Giuseppi. "Lovecraft's Dreamworld Revisited." *Lovecraft Studies* 26 (1992): 23-25.

Lovecraft, Howard Phillips. 2000. *H.P. Lovecraft Omnibus 3: The Haunter of the Dark*. London: HarperCollins.

The Annotated Supernatural Horror in Literature. Edited by S.T. Joshi. New York: Hippocampus Press, 2012.

Lowell, Mark. "Lovecraft's Cthulhu Mythos." *Explicator* 63.1 (2004): 47-50.

Matolcsy, Kálmán. "Naturalizing the Supernatural: H.P. Lovecraft and the Aesthetics of Cosmic Horror." B.A.S.: *British and American Studies/Revista de Studii Britanice și Americane* 9 (2003): 85-91.

Michel, Paul. "Anhang: Einige Grundbegriffe der mittelalterlichen Bibelauslegung." *Tiersymbolik*. Ed. Paul Michel. Schriften zur Symbolforschung 7. Bern: Peter Lang, 1991. 205-217.

Mosig, Dirk W. "H.P. Lovecraft: Mythenschöpfer." *Über H.P. Lovecraft*. Ed. Franz Rottensteiner. Frankfurt am Main: Suhrkamp, 1984. 142-153.

Price, Robert M. "The Lovecraft-Derleth Connection." 1982. http://crypt-of-cthulhu.com/lovecraftderleth.htm, accessed 08 June 2013.

"Lovecraft's "Artificial Mythology"." *An Epicure in the Terrible: A Centennial Anthology of Essays in Honor of H. P. Lovecraft*. Ed. David E. Schultz and S.T. Joshi. First edition 1991. Revised and expanded version. New York: Hippocampus Press, 2011. 259-268.

Rottensteiner, Franz. "Lovecrafts transhumane Transformationen: Geschichten von der Begegnung mit dem maximal Fremden." *Im Labor der Visionen: Anmerkungen zur phantastischen Literatur*. Ed. Franz Rottensteiner. Lüneburg: von Reeken, 2013. 132-150.

Saler, Michael. *As If: Modern Enchantment and the Prehistory of Virtual Reality*. Oxford: Oxford University Press, 2012.

Schultz, David E. "From Microcosm to Macrocosm: The Growth of Lovecraft's Cosmic Vision". *An Epicure in the Terrible: A Centennial Anthology of Essays in Honor of H. P. Lovecraft*. Ed. David E. Schultz and S.T. Joshi. First edition 1991. Revised and expanded version. New York: Hippocampus Press, 2011. 208-229.

Schweitzer, Darrell. "M.R. James and H.P. Lovecraft: The Ghostly and the Cosmic". *Studies in Weird Fiction* 15 (Summer 1994): 12-16.

"Know Your Elder Gods". *Weird Tales*. http://weirdtalesmagazine.com/2012/05/25/know-your-elder-gods-lovecraft/ (accessed 4 July 2013).

SCULL, Christina and Wayne G. HAMMOND. *The J.R.R. Tolkien Companion and Guide. Chronology*. Boston and New York: Houghton Mifflin, 2006.

SHIPPEY, Tom A. *The Road to Middle-earth*. Third edition. First edition 1982. Boston: Houghton Mifflin, 2003.

ST. ARMAND, Barton Levi. *The Roots of Horror in the Fiction of H.P. Lovecraft*. Elizabethtown, NY: Dragon Press, 1977.

ST. PIERE, Ronald. ""Never Fully Realize": Birth of a Mythos, H.P. Lovecraft's "Dagon"." *Shoin Literary Review* 37 (2004): 15-36.

TOLKIEN, John Ronald Reuel. *The Letters of JRR Tolkien*. Edited by Humphrey Carpenter with the assistance of Christopher Tolkien. First published 1981. London: HarperCollins, 1995.

"Mythopoeia". (originally written ca. 1931). *Tree and Leaf.* London: Grafton, 1992. 97-101.

Tolkien On Fairy-stories. (Expanded edition, with commentary and notes; first edition 1947). Edited by Verlyn Flieger and Douglas A. Anderson. London: HarperCollins, 2008.

VANDERBEKE, Dirk and Allan TURNER. "The One or the Many? Authorship, Voice and Corpus." *Sub-creating Middle-earth. Constructions of Authorship and the Work of J.R.R. Tolkien*. Ed. Judith Klinger. Cormarë Series 27. Zurich and Jena: Walking Tree Publishers, 2012. 1-20.

WEINSTEIN, Lee. "William Hope Hodgson. "The First Literary Copernicus"." First published in *Nyctalops* 15 (January 1980). http://williamhopehdgson.wordpress.com/2012/07/23/the-first-literary-copernicus-2 (accessed 26 June 2013).

ZACHRAU, Thekla. L.G. Boba, and S.T. Joshi. "The "Cthulhu Mythos": Between Horror and Science Fiction". *Lovecraft Studies* 19-20 (1989): 56-62.

Dirk Vanderbeke

The Sub-Creation of Sub-London: Neil Gaiman's and China Miéville's Urban Fantasy

Abstract

Fantasy is reputedly an escapist literature for juvenile or immature audiences, set in an ill-defined era between prehistory and fake medievalism, endlessly repeating generic stories about mythical heroes, beasts, elves, dwarves and wizards. This has never been quite true, and fantasy has always addressed serious issues, albeit in metaphorical and symbolic garb. Over the last decades the innovative subgenre of urban fantasy has discarded the stereotypical markers of time and space, heroes and villains, and replaced the traditional versions of the perilous realm by the very real and recognizable cityscapes of the modern metropolis. Drawing on earlier literary explorations of the city as the location of the fantastic and inexplicable, the texts discussed in this paper merge elements of various genres, e.g. fantasy, magic realism and steampunk to create counter-world visions of London that appear simultaneously weird and familiar, appalling and fascinating, unbelievable and eminently political.

Counter-worlds have been an integral element of human storytelling ever since the earliest myths. They include underworlds that the hero has to enter in the course of his quest, islands of immortality, lands of no return, magic wells at the bottom of which you can enter the domain of Mother Hulda or some other female deity, lands of abundance like Cockayne, of eternal youth like Tír na nÓg and the more recent Shangri-La, or even Ivor Novello's "The Land of Might-Have-Been", "far more mercifully planned / than the cruel place we know". Such places may represent the land of death, the vagina of mother Earth (Duerr 30-46), the fantastic dreams of a better life in a carnevalesque world turned upside down (ibid. 90-95), or the timeless abode of the gods or the great goddess, and they can be moulded and adapted to ever new purposes in legends, fairy tales or fantastic literature. Until the middle ages, such counter-worlds were often expected and sometimes even found by those who travelled into unknown regions at the edge of the world, but then spatial distance is not a necessary feature of the fantastic realm, and an entrance can open up just around every corner. Rip van Winkle enters such a mysterious realm when he goes hiking in the Catskill Mountains in an attempt to escape his nagging wife, Tannhäuser spends a year under the Venus Mountain worshipping the goddess of love, and Jack has only to climb an oversized bean-stalk right in front of his door to reach the land of the giant.

Traditionally, such counter-worlds are predominantly set in a pastoral or rural environment. It is the solitary hero on his journey who encounters an entrance into the mysterious realm, the girl who fled from a cruel stepmother, or the never-do-well third son who is sent away from his father's house to make some kind of living in the hostile world. More recently, however, such doorways into a world that is and isn't ours can also appear in the modern city and metropolis, and they lead to regions no less amazing than those of the times of yore, regions that are simultaneously both utterly alien and quite familiar.

Such tales are now subsumed under the umbrella term *urban fantasy*, sharing some aspects with magical realism that also moved from rural settings to urban environments (Faris 183f). As in magical realism, mutually exclusive ontologies collide in such urban fantasies, and what is quite natural and realistic to the inhabitants of one realm is absolutely impossible and incomprehensible to those of the other. In addition we once more find various characteristic literary techniques of magical realism as discussed by Anne Hegerfeldt: a hybridity, resulting from the adaptations of various modes and genres (69ff), a use of ex-centric focalizers (115ff), various forms of literalization (235ff), and in general an inversion of Western concepts of knowledge, of the real and the fantastic (157ff).

Urban fantasy seems to be a fairly recent denomination for a literary phenomenon that builds on traditions of long standing. Walter Benjamin acknowledged the similarities between mythological landscapes and the modern cities when he wrote about the two faces of Paris:

> [o]ne knew of places in ancient Greece where the way led down into the underworld. Our waking existence likewise is a land which, at certain hidden points, leads down into the underworld – a land full of inconspicuous places from which dreams arise. All day long, suspecting nothing, we pass them by but no sooner has sleep come than we are eagerly groping our way back to lose ourselves in the dark corridors. By day the labyrinth of urban dwellings resembles consciousness; the arcades (which are galleries leading into the city's past) issue unremarked onto the streets.

> At night, however, under the tenebrous mass of the houses, their denser darkness protrudes like a threat, and the nocturnal pedestrian hurries past – unless, that is, we have emboldened him to turn into the narrow lane. (Benjamin 84)[1]

The fantastic potential of such an urban environment was quickly recognized in literary works such as Louis Aragon's *Le Paysan de Paris* of 1926 which fused realist and surrealist elements in its depiction of the modern city. Literary cities are frequently labyrinthine and uncontrollable; they seem to have a life of their own and are not always hospitable to their inhabitants; they can change rapidly and their "lanes as dark as death" (Alfred Douglas, "Impression de Nuit", quoted from Goetsch 149) can lead the unwary traveller as quickly into danger and despair as any bog or swamp. The secret streets and quarters of Rome, Venice, Paris and London have frequently been explored as places that are no less mysterious and perilous than any exotic region or island. Moreover, it is not only the city that presents the traveller with uncanny experiences; the inhabitants and their customs and manners can be just as unfamiliar as those of any foreign tribe. Famously, Eugene Sue took his main inspiration for *The Mysteries of Paris* from James Fenimore Cooper's *Leatherstocking Tales*, and "the city replaced the forest, the underworld gang replaced the evil Indians" (Lehan 55). In particular the slums were for many writers "a site comparable to the jungle, the wilderness, or the interior of Africa" (Goetsch 150). In his *Confessions of an English Opium Eater* (1821), Thomas de Quincey writes about his ramblings through London in terms of a geographical expedition into foreign territories:

> sometimes in my attempts to steer homewards, upon nautical principles, by fixing my eye on the pole-star, and seeking ambitiously for a north-west passage, instead of circumnavigating all the capes and head-lands I had doubled in my outward voyage, I came suddenly upon such knotty problems of alleys, such enigmatical entries, and such sphynx's riddles of streets without thoroughfares, as must, I conceive, baffle the audacity of porters and confound the intellects of hackney-coachmen. I could almost have believed at times that I must be the first discoverer of some of these *terræ incognitæ*, and doubted whether they had yet been laid down in the modern charts of London. (de Quincey 192, cf. also Goetsch 150)

---

[1] I want to thank Isabel Vila Cabanes who brought this passage to my attention.

And, of course, cities have also been the location of supernatural intrusions and epistemological uncertainty. In Dublin's nighttown, hallucinations rule, and a man can easily succumb to the spell of a madam who is not only running a brothel but also appears to be the incarnation of Circe (Joyce, chapter 15 passim), the sorceress. In Venice, there is "a city within the city that is the knowledge of a few" (Winterson 53). "This city enfolds upon itself. Canals hide other canals, alley-ways cross and crisscross so that you will not know which is which until you have lived here all your life" (Winterson, 113). Here Boatmen are born with webbed feet so that they can walk on the water, and "the laws of the real world are suspended" (Winterson 76).

But then the ancestors of urban fantastic are not restricted to the old world. The clash of simultaneously familiar and unfamiliar elements has become an important feature in American urban and suburban literature. In Thomas Pynchon's *V.* (1963), one of the main characters joins a patrol that hunts alligators in the sewers of New York, the offspring of baby alligators sold as pets but then flushed down the toilets once the kids got bored of them. He learns about a priest who lived in the sewers in the 1930s. Convinced that the rats would take over New York he was trying to convert them to Roman Catholicism, and indeed he not only succeeded with one particular batch but even finds a female rat who wants to take up holy orders (Pynchon, *V.* 118-121). In addition to such modern urban legends, the past can also be part of the fantasy, and H.P. Lovecraft's stories imagine a long history for his fictional city Arkham, a kind of fake medieval past, and the layers of this city can then be explored by characters like Walter Gilman ("The Dreams in the Witch House"), frequently with fatal results. Since the 1950s, the modern suburbia has also developed its own kinds of anxieties or horror, and Pleasantville or Smallville can easily turn into Stepford (Ira Levin, *The Stepford Wives*) or Castle Rock (Steven King, *Needful Things*).

Still, the city that seems to be most often associated with an entanglement of archaeological investigation and fantastic narration is unquestionably London, a city where almost everyone frequently, if not daily, enters an intricate web of tunnels and tracks underground, if only to commute to work. It is the ready-made location for narrations of urban anxieties, conflicts, contradictions, marginalization and strife, and it offers itself to fantastic visions and nightmares, to strategies of literalization and metaphorization, to realistic stories and tales of magic.

In *London Under*, his recent supplement to the huge volume *London. A Biography* (2000), Peter Ackroyd explores the world beneath the surface of the metropolis. This subterranean realm consists of tunnels and sewers, of "Forgotten Streams" and "The Pipes of London" (*London Under* 38 and 88), of the London Underground and the dead ends of abandoned stations. It is a world of detritus and waste, of excrement and filth, but also of the hopes for lost treasures, of safety in war times, of intense human contact during the daily travels on the tube, and ultimately also of fantastic dreams.

As the subtitle of the earlier volume, *A Biography*, indicates, Ackroyd perceives the city as an organism or even a sentient being; and its development from the early beginnings to the present can be described in analogy to a human life.[2] The very first words of the book confirm this assumption. Ackroyd writes: "The image of London as a human body is striking and singular" (Ackroyd, *London* 1), and he then goes on to offer two contradictory perspectives. On the one hand, "London has been envisaged in the form of a young man with his arms outstretched in a gesture of liberation" (ibid.), but on the other hand "it has been commonly portrayed in monstrous form, a swollen and dropsical giant which kills more than it breeds" (ibid.). But no matter which of the two images seems to be more accurate:

> Whether we consider London as a young man refreshed and risen from sleep [...] or whether we lament its condition as a deformed giant, we must regard it as a human shape with its own laws of life and growth. (Ackroyd, *London* 2)

In *London Under*, Ackroyd once more emphasises the analogy of the city and an organism when he suggests that "[l]ike the nerves within the human body, the underworld controls the life of the surface" (Ackroyd, *London Under* 2). But then he also immediately conjures the images of danger, of forbidden zones, of mythological labyrinths and their inhabitants: "Yet, there may be monsters.

---

2 Peter Droege's anthology on *Intelligent Environments* goes one step further, attributing to the developing cities of our times not only organic phenomena akin to biological processes, but also cognitive abilities (see in particular Chun Wei Choo's essay on "IT 2000: Singapore's Vision of an Intelligent Island" and Marcos Novak's "Cognitive Cities: Intelligence, Environment and Space").

The lower depths have been the object of superstitions and of legend as long as there have been men and women to wonder" (ibid. 3).

But then the journey into the metropolitan underworld includes not only a spatial movement, it is also a return to the past, as "all of [London's] history from the prehistoric settlers to the present day [is] packed within 24 feet of earthen fabric" (Ackroyd, *London Under* 1).[3] Ackroyd indeed has always been fascinated by London's past, which in his novels regularly reaches out and touches our present lives in inexplicable and fantastic ways. In *Hawksmoor* (1985), some human sacrifices committed by a satanic architect of the early 18th century seem to resonate in similar murders in modern London; in *The House of Dr. Dee* (1993), the house of the alchemist seems to merge the present and the past, and some incidents take place in both times simultaneously. Age certainly contributes to the potential for magic and mystery, for fear and terror. Accordingly, Alexander Irvine suggests that "the fantastic city is old, if not in its current incarnation then by virtue of being built on the remnants of preceding cities (and previous narratives)" (Irvine 212). Similarly, Hadas Elber-Aviram argues that the genre of urban fantasy "correlates with urban archaeology through a shared concern with the material history of the city" (forthcoming); the protagonists are thus cast "into the symbolic role of archaeologists who descend into the urban underworld to recover the city's forgotten past" (ibid.)

In the final chapter of his book, Ackroyd turns to literature that explores the world below London. He repeatedly mentions H.G. Wells and his visions of underground futures in *The War of the Worlds, The Time Machine* and *When the Sleeper Wakes*, but also Michael Moorcock's more recent novel *Mother London*, in which one of the characters, David Mummery, self proclaimed "urban anthropologist, and with an impressive record of mental illness" (Moorcock 5), is working on a book on London's underground waterways:

---

3   His assessment echoes Benjamin's depiction of his chosen modern city when he wrote: "Paris is built over a system of caverns from which the din of Métro and railroad mounts to the surface, and in which every passing omnibus or truck sets up a prolonged echo. And this great technological system of tunnels and thoroughfares interconnects with the ancient vaults, the limestone quarries, the grottoes and catacombs which, since the early Middle Ages, have time and again been reentered and traversed" (Benjamin 85).

He first went down several years ago in search of the legendary subterraneans. The Fleet's pig herd was rumoured to be moving back to its old pastures, inhabiting the river just below Holborn Viaduct, having gone wild since the early 19th century. (Moorcock 18)

Mummery later writes on hospital stationary:

I discovered evidence that London was interlaced with connecting tunnels, home of a forgotten troglodytic race that had gone underground at the time of the Great Fire, whose ranks had been added to periodically by thieves, vagabonds and escaped prisoners, receiving many fresh recruits during the Blitz when so many of us sought the safety of the tubes. (Moorcock 344, see also Ackroyd, *London Under* 177)

Subterranean London is thus a location of legend and rumour, of delusionary dreams and wild fantasy, the urban equivalent to Coleridge's "caverns measureless to men" under "the stately pleasure domes" of the metropolis. And should London indeed be a sentient organism, its underside is not only the urban bowels and organs of excretion but also the city's untamed unconscious, the place of repressed desires and uncontrollable instincts.

*

In his chapter on literature in *London Under*, Peter Ackroyd mentions neither Neil Gaiman nor China Miéville, an omission that seems all the more striking as Neil Gaiman's *Neverwhere* is mostly set in a "London Below",[4] China Miéville wrote not only *King Rat*, but also about an UnLondon in *Un Lun Dun*, and these novels may well have contributed to Ackroyd's selection of his topic as well as influenced the choice of a title for his book.

In spite of various differences, there is a lot of overlap between Miéville and Gaiman, an interdependency both authors freely acknowledge. Both present cities that blend realist and fantastic or weird elements; both draw on myth and fairy tales as sources for their stories; both use unexceptional protagonists as heroes; both introduce sentient animals and animistic deities like the king of the rats or the spider king or god Anansi, both partly set their narratives in the sewers and underground tunnels of London, and, most importantly, both

---

4 In urban fantasy, the counter-cities have various names. In the course of this paper I will use "London Below" not only in reference to Gaiman's *Neverwhere*, but also as an umbrella term for such locations, even if they are not always and necessarily underground.

have a particular fondness for the motif of divided worlds. The barriers as well as the entrances or gates to the Otherworld are varied. Gaiman has used rather traditional options like magical books and mirrors (*Mirrormask*), different kinds of walls (*Stardust, The Wolves in the Wall*), various doors (*Coraline, Neverwhere*), and dreams (*Sandman*), but while Miéville in his young adult book *Un Lun Dun* has also used a rather common door as the passageway for his heroine, he has more often turned to divisionary lines that at the same time seem more plausible and more strange, as for example language (*Embassytown*) or social and political conventions (*The City & the City*).

No matter which form of separation and possibility for contact or intrusion is chosen, the division is always marked by hierarchies. London Above is the affluent, capitalist and consumerist world of our daily experience, the sphere in which the inhabitants have to work in shops and offices, where money is the usual means of trade and commerce, where machines work, where information technologies increasingly structure interpersonal communication and relationships, and where digital media inform us about the world and external reality. In contrast, the other London, London Below or UnLondon, is the world of those who have "fallen through the cracks" (Gaiman, *Neverwhere* 136). These locations are heterotopias of deviation as analyzed by Michel Foucault, places "in which individuals whose behaviour is deviant in relation to the required mean or norm are placed" (Foucault n.p.). Foucault names asylums and prisons as such heterotopias of deviation, retirement homes may also belong in this category and even cemeteries. The urban counter-worlds are inhabited by potential inmates of all these institutions or locations, sometimes including ghosts or the undead, but also those who are economically destitute and thus not able to follow the normative behaviour in a consumerist world. In *Un Lun Dun* this includes not only people "crossing down, or up, or sideways, from there to here" (60), but also broken or discarded objects which seep through and now appear as sentient beings – and one of the heroines quickly acquires a crumpled milk carton as a kind of pet. In a world in which performance extends to consumerist goods, the junk yard needs to be added to the places of deviant behaviour.[5]

*

The challenges to common norms and codes of behaviour also include a re-valuation of traditional conventions and of the "system of associated commonplaces" (Black 287) that is part and parcel of our cognitive approach to, and intuitive assessment of, experiences. Together with the protagonists, the readers undergo a thorough process of defamiliarization, in which we do not only have to assimilate supernatural and magical aspects into a seemingly realist world, but also modify our acquired views on magic. If the world we encounter in urban fantasy presents us with the darker and less pleasant aspects of our environment, this also applies to the magic involved, a magic that is not particularly appealing, wonderful or marvellous.

> Magic had entered Saul's life. It didn't matter any more that he didn't understand. This was a million miles from the tawdry world of conjuring tricks. His life was in thrall to another hex, a power which had crept into his police cell and claimed him, a dirty, raw magic, a spell that stank of piss. This was urban voodoo, fuelled by the sacrifices of road deaths, of cats and people dying on the tarmac, an I Ching of spilled and stolen groceries, a Cabbala of road signs. (Miéville, *King Rat* 120)

The first thing Saul learns after he has been freed from prison by King Rat is that he himself is half rat and thus it is not in his nature to become sick. He can feed on anything, including "pigeon-meat scraped off a car wheel" (59), and he immediately puts his new knowledge into practice and gorges himself on a half eaten hamburger pulled from a trash sack. Uncommon and possibly nauseating food is also introduced in *Neverwhere*, and when Richard Mayhew admits to a girl that he does like cats, "Anaesthesia looked relieved. 'Thigh?' she asked, 'Or breast?'" (78).

---

[5] This inclusion also recalls Thomas Pynchon's W.A.S.T.E., the alternative mail system that links all the different undergrounds of the metropolis and all those that have been disinherited and now reject the usual channels of communication: "It was not an act of treason, nor possibly even of defiance. But it was a calculated withdrawal, from the life of the Republic, from its machinery. Whatever else was being denied them out of hate, indifference to the power of their vote, loopholes, simple ignorance, this withdrawal was their own, unpublicized, private. Since they could not have withdrawn into a vacuum (could they?), there had to exist the separate, silent, unsuspected world" (Pynchon, *The Crying of Lot 49* 92).

In *Un Lun Dun*, the forces of evil are ruled by the Smog that has self-organized into a sentient entity:

> There were so many chemicals swilling around in it that they reacted together. These gases and liquid vapour and brick dust and bone dust and acids and alkalis, fired through by lightning, heated up and cooled down, tickled by electric wires and stirred up by the wind – he reacted together and made an enormous, diffuse, cloud brain. (110)

The servants of the Smog include stink junkies, "people that Smog had caught and, horribly, forced to breathe it" (123), but then the "abcity" as such is chiefly made of junk and rubbish, and a smelly empty milk carton also seems to be a rather unusual pet.

If *Alice in Wonderland* was the innocent, but also mendacious dream of a Victorian garden without industrialization, poverty and filth, urban fantasy in some of its elements presents us with the nightmare of late capitalism, a world made of our own waste. Science fiction has for a long time told us tales of war between mankind and its own technological products, wars in which the odds are against us because we are neither as powerful nor as efficient as our machinery, in particular the machinery explicitly developed for the purpose of battle and warfare. Now we are under attack from our own waste, while more loyal objects are coming to our aids – the revival of a motif well-known from the Western and Science Fiction, where hostile Indians and aliens are fought with the help of slightly inferior and also funny Indian or alien sidekicks.

*

Inversion with a re-valuation of traditional hierarchies and associated commonplaces are also very much at the core of the depiction of the urban biological Other, the animal populations that have been inevitably and ineradicably our unwelcome neighbours since the earliest human settlements. Most important in this respect is the rat, feared and loathed as a transmitter of filth and disease, in many places a serious danger to new-born infants and, of course, the subject of innumerable urban legends. In *Neverwhere*'s London Below, the rat is on top of the social hierarchy. Rats are served by rat-speakers who can communicate with them and carry out their wishes and orders. In *King Rat*, very much darker than Gaiman's novel, the rodents are similarly intelligent and able to communicate. They are ruled by a humanoid king who fathered the protagonist Saul by raping his mother. Because of his mixed heritage, Saul is able to resist the almost invincible villain of the novel, the pied piper of Hamelin who turns out to be a sadistic sociopath, using his music to gain absolute power. The ability to manipulate crowds and vast audiences with music is here fused with the fairy tale, and by the use of electronic devices the piper can reach and control the frenzied masses of humans and animals alike. In the end, not only the pied piper is subdued, possibly killed, and sent back to the mystical realm from where he had emerged, but also the Rat King who has lost his kingdom and subjects to Saul. The novel ends with Saul abdicating and proclaiming "Year One of the Rat Republic" (Miéville, *King Rat* 420), a solution that is equally utopian and absurd and thus indicates the utter impossibility of a harmonious political conclusion even in a completely fantastical urban environment.

The second animal that frequently takes up a new garb in urban fantasy is the spider. Equally feared and abhorred as the rat, the spider is now also elevated to a royal or even divine status. In popular culture, this re-valuation has a longer history, Spiderman having roamed the comics ever since the early 1960s, defending a usually ungrateful New York population against criminals and supervillains. In *Harry Potter and the Chamber of Secrets*, Harry and his friends encounter a colony of sentient giant spiders fathered by Aragog, one of Hagrid's previous pets. In urban fantasy, Miéville turned to the West African trickster Anansi who frequently appears as a spider and is famed for his knowledge and his enormous hoard of stories.[6] Anansi features as the Spider King in *King Rat* where he is by far more sympathetic and affable than the eponymous rodent. Both Anansi and Loplop the Bird King borrowed from Max Ernst are allies against, and eventually victims of, the pied piper, and in general they appear as gentle and supportive characters, in contrast to the more ruthless and violent Rat King.

In *Perdido Street Station*, the Weaver is one of the strangest figures in a novel filled with weird beings: a multi-dimensional entity in the shape of a giant spider that communicates in an endless stream of free verse. Weavers are able to manipulate the worldweb, "metareal filaments connecting every moment to every

---

6 Anansi had already been introduced to Western audiences in various tales, e.g. in Gerald McDermott's short film *Anansi the Spider* (1969), which was later turned into a book for children.

other" (Miéville, *Perdido Street Station* 576). Asked for assistance only after the Ambassador of Hell has declined to help the city against a seemingly invincible enemy, the Weaver agrees, but less out of pity than according to aesthetic principles.

> Old stories told how Weavers would kill each other over aesthetic disagreements, such as whether it was prettier to destroy an army of a thousand men or to leave it be, or whether a particular dandelion should or should not be plucked. For a Weaver, to think was to think aesthetically. To act – to Weave – was to bring about more pleasing patterns. They did not eat physical food: they seemed to subsist on the appreciation of beauty. (ibid. 290)

In a world of uncertainties and ambiguities, aesthetic perception offers a seemingly arbitrary, but still functional basis for valuation, and it seems as if Weaver decides to help not out of moral considerations but because this course of action offers new aesthetic possibilities. In a crucial situation, he first hesitates and tells the protagonist:

> … YOU WORK WITH FINESSE I GRANT AND GIVE YOU BUT THIS SIPHONING OF PHANTASMS FROM MY SOLE SOUL LEAVES ME MELANCHOLIC SEE PATTERN INHERE EVEN IN THESE THE VORACIOUS ONES PERHAPS I JUDGE QUICK AND SLICK TASTES FALTER AND ALTER AND I AM UNSURE …
> (Miéville, *Perdido Street Station* 573)

But then, being told that his help allowed him "to judge and weave" (ibid.) and that further assistance is now needed, Weaver once more becomes decisive:

> … BY GOODNESS ME YOU CONVINCE […] LOOK AT THE INTRICATE SKEIN AND THREADLINES WE CORRECT WHERE THE DEADLINGS RAVED WE CAN RESHUFFLE AND SPIN AND FIX IT UP NICELY …
> (ibid.)

Neil Gaiman introduced Anansi as one of his *American Gods* and then used the figure again in *Anansi Boys*, a novel about one of his everyday protagonists, Charles Nancy,[7] who finds out that his father was, in fact, the incarnation of the spider god. Unfortunately, the divine powers seem to have all gone to an up to this point unknown brother, Spider, who acts as a trickster and

---

7 In China Miéville's *The City & the City*, there is an archaeologist with the name Isabelle Nancy. This may well indicate another emanation of the spider god, but I have been unable to figure out to what extent this rather minor character actually pulls any strings or otherwise fulfils the role of a divine arachnid.

doppelganger to Charlie. Ultimately, Charlie has to learn that originally he and Spider had been one person which was split into two by a witch's spell, and by telling stories he can exert the power of the spider god and manipulate not only other people and sentient animals but also reality.

Quite obviously, sentient rats and spiders have become stock figures in urban fantasy, and their new incarnations replace previous stereotypes that served horror movies from *Tarantula* (1955) and *Arachnophobia* (1990) to *Willard* (1971) and *Deadly Eyes* (1982). Such re-valuations have become rather common since the 1960s, and there are hardly any epitomes of evil or terror that have not been recast as heroes or victims of prejudice and superstition. The vampire, the werewolf, the dragon or oversized animals like King Kong have been revealed as endangered species and as suffering creatures, deserving our pity and compassion, and even the prince of darkness himself found apologists when the Rolling Stones asked for "Sympathy for the Devil". Both rat and spider have also become important in punk and gothic iconography and as alternative pets. In urban fantasy, the counter-world is a place where our fears and anxieties are re-negotiated, where our instinctive responses of terror and disgust are simultaneously tested and challenged, and where the repugnant and repulsive are revealed as integral parts of our world and as potentially pleasing. The texts thus position themselves in traditions of the carnevalesque with its emphasis on the grotesque, but also within the "aesthetics of ugliness", examples of which we can find in particular in earlier urban literature as for example the poetry of Charles Baudelaire or James Joyce's *Ulysses*.

In *Perdido Street Station* this is brought to a sort of climax when early in the novel the reader is presented with a highly erotic encounter between the protagonist and his lover, only to realize after some explicit passages about their nude bodies that the female is actually a khepri, i.e. the mixture of a human body and a scarab beetle's head. Surprisingly, while this certainly evokes some variant of the hesitation on part of the reader that is a significant element in the appreciation and conceptualization of fantastic literature (Todorov 31; Hegerfeldt 55), it does not break the erotic tension of the passage, and the inter-species intercourse continues with the tenderness and desire of well-written erotic literature. Beauty is certainly in the eye of the beholder, and urban fantasy forces us to modify our modes of perception and to readjust our aesthetic principles.

*

One of the most important aspects of the urban counter-world is the question of visibility. Almost all the texts involve different degrees and modes of invisibility, ranging from the wilful dismissal of an undesirable or improper sight[8] to the complete inability to see what is right in front of the eyes. In Salman Rushdie's *The Satanic Verses*, chapter V is titled "A City Visible but Unseen", and in an interview Rushdie argued that at the time when he wrote the novel the Indian community was indeed unseen:

> It was there and nobody knew it was there. And I was very struck by how often, when one would talk to white English people about what was going on, you could actually take them to these streets and point to these phenomena, and they would somehow still reject this information. (Rushdie, "Interview" 210)

He then suggested that the eyesight of people may have improved and that "at the level of the city which was unseen" (ibid.) things could be different now, but each of the works discussed here makes the point that this is, in fact, not the case. When in *Neverwhere* Richard Mayhew becomes part of London Below for no other reason than helping an injured girl who belongs to the counter-world, he simply disappears to his previous colleagues, friends and even his fiancée – it seems as if in our world altruism already counts as deviant behaviour. Moreover, his credit card is no longer accepted by ATM machines, taxis will not stop for him, and if he tries to force himself onto anyone's attention he is not recognized and immediately forgotten. His situation is summed up as: "You can't go back to your old home or your old life. [...] None of those things exist. Up there, you don't exist" (Gaiman, *Neverwhere* 127; on invisibility in this novel, cf. Beaudry passim). In *King Rat*, Saul Garamond is shown a man staring out of a window, and then his new guide tells him:

---

[8] This is most importantly realized in Miéville's *The City & the City*, in which two cities are interwoven, but any mutual contact or even recognition is strictly prohibited. While there is no actual magical or supernatural element at work, this construct may well seem even more fantastic to readers than the more common inventions of counter-worlds or hidden cities – until the realization that split cities did and still do exist (e.g. Berlin or Belfast) and that reality may be more unbelievable than the wild creations of our fantasy (cf. Vanderbeke passim).

> That geezer there, stopping and staring, that's as close as you ever got to this before. The place he's looking at now – no, he's not looking at it, he's caught *a glimpse*, a *hint*, it's teasing him out of the corner of his eye – that's your gaff now, me old son. [...] The rest of it, that's just in between for you now. All the main streets, the front rooms and the rest of it, that's just filler, that's just *chaff*, that ain't the real city. [...] All the vacant lots and all – that's your stomping ground now, your pad, your burrow. That's London. You can't go back *now*, can you? (Miéville, *King Rat* 45-46, italics in the original)

Even the urban passages of *Harry Potter* employ this motif, and standing in front of the Leaky Cauldron, the entrance to Diagon Alley, Harry notices that:

> The people hurrying by didn't glance at it. Their eyes slid from the big book shop on one side to the record store on the other as if they couldn't see the Leaky Cauldron at all. In fact, Harry had the most peculiar feeling that only he and Hagrid could see it. (Rowling, *Philosopher's Stone* 78)

Invisibility, of course, is one of the oldest and most familiar magical features in myth and fairy tales, but now it gains unmistakable political, social and psychological dimensions. If the "gaze" always includes power relations and objectifies those that are under surveillance, the exclusion from all notice indicates an even stronger imbalance. Momentary and active invisibility may serve mythical heroes like Perseus or Siegfried or some more recent superheroes well, and the cloak of invisibility is certainly quite useful for Harry Potter, but for the passive victim of a social practice invisibility indicates the ultimate form of ostracism and, literally, disregard. The Othercity or the urban underworld thus literalizes the distinction between the decent and prosperous quarters and the no-go-areas or slums. The metropolis appears as an oversized variant of the Potemkin village in which the less reputable sights are hidden and rendered invisible by the gaudy façades.

*

It is, however, not only poverty and destitution that is hidden by the literalized invisibility, but also the urban history. As indicated above, the descent into the counter-world is also an archaeological journey into the city's past, into the layers on which the present day metropolis has been erected. Those layers are not only the material remnants of the past but also involve the social relationships of various previous eras which have persisted in the niches of London Below. Many characters in *Neverwhere* seem to have been taken straight out of Henry

Mayhew's *London Labour and the London Poor* – in fact, Gaiman has admitted that he chose the name of his protagonist as an allusion to the 19th century social researcher (Gaiman, FAQs n.p.). In addition, the economy is based on pre-modern principles, barter seemingly being the preferred mode of exchange.

The histories of the counter-cities are, however, not the official histories that can be found in the upper regions. If postmodern literature and in particular magical realism employ strategies of historiographic metafiction to challenge traditional concepts of history by the intrusions of alternative versions and subjective memories, often of a fantastic nature, urban fantasy presents the reader with remnants that are supposedly still in existence, but once more highly imaginative modifications and twists are added to subvert the allegedly objective modes of historiography.

In his delightful and outrageously inaccurate novel about *The Late Mr Shakespeare*, Robert Nye's narrator makes a distinction between town history and country history, and even though the urban fantasy never really leaves the city, the dichotomy also applies to the respective histories of London Above and Below.

> Town history is cynical and exact. It is written by wits and it orders and limits what it talks about. It relies on facts and figures. It is knowing. Dry and sceptical and clever, it is ruled by the head. Beginning in the shadow of the law courts, at the end of the day your town history tends to the universities – it becomes academic. Town history is believable and reliable. Offering proofs, it never strains credulity. But sometimes it can't see the Forest of Arden for the trees. [...]
>
> Your country history is a different matter. Country history is faithful and open-ended. It is a tale told by various idiots on the village green, all busy contradicting themselves in the name of a common truth. It exaggerates and enflames what it talks about. It delights in lies and gossip. It is unwise. Wild and mystical and passionate, it is ruled by the heart. Beginning by the glow of the hearth, at the end of the night your country history tends to pass into balladry and legend – it becomes poetic. Country history is fanciful and maggoty. Easy to mock, it always strains belief. But sometimes it catches the ghostly coat-tails of what is otherwise ungraspable. (Nye 67-68)

In London Above, the past is relegated to museums where things are neatly catalogued and put on display for sponsored exhibitions, show events that need to be organized and contribute enormously to the prestige of the affluent, but not particularly well-meaning benefactor.

In London Below, the past is still alive, but it is not quite the past that can be learned from history books. Thus, there are not only fiefdoms and baronies, but also an earl's court, located in a tube carriage that can only be seen and entered by the inhabitants of London Below at Earl's Court Station. Even earlier ages seem to have survived in more remote places. In fact, we are told that "there are still some Roman soldiers camped out by the Kilburn River" (Gaiman, *Neverwhere* 89). And deep down there is the labyrinth which holds the beast of London, a monstrously huge animal of uncertain origin, akin to the "great blind white alligator king" (ibid. 226-227) in the sewers of New York, "the bear that stalked the city beneath Berlin" (ibid. 227) or the "black tiger in the undercity of Calcutta" (ibid.); Richard will eventually have to fight it in the course of his quest.

One of the strategies by which the past is resurrected, but also supplemented by fictitious and fantastic invention is the re-literalization of the tube's station names. In London Below there are still black friars under Blackfriars Station and shepherds under Shepherd's Bush, but then the latter may not be quite what the word suggests, for Richard Mayhew is warned: "Pray you never meet them" (ibid. 137). And finally, there is a real angel Islington, albeit one of the malignant variety who wants to sacrifice London in order to revenge itself and gain power over the hosts of Heaven.

In *Un Lun Dun*, one of the city's quarters is Wraithtown, in which the houses themselves are phantoms of their previous existences.

> Each of the houses, halls, shops, factories, churches and temples was a core of brick, wood, concrete or whatever surrounded by a wispy corona of earlier versions of itself. Every extension that had ever been built and knocked down, every smaller, squatter outline, every different design: all hung on to existence as spectres. (Miéville, *Un Lun Dun* 202)

This, of course, then also extends to the inhabitants, the ghosts of UnLondon who are dressed "in costumes from throughout history. Some looked like Londoners, in antique wigs and old-fashioned coats. Some looked [...] more like UnLondoners in their peculiar outfits" (Miéville, *Un Lun Dun* 203). In Wraithtown's Council then, in search of a list of the dead, "Deeba entered many layers of history" (210). But then the repression of the past reaches a second level, and while UnLondon itself is made up of the discarded and broken old objects and thus inevitably linked to London's past, Wraithtown is, in a sense, the repressed of the repressed, rejected and viewed with suspicion by the other UnLondoners. Unsurprisingly, one of the inhabitants of Wraithtown, son of a living UnLondon Father and a London ghost mother and thus yet another hybrid between ontological exclusives, has to prove himself against prejudices and anxieties within his own world, but is quickly accepted by the heroine and helps to save UnLondon from the Smog.

*

In the course of this paper, it must have become evident that urban fantasy is not only extremely bewildering and entertaining but also highly political. One of the persistent accusations against fantastic literature proclaims that this genre merely serves escapist pleasures and that it thus needs to be banished from the higher echelons of serious literature. Of course, such a view is untenable, and the battle between good and evil is quite regularly also political in nature. While it makes a significant difference whether the conflict is between the powers that be and the oppressed in a dystopian status quo or whether a rightful monarch or ruler has to be reinstalled after his position has been usurped by an evil intruder and the happy ending is marked by the return to a former equilibrium, both versions have ineluctable political dimensions and transmit affirmative or dissenting ideologies. The quests and battles are then frequently imaginative allegorizations of very real human conflicts and psychological dilemmas.

Urban fantasy is far more explicit in its political concerns. The dichotomies are regularly metaphorizations of the internal political and social fault lines and contradictions of our societies, and the topics that are imaginatively represented in a fantastic garb are topical and controversial issues of the political debate. This, of course, requires the negotiation of the local power relations – as mentioned above, the otherworld is steeped not only in one but often in various competing pasts and thus no superior alternative to London Above. It is rather more hostile, bleak and violent, as it is the place where internal inconsistencies and the allegedly tacit assumptions and unspoken codes of conduct of the upper world become visible and refuse to be repressed. By entering London Below, the hero or heroine leaves the world we know, but by entering the invisible sphere he or she also joins marginalized and silenced segments of our society. This always includes the immersion into new discourses and knowledge systems. The othercity is an ontologically different realm, governed by unfamiliar and frequently fantastic physical laws, and in consequence it also requires unusual epistemologies and discursive codes and conventions. Knowledge is not universal, but local, and different places require not only different behaviour but also different approaches to external reality. Nevertheless, principles of inclusion and exclusion, of status and hierarchies, of appropriate address and adequate deportment govern not only all social interaction but also the production and transmission of knowledge in the fantastic realm no less than in our world. Their very difference now also emphasizes the artificiality of such normative constructs, and, similarly, the alternative economies and social stratifications serve as a distorting mirror that draws attention to political and social inequality and injustice in the world that we make and live in. The raw and often physical aggression within the othercity replaces, but also reveals hidden or concealed modes of violence and institutionalized exertions of power, and the seemingly invincible foe shares characteristics with self-indulgent and indifferent political or economic elites.

The counter-city is thus simultaneously an inversion and an imaginative reflection of our world, a satirical exaggeration and an alternative vision. It merges utopian and dystopian aspects, offering possibilities for agency but also pre-modern forms of authority and legislation. It questions modern concepts of political participation but withholds any consistent alternatives. The counter-worlds are on the one hand inhabited by survival specialists and thus they have managed to persist in their respective niches and realms into our times, but then they are also urban landscapes of decay and waste.

This last point deserves some further elaboration. London Above and London Below are marked by different levels of order and entropy, and the motif thus takes up some concepts that have been prominent in literature for some time (Freese, passim). The two faces of our economic medal, with the glamorous sphere of consumerism on one side and the wastelands that result from unrestricted consumption on the other, have been topical in literature ever since *The Great Gatsby* addressed the contrast between West Egg and the Valley of the Ashes. In *King Rat*, the thoroughly disgusting passage in which Saul realizes his inordinate fondness for the half-rotten food which the streets and trash sacks of

London offer in abundance depicts a society of mindless consumption and the waste of life sustaining resources. *Neverwhere*, as usual, is less bleak in its vision of the counter-world; the economy of London Below seems to be based at least to some extent on the debris from London Above, which is recycled and then traded on the Floating Market. Here we find an alternative to the throwaway society, and the entropic processes are possibly slowed down when everything can still serve some old or new purpose and new order is created from disorder. In UnLondon the discarded objects are narratively salvaged from the dust heaps of our world and literally infused with new life – and the othercity is riddled with "binja"-warriors (martial art rubbish bins), "unbrellas" (broken umbrellas that may serve as a defence against the Smog), and, of course, the evil Smog itself. Evan Calder Williams has coined the term "salvagepunk" for a genre – possibly also for a practice – that is concerned with wreckage and recuperation in late capitalism and cast within post-apocalyptic settings:

> *salvagepunk*: the post-apocalyptic vision of a broken and dead world, strewn with both the dream residues and real junk of the world that was, and shot through with the hard work of salvaging, repurposing, detouring and scrapping. (Williams 19)

This, of course, applies to urban fantasy in general; Calder himself names Miéville's New Crobuzon novels (*Perdido Street Station*, *The Scar*, *Iron Council*) as examples of salvagepunk. In New Crobuzon, a city that feels like an urban underworld[9] without its sunny counterpart, discarded machinery has self-assembled into the artificial intelligence Construct Council, "born of random power and virus and chance" (Miéville, *Perdido Street Station* 397), and it is now worshipped by the dustmen and their "Godmech Gog, with their doctrine of the mechanized cosmos" (ibid. 397-398). For reasons that are not quite clear, the Construct Council was not able to develop some kind of microphone or loudspeaker, and so it uses the dead or semi-dead body of a man to speak for it. The image may be weird, but the metaphor is not. We may encounter here a radicalization of the phenomenon that Günther Anders has discussed in his

---

9 When Miéville was asked in an interview about his inspiration for New Crobuzon, he answered: "London's the obvious one, but London as filtered through art, really, as much as the real London. It's almost like two cities: there's London where I've always lived, which is a big influence, and there's also Michael Moorcock's London and Iain Sinclair's London and Charles Dickens's London and Thomas de Quincey's London and Neil Gaiman's London. For some reason London is a city that refracts particularly intensely and hallucinatorily through fiction" (Miéville, "The Lit Interview", n.p.).

book on "The Obsolescence of Mankind" (*Die Antiquiertheit des Menschen*)[10] as the "Promethean shame". It is a feeling of inferiority in the face of our own technological products which are more durable and efficient than their creators and the workings of which we are no longer really able to understand. Now, in the junk yards of the urban counter-world, it is no longer the new and innovative technological commodity that causes anxiety and embarrassment, but the discarded and dysfunctional debris that haunts us and refuses to rot in peace. The human body in its very materiality is now salvaged and serves as a tool for the machine, ready to be discarded and replaced if its decay renders it no longer functional.

A further aspect is added in *Un Lun Dun*: a unidirectional transfer of waste and pollution between the different spheres is directly addressed in the practice of sending the smog from London to Unlondon,[11] an obvious reference to similar policies by which industrial waste, often of a toxic nature, is shipped to third world countries for processing or disposal – out of sight, out of mind, at least for those gifted with the short attention span of politicians and voters. The narrative answer to the ecological disaster – the smog is condensed and packed into the barrels of an UnGun, a truly magical weapon – fulfils the generic demands for a happy ending in fantasy and, in particular, in fantasy for a young audience, but its very absurdity also emphasizes the impossibility of any easy solution.

*

As demonstrated, urban fantasy is a hybrid genre, merging elements of fantasy, magical realism, satire, utopia and dystopia, allegory, urban fiction, science fiction, steampunk, salvagepunk and a few other genres. But then the two authors discussed here are themselves at home in various fields and artistic modes. Neil Gaiman started out as a journalist before he became the acclaimed author of graphic novels, screenplays and novels. China Miéville is well known for his Marxist politics; he completed a PhD in International Relations at the London

---

10 The book has never been translated and several possible English titles are used with reference to the original.
11 Isaac Asimov explored a similar idea in his science fiction novel *The Gods Themselves*, in which an "Electron Pump" is employed to exchange energy and matter with a parallel universe – with disastrous consequences for the inhabitants of that universe. The novel is dedicated "[t]o Mankind. And the hope that the war against folly may someday be won, after all".

School of Economics on a Marxist Theory of International Law, and stood for the Socialist Alliance in the general elections of 2001. Apart from his literary work, including a comic and a graphic novel, he also published his PhD thesis and academic essays on politics and law, but also on science fiction theory and his own chosen field of fiction. Urban fiction is then a nodal point at which several interests seem to meet: a fascination with the popular genres that were long rejected but have found support and acclaim in the late 20th century, a decidedly political perception of art and literature and the belief that storytelling is a form of political action, a fondness of strong visual imagery both in the graphic arts and in literature, a deep respect for the readers of popular literature and their ability to engage in complex and multi-levelled narration, a highly ambivalent love for London and its history, and, quite obviously, one hell of a lot of fun in the creation of weird and unbelievably strange worlds and their inhabitants.

About the author

DIRK VANDERBEKE studied German and English Literature at the University of Frankfurt/Main. His doctoral thesis, Worüber man nicht sprechen kann (Whereof One Cannot Speak), deals with aspects of the unrepresentable in philosophy, science and literature. His habilitation study, *Theoretische Welten und literarische Transformationen (Theoretical Worlds and Literary Transformations)* examines the recent debate about 'science and literature' and science's role(s) in contemporary literature. He has also published on a variety of topics, e.g. Joyce, Pynchon, science fiction, self-similarity and vampires. Dirk Vanderbeke has taught at several universities in Germany and the USA; he is currently holding the Chair for Modern English Literature at the Friedrich-Schiller-University Jena, Germany, and a permanent guest-professorship at the University of Zielona Góra, Poland.

Bibliography

Ackroyd, Peter. *London: A Biography*. London: Vintage, 2001.

—. *London Under*. London: Vintage, 2011.

—. *Hawksmoor*. London: Abacus, 1986.

—. *The House of Dr. Dee*. London: Penguin, 1994.

Anders, Günther. *Die Antiquiertheit des Menschen*. [1956] München: C.H. Beck, 1980.

Asimov, Isaac. *The Gods Themselves*. New York: Fawcett Crest, 1972.

Beaudry, Jonas-Sébastien. "Apologizing to a Rat." *Neil Gaiman and Philosophy: Gods Gone Wild*. Eds. Tracey L. Bealer, Rachel Luria and Wayne Yuen. Chicago and LaSalle IL: Open Court, 2012. 71-84.

Benjamin, Walter. *The Arcades Project*. Translated by Howard Eiland and Kevin McLaughlin. Massachusetts and London: The Belknap Press of Harvard University Press, 1999.

Black, Max. "Metaphor". *Proceedings of the Aristotelian Society*, New Series, vol. 55 (1954-1955): 273-294.

Choo, Chun Wei. "IT 2000. Singapore's Vision of an Intelligent Island." *Intelligent Environments: Spatial Aspects of the Information Revolution*. Ed. Peter Droege. Amsterdam et al.: Elsevier, 1997. 49-65.

Duerr, Hans-Peter. *Traumzeit. Über die Grenzen zwischen Wildnis und Zivilisation*. Frankfurt: Syndikat, 1978.

Elber-Aviram, Hadas. "'A Statement of Attitude as Well as Geography': Urban Fantasy and the Recovery of Suppressed History." *Papers from the Institute of Archaeology*, forthcoming.

Faris, Wendy B. "Scheherezade's Children: Magic Realism and Postmodern Fiction." *Magical Realism. Theory, History, Community*. Eds. Lois Parkinson Zamora and Wendy B. Faris. Durham and London: Duke University Press, 1995. 163-190.

Fitzgerald, F. Scott. *The Great Gatsby*. [1925] London: Penguin Modern Classics, 2000.

Foucault, Michel. "Of Other Spaces: Utopias and Heterotopias." *Architecture/Movement/Continuité*, October 1984. ["Des Espace Autres". March 1967. Transl. Jay Miskoviec]. Reprint available online at http://web.mit.edu/allanmc/www/foucault1.pdf, accessed 9 June 2013.

FREESE, Peter. *From Apocalypse to Entropy and Beyond: The Second Law of Thermodynamics in Post-War American Fiction*. Essen: Blaue Eule, 1997.

GAIMAN, Neil. *Neverwhere*. [1997] New York: HarperTorch, 2001.

— et al. *Sandman*, 10 vols. New York: Vertigo, 1988-1996.

— *Stardust*. New York: Avon Books, 1999.

— *Coraline*. London: Bloomsbury, 2002.

— *American Gods*. [2001] New York: HarperTorch, 2002.

— *Anansi Boys*. [2005] New York: HarperTorch, 2006.

— *Mirrormask*. Dir. David McKean. 2005.

— "FAQs. Books, Short Stories and Films." Available online at http://www.neilgaiman.com/p/FAQs/Books,_Short_Stories,_and_Films, accessed 9 June 2013.

— and Dave MCKEAN. *The Wolves in the Wall*. New York: HarperCollins, 2003.

GOETSCH, Paul. *Monsters in English Literature: From the Romantic Age to the First World War*. Frankfurt: Peter Lang, 2002.

HEGERFELDT, Anne. *Lies that Tell the Truth: Magic Realism Seen Through Contemporary Fiction From Britain*. Amsterdam and New York: Rodopi, 2005.

IRVINE, Alexancer C. "Urban Fantasy." *The Cambridge Companion to Fantasy Literature*. Eds. Edward James and Farah Mendlesohn. Cambridge: Cambridge University Press, 2012. 200-213.

JOYCE, James. *Ulysses*. [1922] Eds. Hans Gabler et al. New York: Vintage, 1986.

KING, Stephen. *Needful Things*. New York: Viking, 1991.

LEHAN, Richard Daniel. *The City in Literature: An Intellectual and Cultural History*. Berkeley and Los Angeles: University of California Press, 1998.

LEVIN, Ira. *The Stepford Wives*. [1972] New York: Signet Books, 1994.

LOVECRAFT, Howard Phillips. "The Dreams in the Witch House." [1933] *At the Mountains of Madness*. New York: Del Ray, 1971. 139-177.

MIÉVILLE, China. *King Rat*. [1998] London: Pan Books, 1999.

— *Perdido Street Station*. [2000] New York: Del Rey, 2003.

— *Un Lun Dun*. [2007] London: Macmillan, 2008.

— *The City and the City*. [2009] London: Pan Books, 2011.

— *Embassytown*. [2011] London: Pan Books, 2012.

"The Lit interview: China Miéville, A young British writer dons the robes of the un-Tolkien." (Interview in the *San Francisco Bay Guardian* with A.C. Thompson and David Martinez) http://www.sfbg.com/38/48/lit_mieville.html (June 9, 2013).

Moorcock, Michael. *Mother London*. London: Penguin, 1989.

Novak, Marcos. "Cognitive Cities: Intelligence, Environment and Space." *Intelligent Environments: Spatial Aspects of the Information Revolution*. Ed. Peter Droege, Amsterdam: Elsevier, 1997. 386-419.

Nye, Robert. *The Late Mr. Shakespeare*. [1998] London: Penguin, 2000.

Pynchon, Thomas. *The Crying of Lot 49*. [1966] New York: Bantam Books, 1980.

V. [1963] London: Picador, 1975.

Quincey, Thomas de. *Confessions of an English Opium Eater*. [1821] London: Everyman's Library, 1972.

Rowling, Joanne K. *Harry Potter and the Philosopher's Stone*. [1997] London: Bloomsbury, 2000.

Harry Potter and the Chamber of Secrets. [1998] London: Bloomsbury, 2000.

Rushdie, Salman. *The Satanic Verses*. New York: Viking, 1988.

"Interview: Salman Rushdie talks to the London Consortium about the Satanic Verses." *Salman Rushdie. Critical Essays*. Vol. 2. Eds. Mohit Kumar Ray and Rama Kundu. New Delhi: Atlantic Publishers and Distributors, 2006. 188-211.

Todorov, Tzvetan. *The Fantastic. A Structural Approach to a Literary Genre*. [*Introduction à la litterature fantastique*. 1970. Transl. Richard Howard.] Ithaka NY: Cornell University Press, 1975.

Vanderbeke, Dirk. "Haven't I been here before? China Miéville's Uncanny Cities". *The Politics of Contemporary Fantasy*. Eds. Gerold Sedlmayr, Nicole Waller and Angela Sedlmaier. Jefferson NC: McFarland, forthcoming.

Williams, Evan Calder. *Combined and Uneven Apocalypse*. Ropley: Zero Books, 2010.

Winterson, Jeanette. *The Passion*. [1987] New York: Grove Press, 1997.

Walking Tree Publishers
Zurich and Jena

Walking Tree Publishers was founded in 1997 as a forum for publication of material (books, videos, CDs, etc.) related to Tolkien and Middle-earth studies. Manuscripts and project proposals can be submitted to the board of editors (please include an SAE):

Walking Tree Publishers
CH-3052 Zollikofen, Switzerland
e-mail: info@walking-tree.org
http://www.walking-tree.org

Cormarë Series

The *Cormarë Series* collects papers and studies dedicated exclusively to the exploration of Tolkien's work. It comprises monographs, thematic collections of essays, conference volumes, and reprints of important yet no longer (easily) accessible papers by leading scholars in the field. Manuscripts and project proposals are evaluated by members of an independent board of advisors who support the series editors in their endeavour to provide the readers with qualitatively superior yet accessible studies on Tolkien and his work.

News from the Shire and Beyond. Studies on Tolkien
Peter Buchs and Thomas Honegger (eds.), Zurich and Berne 2004, Reprint, First edition 1997 (Cormarë Series 1), ISBN 978-3-9521424-5-5

Root and Branch. Approaches Towards Understanding Tolkien
Thomas Honegger (ed.), Zurich and Berne 2005, Reprint, First edition 1999 (Cormarë Series 2), ISBN 978-3-905703-01-6

Richard Sturch, *Four Christian Fantasists. A Study of the Fantastic Writings of George MacDonald, Charles Williams, C.S. Lewis and J.R.R. Tolkien*
Zurich and Berne 2007, Reprint, First edition 2001 (Cormarë Series 3), ISBN 978-3-905703-04-7

Tolkien in Translation
Thomas Honegger (ed.), Zurich and Jena 2011, Reprint, First edition 2003 (Cormarë Series 4), ISBN 978-3-905703-15-3

Mark T. Hooker, *Tolkien Through Russian Eyes*
Zurich and Berne 2003 (Cormarë Series 5), ISBN 978-3-9521424-7-9

Translating Tolkien: Text and Film
Thomas Honegger (ed.), Zurich and Jena 2011, Reprint, First edition 2004 (Cormarë Series 6), ISBN 978-3-905703-16-0

Christopher Garbowski, *Recovery and Transcendence for the Contemporary Mythmaker. The Spiritual Dimension in the Works of J.R.R. Tolkien*
Zurich and Berne 2004, Reprint, First Edition by Marie Curie Sklodowska, University Press, Lublin 2000, (Cormarë Series 7), ISBN 978-3-9521424-8-6

Reconsidering Tolkien
Thomas Honegger (ed.), Zurich and Berne 2005 (Cormarë Series 8),
ISBN 978-3-905703-00-9

Tolkien and Modernity 1
Frank Weinreich and Thomas Honegger (eds.), Zurich and Berne 2006 (Cormarë Series 9), ISBN 978-3-905703-02-3

Tolkien and Modernity 2
Thomas Honegger and Frank Weinreich (eds.), Zurich and Berne 2006 (Cormarë Series 10), ISBN 978-3-905703-03-0

Tom Shippey, *Roots and Branches. Selected Papers on Tolkien by Tom Shippey*
Zurich and Berne 2007 (Cormarë Series 11), ISBN 978-3-905703-05-4

Ross Smith, *Inside Language. Linguistic and Aesthetic Theory in Tolkien*
Zurich and Jena 2011, Reprint, First edition 2007 (Cormarë Series 12),
ISBN 978-3-905703-20-7

How We Became Middle-earth. A Collection of Essays on The Lord of the Rings
Adam Lam and Nataliya Oryshchuk (eds.), Zurich and Berne 2007 (Cormarë Series 13), ISBN 978-3-905703-07-8

Myth and Magic. Art According to the Inklings
Eduardo Segura and Thomas Honegger (eds.), Zurich and Berne 2007 (Cormarë Series 14), ISBN 978-3-905703-08-5

The Silmarillion - Thirty Years On
Allan Turner (ed.), Zurich and Berne 2007 (Cormarë Series 15),
ISBN 978-3-905703-10-8

Martin Simonson, *The Lord of the Rings and the Western Narrative Tradition*
Zurich and Jena 2008 (Cormarë Series 16), ISBN 978-3-905703-09-2

Tolkien's Shorter Works. Proceedings of the 4th Seminar of the Deutsche Tolkien Gesellschaft & Walking Tree Publishers Decennial Conference
Margaret Hiley and Frank Weinreich (eds.), Zurich and Jena 2008 (Cormarë Series 17), ISBN 978-3-905703-11-5

Tolkien's The Lord of the Rings: Sources of Inspiration
Stratford Caldecott and Thomas Honegger (eds.), Zurich and Jena 2008 (Cormarë Series 18), ISBN 978-3-905703-12-2

J.S. Ryan, *Tolkien's View: Windows into his World*
Zurich and Jena 2009 (Cormarë Series 19), ISBN 978-3-905703-13-9

Music in Middle-earth
Heidi Steimel and Friedhelm Schneidewind (eds.), Zurich and Jena 2010 (Cormarë Series 20), ISBN 978-3-905703-14-6

Liam Campbell, *The Ecological Augury in the Works of JRR Tolkien*
Zurich and Jena 2011 (Cormarë Series 21), ISBN 978-3-905703-18-4

Margaret Hiley, *The Loss and the Silence. Aspects of Modernism in the Works of C.S. Lewis, J.R.R. Tolkien and Charles Williams*
Zurich and Jena 2011 (Cormarë Series 22), ISBN 978-3-905703-19-1

Rainer Nagel, *Hobbit Place-names. A Linguistic Excursion through the Shire*
Zurich and Jena 2012 (Cormarë Series 23), ISBN 978-3-905703-22-1

Christopher MacLachlan, *Tolkien and Wagner: The Ring and Der Ring*
Zurich and Jena 2012 (Cormarë Series 24), ISBN 978-3-905703-21-4

Renée Vink, *Wagner and Tolkien: Mythmakers*
Zurich and Jena 2012 (Cormarë Series 25), ISBN 978-3-905703-25-2

The Broken Scythe. Death and Immortality in the Works of J.R.R. Tolkien
Roberto Arduini and Claudio Antonio Testi (eds.), Zurich and Jena 2012
(Cormarë Series 26), ISBN 978-3-905703-26-9

Sub-creating Middle-earth: Constructions of Authorship and the Works of J.R.R. Tolkien
Judith Klinger (ed.), Zurich and Jena 2012 (Cormarë Series 27),
ISBN 978-3-905703-27-6

Tolkien's Poetry
Julian Eilmann and Allan Turner (eds.), Zurich and Jena 2013
(Cormarë Series 28), ISBN 978-3-905703-28-3

O, What a Tangled Web? Tolkien and Medieval Literature. A View from Poland
Barbara Kowalik (ed.), Zurich and Jena 2013, (Cormarë Series 29),
ISBN 978-3-905703-29-0

J.S. Ryan, *In the Nameless Wood. Explorations in the Philological Hinterland of Tolkien's Literary Creations*
Zurich and Jena 2013, (Cormarë Series 30), ISBN 978-3-905703-30-6

Paul H. Kocher, *The Three Ages of Middle-earth*
Zurich and Jena, forthcoming

Beowulf and the Dragon

The original Old English text of the 'Dragon Episode' of *Beowulf* is set in an authentic

font and printed and bound in hardback creating a high quality art book. The text is illustrated by Anke Eissmann and accompanied by John Porter's translation. The introduction is by Tom Shippey. Limited first edition of 500 copies. 84 pages.

This high-quality book will please both Tolkien fans and those interested in mythology and Old English. It is also well suited as a gift.

Selected pages can be previewed on: www.walking-tree.org/beowulf

Beowulf and the Dragon
Zurich and Jena 2009,
ISBN 978-3-905703-17-7

Tales of Yore Series

The *Tales of Yore Series* grew out of the desire to share Kay Woollard's whimsical stories and drawings with a wider audience. The series aims at providing a platform for qualitatively superior fiction that will appeal to readers familiar with Tolkien's world.

Kay Woollard, *The Terror of Tatty Walk. A Frightener*
CD and Booklet, Zurich and Berne 2000, ISBN 978-3-9521424-2-4

Kay Woollard, *Wilmot's Very Strange Stone or What came of building "snobbits"*
CD and booklet, Zurich and Berne 2001, ISBN 978-3-9521424-4-8

www.ingramcontent.com/pod-product-compliance
Lightning Source LLC
Chambersburg PA
CBHW050803160426
43192CB00010B/1629